The
South Atlantic
Quarterly

SAQ

T0341601

116:1 · January 2017

Climate Change and the Production of Knowledge

Ian Baucom and Matthew Omelsky, Special Issue Editors

AGAINST the DAY

Environmental Activism across the Pacific
Teresa Shewry, Editor

Ian Baucom and Matthew Omelsky

Knowledge in the Age of Climate Change

By now, the facts and futures of human-induced climate change have been well rehearsed. Before the end of this century, global temperatures could approach 3 degrees Celsius warmer than average temperatures in the 1990s. Sea levels could rise up to a meter or more, threatening millions living in coastal areas. In these conditions diseases will likely spread more rapidly, food will become more and more scarce with anticipated population explosions, and droughts and storms will be increasingly severe. Mass-scale climate migrations will come to dominate our news cycles. And, of course, all of this will be felt most acutely in less developed countries. The implications of these projections produced by the Intergovernmental Panel on Climate Change (IPCC) nearly three decades ago were and continue to be all encompassing. They saturate the air we breathe, the water we drink, the food we eat, and the objects we use. They are, in short, deeply connected to what it means to be human on earth in the twenty-first century. Even if momentarily, it is not difficult to imagine the subtle ways we live and experience the material effects of climate change every day. Perhaps more difficult to conceive, though, are the ways climate change affects how we *think*

The South Atlantic Quarterly 116:1, January 2017
DOI 10.1215/00382876-3749271 © 2017 Duke University Press

and how we organize that thinking. How do these dire projections—their facticity, as Martin Heidegger would put it, but also simply our lived experience of what those projections portend—affect how we make meaning of ourselves and our world? What does it mean to generate knowledge in the age of climate change?

This issue is an attempt to map some of the epistemological shifts we have witnessed in these times of ubiquitous change. These essays begin to chart some of the ways in which climate change discourses have reshaped the contemporary architecture of knowledge itself, reconstituting intellectual disciplines and artistic practices, redrawing and dissolving boundaries, but also reframing how knowledge is represented and disseminated. The essays that follow roughly fall into three larger categories. The first focuses on the shape of global warming discourse as it has emerged *within* particular disciplines in recent years, such as history, journalism, anthropology, and the visual arts. How is climate change renovating these fields, perhaps necessitating a turn toward material science and experience? How, inversely, have particular disciplines influenced the language and discourse of climate change? The second category concerns what we're calling "interdisciplinarity 2.0." If in the 1980s and 1990s we witnessed a turn to interdisciplinarity among proximate disciplines in the humanities and social sciences—such as the convergence of political economy, literary studies, and sociology that we find in postcolonial studies, as well as gender and sexuality studies, for instance—then for the past decade or so we have witnessed a new kind of interdisciplinarity, in which the material sciences have had a pervasive influence on those already interdisciplinary human sciences. Scholars like Donna Haraway and Bruno Latour, of course, have been doing this kind of work for decades, but twenty-first-century developments in ecocriticism, object-oriented ontology, posthumanism, and the neurohumanities have brought an enduring materialism to the human sciences. Given this rebooted intellectual landscape, our interest lies in how climate change science and discourse have further dissolved the barriers between established fields of knowledge. Just as critical are the ways the human and social sciences are in turn reshaping the production of climate change knowledge. The third category emerges from these others, focusing on the forms of representation and dissemination in this new epistemological landscape. What formal strategies do music composers, novelists, and sculptors take up so that climate change might somehow be represented? How have emergent platforms and media—such as small-scale popular science journalism, open access publication, and online curation—engaged new audiences and disseminated climate-related work? The combination of these three categories is our way of taking the temperature, as it were, of the contemporary order of knowledge and how that order has been deeply affected by the climatic shifts that we live and experience each day.

It should be clear, then, that the articles in this issue are part of a growing constellation of contemporary voices and texts. Of the many acknowledged and implied interlocutors in this collection, perhaps the most visible are the widely disseminated documents recently produced by world leaders. The agreement set at the twenty-first session of the Conference of the Parties (COP21) to the United Nations Framework Convention on Climate Change in Paris in December 2015 is of course the latest installment in a decades-long affair to reduce global carbon emissions and to provide assistance to those countries least prepared for a warmer world (United Nations 2015). The contributors to this collection provide a range of responses to COP21, principally critiques of its insufficiencies, its omissions, and its dissimulations. Given the continued prominence of religious faiths in our world, we cannot ignore the discursive force of religious leaders as they weigh in on the debate. Issued ahead of the Paris talks, Pope Francis's *Laudato Si'* (2015) and the "Islamic Declaration on Global Climate Change" (IICCS 2015) are ambitious statements made by the leaders of two of the world's most influential religions, both documents employing a combination of anticapitalism and religious naturalism in their call for an end to fossil fuel consumption altogether.

Crucial, too, in the contemporary landscape of climate change knowledge are the nonfiction works written to be more accessible to the public but no less rigorous in their critical engagement. Particularly influential in recent years are Naomi Klein's *This Changes Everything* (2014) and Elizabeth Kolbert's *The Sixth Extinction* (2014), the former attending to the ways neoliberal capital simultaneously drives changing climates and prevents systematic action, and the latter situating our current climatic and ecological crises in a long history of mass extinctions on earth. These prize-winning works employ analogy, extended anecdote, and empirical evidence to galvanize a sense of shared urgency of our lived moment and anticipated futures. The concluding thoughts to Kolbert's book (2014: 38) demonstrate the strategies of the genre well: "By disrupting these systems—cutting down tropical rainforests, altering the composition of the atmosphere, acidifying oceans—we're putting our own survival in danger. Among the many lessons that emerge from the geologic record, perhaps the most sobering is that in life, as in mutual funds, past performance is no guarantee of future results. When a mass extinction occurs, it takes out the weak and also lays low the strong."

Indeed, this kind of straightforward and lucid prose style is part of what makes these works best sellers, no doubt reaching far wider audiences than most academic publications. Texts like these are pivotal to contemporary knowledge production, and these two in particular are not lost in this collection. In fact, tracing the varied uses of Klein's and Kolbert's books in this issue—especially in the contributions by Michael Segal, Noel Castree, Gary Tomlinson, and Claire Colebrook and Tom Cohen—affords a momentary taste of the decidedly heterogeneous nature of climate change discourse today.

Amid this density and diversity of climate discourse are also several recent influential texts in the humanities and social sciences. Unsurprisingly, the works that have gained the most traction among scholars and the broader public have been interdisciplinary patchworks, some combination of climate science, history, critical theory, aesthetic representation, and political activism. The focuses of these texts vary widely, from genealogical investigations, to studies of different scales of time, to close readings of geographically distinct crises. In *The Shock of the Anthropocene*, Christophe Bonneuil and Jean-Baptist Fressoz (2016: xiii–xiv) take the genealogical approach, reading an array of thinkers, from Henri de Saint-Simon to Charles Fourier, Fernand Braudel to Bruno Latour, to construct a sprawling intellectual history intended to "help us change our world-views and inhabit the Anthropocene more lucidly, respectfully and equitably." In contrast, *The Conflict Shoreline*, a collaboration between forensic architect Eyal Weizman and photographer Fazal Sheikh (2015), is a recent notable example of a more geographically specific text. Through a counterpoint of rigorous historical and political analysis and dozens of aerial photographs, satellite images, and maps, the book chronicles how climate change–induced desertification has exacerbated the Israeli state's decades-long expulsion of Bedouin indigenous to the Negev for the purpose of transforming the expanding desert into Jewish settlements, forests, and fields. Also focusing on populations most vulnerable to ecological crisis is Rob Nixon's American Book Award–winning *Slow Violence and the Environmentalism of the Poor*. Nixon (2013: 2) suggests that climate change, nuclear contamination, and other forms of environmental devastation enact a kind of "violence that occurs gradually and out of sight, a violence of delayed destruction that is dispersed across time and space." The most impoverished of the "global South," Nixon contends, are most threatened by what he calls "slow violence," and the challenge lies in locating those memoirs, novels, films, and other media that can best make visible what so often remains invisible.

While many of these works mentioned to this point have some kind of presence in this issue, one essay stands out as the most widely engaged. That Dipesh Chakrabarty's "The Climate of History: Four Theses" is closely read by several contributors should come as no surprise, given the influence the article has had on a range of fields since its 2009 publication. In the essay Chakrabarty suggests that the crisis of climate change is larger in time and space than the crises of national belonging or global capital. The Anthropocene demands that we think in terms of a deeper history of life on earth (recorded as well as prerecorded geological histories) and that we move past our human exceptionalism to think of ourselves as one among innumerable interdependent species on earth, all threatened in some way in this newly named epoch. "Climate change," he says in the essay's conclusion, "poses for us a question of a human collectivity, an us, pointing to a figure of the universal that escapes our capacity to experience the world" (Chakrabarty 2009: 222). The contributors to this collection take up these questions of (in) experientiality, deep time, and species thinking in our moment of global warming, bringing them to bear on neuroscience, religious studies, food studies, and scientific modeling, among other diverse fields of knowledge.

Another pervasive question that animates this collection, one crucial to the broader climate change intellectual landscape, concerns aesthetic representation. As recently as 2005, Bill McKibben famously asked, "Where are the books? The poems? The plays?," noting what he observed as a dearth of climate change–engaged art. "Art," he continues, "is one of the ways we digest what is happening to us, make the sense out of it that proceeds to action" (McKibben 2005). His call, it turned out, was timely. A global creative "digestion" was indeed coming into its own. "Moving images and sounds and words," McKibben (2009) wrote four years later, revisiting the subject, "have been flooding out into the world." And this aquatic metaphor, it appears, was also prescient of much of the creative work to come. Water—its devastating excess, but also its haunting absence—has become central to climate change aesthetics globally since the turn of the century. Take, for instance, Vincent Huang's interactive installation in the Tuvalu Pavilion at the 2015 Venice Biennale. Visitors walked through the pavilion on wooden platforms floating on a shallow pool of water. As more weight bore down, water subtly seeped onto the platforms, soaking the bottoms of visitors' shoes—an allegorical experience for the ecological impact of humans on the vanishing Pacific island nation of Tuvalu. In another form, we find a kind of literary analogue to this interactive experience in Amitav Ghosh's 2004 novel *The Hungry Tide* (2004: 37), in the narrator's description of the precarious position of an island in the Sundarbans region of Bangladesh: "At low tide, when the embankment, or *bādh*, was riding high on the water, Lusibari looked like some gigantic earthen ark, floating serenely above its surroundings. Only at high tide was it evident that the interior of the island lay below the level of the water. At such times the unsinkable ship of a few hours before took on the appearance of a flimsy saucer that could tip over at any moment and go circling down into the depths."

The simultaneous aesthetic beauty and imminent devastation of these images is a hallmark of some of the best climate change–inflected aesthetics to date. If Huang achieves this dialectic through installation, and Ghosh through narrative, composer John Luther Adams does it through sound in his Pulitzer Prize–winning symphony *Become Ocean*. "Life on this earth first emerged from the sea," he writes in the album's liner notes. "Today, as the polar ice melts and sea level rises, we humans face the prospect that we may once again, quite literally, become ocean" (Adams 2014). Adams transposes this sense of "becoming" into a minimalist ebb and flow of sound that washes over the listener, a series of gradual swellings and releases built through brass, woodwinds, piano, and strings. At its quietest, the symphony is whimsical and utterly sublime; at its peaks, the work is soaring, massive, and heaving. Rounding out this snippet view of climate-aquatic aesthetics is yet another vector in Nnedi Okorafor's speculative fiction. To read her 2015 cyberpunk novel *The Book of Phoenix* is to enter a dystopian world in which global warming has advanced far into the IPCC's projected future. New York City has become tropical: mango trees and palm trees line the streets, a new strand of malaria plagues the city, and "the poor and illegal" inhabit the now partially submerged skyscrapers of Lower Manhattan, "commut[ing] to the city using boat services provided by New York's government" (Okorafor 2015: 57). The shock of such a transfigured familiar landscape evokes an uneasy melding of horror, wonder, and curiosity, very much in line with the aquatic forms of Adams, Ghosh, and Huang.

This growth of engagement with climate change that we find in contemporary artistic practice, and certainly in the earlier mentioned best sellers, declarations, and critical investigations, is of course not without precedent. We may have witnessed an explosion of participation in climate discourses in the past two decades, but those discourses indeed have a long and variegated history. Briefly, we want to sketch a version of that history, providing a few of what we're calling "threshold texts" that chart a certain historical movement of climate change thought and expression. We prefer this term because our aim is not to be comprehensive or to make grand claims about foundational texts or ideas but instead to chronicle a series of paradigm shifts in the architecture of knowledge that is particular to the disciplinary constellation in this issue. Each of the following texts marks in some way a kind of "threshold moment" in the evolution of climate change knowledge as it manifests in the articles in this collection and the contemporary epistemological landscape presented here.

═══

As all the essays in this collection are in some way concerned with a certain "cultural processing" of anthropogenic climate change, we might begin this sketch by turning to a few relatively early texts to participate in that processing. The first we have in mind is, and is not, about climate change. It is a summary of arguments published in London's *Star* newspaper in 1799 of the trial of *Hornblower v. Boulton and Watt.* Watt, unsurprisingly, refers to James Watt, inventor of the Watt steam engine patented in 1784, a machine considered pivotal to the expansion of the Industrial Revolution. In the article's recounting of the case, we find that Watt has taken Jonathan Hornblower to court for violating his patent, the latter claiming that the patent applied only to an abstract idea, not to an actual machine: "He [Watt's attorney] contended that this invention of Mr. Watt was the greatest practical advance ever made in the arts, and was universally admired through every part of Europe. By it a single bushel of coals would raise one foot high thirty millions of pounds weight. It possessed a force more than double the power of gunpowder. Could this operation be performed by a mere abstract idea— by a thing not tangible?" (*Star* 1799).

The lawyer's language, of course, is hyperbolic, but for his argument to be taken seriously (which it was) that hyperbole had to have been grounded in some common understanding of the invention's significance. The historicist language is striking: "the greatest practical advance ever made in the arts." The machine, the logic goes, will bring progress, making culture and society more perfect as time moves on. The optimism, the celebration of power, and certainly the reference to the "single bushel of coals" is almost haunting from our twenty-first-century vantage point. It is a telling, albeit small, window into the ideology of a particular moment in Britain's history, a moment that in retrospect we have come to see as the first great historical acceleration of the burning of fossil fuels. If this document tells us anything, it's that the earliest days of human-caused climate change were (at least in part) days of elation, confidence, and hope for the future.

Watt's engine gestures to one principal method of placing carbon dioxide (CO_2) into the atmosphere, and a half century later we find another in the work of George Perkins Marsh. Prior to the publication of his celebrated *Man and Nature* in 1864, Marsh delivered a now well-known speech in 1847 to the Agricultural Society of Rutland, Vermont, in which he claimed that "climate itself has in many instances been gradually changed and ameliorated or deteriorated by human action": "The draining of swamps and the clearing of forests perceptibly effect the evaporation from the earth, and of course the mean quantity of moisture suspended in the air. The same causes modify the electrical condition of the atmosphere and the power of the surface to reflect, absorb and radiate the rays of the sun, and consequently influence the distribution of light and heat, and the force and direction of the winds" (Marsh 1847).

This claim of the effects of "human action" on the climate very much resembles our contemporary Anthropocene discourse, that humans have become a geological force in their capacity to alter the earth's surface, atmosphere, and life-forms. And without naming it as such, Marsh early on managed to identify the role of deforestation in changing climates. Deforestation was crucial to his understanding of warming temperatures produced by the interrelation of the sun, the atmosphere, and the earth's surface, effectively prefiguring what would be more empirically substantiated in the final years of the nineteenth century by Swedish chemist Svante Arrhenius, who all but coined the term *greenhouse effect.*

Moving into the twentieth century, the next critical threshold of climate change knowledge centers on CO_2. The transfer of CO_2 from inside the earth into the atmosphere, of course, had been well under way by the end of the nineteenth century, as the Watt trial summary demonstrates, but the idea that CO_2 had somehow accelerated the change of climates was not yet common knowledge (Fleming 1998: 107). Appropriately enough, a British steam engineer was one of the first to be taken seriously about the effects of CO_2. In his essay, "The Composition of the Atmosphere through the Ages," Guy Callendar (1939: 38) estimates that "some 9,000 tons of carbon dioxide [are transferred] into the air each minute":

> This great stream of gas results from the combustion of fossil carbon (coal, oil, peat, etc.). . . . As man is now changing the composition of the atmosphere at a rate which must be very exceptional on the geological time scale, it is natural to seek for the probable effects of such a change. From the best laboratory observations it appears that the principal result of increasing atmospheric carbon dioxide . . . would be a gradual increase in the mean temperature of the colder regions of the earth.

Callendar is certainly getting closer to the heart of the matter, but he never actually suggests that these atmospheric and climatic changes may be detrimental. In fact, Callendar, as well as Arrhenius, speculated that global warming might even benefit certain societies, providing more land for cultivation, among other potential advantages (Fleming 1998: 115). Telling, too, is Callendar's emphasis on the "colder regions of the earth," and the apparent elision of those that were likely already quite warm in 1939, regions that would presumably *not* benefit from increased temperatures.

The same year Callendar published his essay, *Time* magazine published an article on what must have been bizarre news of a "warming world," giving us an early window into how climate change knowledge initially reached the general public. The four-paragraph article cites figures provided by a few noted meteorologists and gives a sweeping tour of thumbnail anecdotes about the "retreating" ice sheets of Greenland and the warming Arctic Sea. Despite its claim of a warming world, however, the article remains uncertain: "The reason for such climate changes is obscure. . . . Meteorologists do not know whether the present warm trend is likely to last 20 years or 20,000 years" (*Time* 1939: 27). The article, we should note, remains neutral on change, reading it as neither beneficial nor harmful. Indeed, the article almost seems symptomatic of some kind of fracture in the climate change discourse of the time, either among climatologists themselves about the reasons for change or in the communication channels between scientists and journalists. What is clear, though, is that journalists were some of the earliest mediators between climate change scientists and the general public, distilling knowledge to make it palatable and understandable to a lay audience. Interestingly, the uncertainty we find in this *Time* article is still not entirely straightened out a decade later in the *Saturday Evening Post*, at the time a weekly cultural magazine. The 1950 *Post* article is several times longer than the *Time* article, but its discursive strategy is similar: it surveys evidence of hotter temperatures from Boston to Greenland to Kenya, comparing this with anecdotal evidence of cold climes in the decades and centuries prior, and short quotations from a geographer at the University of Stockholm are used to authorize the evidence. In contrast to the 1939 *Time* article, however, the *Post* article seems a bit more sure of its knowledge: it suggests that "this is more than a brief, superficial change" and, intriguingly, that the "most reasonable conclusion is that the earth is emerging from the last lingering chill of one of a succession of little ice ages." And in contrast to the 1939 piece, the latter does begin to read the changes negatively, as one of its image captions demonstrates: "The choking dust storms of America's Midwest, the 'freak' New England hurricane of 1938, the fact that Utah's Great Salt Lake is rapidly drying up—all these point toward a definite climatic upheaval"

(Abarbanel and McClusky 1950: 23). We have finally encountered a cultural response that more closely resembles our discourse of crisis in the twenty-first century. But the article is still silent on carbon, insisting on foregrounding a kind of "natural process" argument over an anthropogenic one.

A few decades further into the century, art and literature begin to make up for this midcentury silence on human action. One unequivocal threshold artwork is Robert Smithson's 1970 earthwork *Spiral Jetty*. Sitting in the pink-hued waters of Utah's Great Salt Lake, the sculpture jets out from the shore in a 1,500-foot-long, 15-foot-wide coil. Made of basalt rock, mud, and salt crystal from the immediate area, the earthwork remains nearly fifty years later, having become a kind of allegory for the human's geological impact in our Anthropocenic moment. The work was also built to register climate fluctuations, surfacing in the water when the lake is in drought and sitting just below the water's surface when the rains from the nearby mountains run in. Published just one year after Smithson built *Spiral Jetty*, Ursula Le Guin's sci-fi novel *The Lathe of Heaven* is another pivotal early climate change aesthetic piece. A futuristic work set in 2002 in Oregon, the novel takes a far less subtle approach:

> Rain was an old Portland tradition, but the warmth—70° F. on the second of March—was modern, a result of air pollution. Urban and industrial effluvia had not been controlled soon enough to reverse the cumulative trends already at work in the mid-Twentieth Century; it would take centuries for the CO_2 to clear out of the air, if it ever did. New York was going to be one of the larger casualties of the Greenhouse Effect, as the polar ice kept melting and the sea kept rising. (Le Guin 1971: 31)

Removed from narrative context, of course, this climate description feels didactic, even belabored, rehearsing a story very much familiar to us today. But what reads as normal now was likely a jarring, alienating reading experience in 1971, a shock to the system that we perhaps have become increasingly immune to today. With the publication of Le Guin's novel, CO_2 now inches closer to widespread acceptance among most media, elected officials, and the public as the primary climate change causing greenhouse gas. Her novel brings us to the edge of our contemporary era of global warming discourse.

That contemporary discursive era begins in earnest in the late 1980s. A brief 1988 *New York Times* report documents a landmark event signaling this new era of protocols, policy, and crisis management. The event was the testimony of National Aeronautics and Space Administration (NASA) climatologist James Hansen before the US Senate Energy and Natural Resources Committee. He announced to receptive lawmakers and the global media that NASA was "99 percent certain" that climate change was real and imminent (Shabecoff 1988). The article reads much like something written today: it goes back to basics to explain the greenhouse effect; it cites mathematical models and experts; it discusses melting polar ice sheets *and* rising sea levels; it identifies CO_2 as the biggest atmospheric pollutant, the result of burning fossil fuels and destroying forests. Hansen's testimony finally put climate change on the agenda of policy makers and elected officials. The media had latched on and the public started to take the issue seriously (Besel 2013: 138). That same year, the United Nations formed the IPCC, which published its first assessment report in 1990, highlighting the scientific, technical, and socioeconomic urgencies of global warming. The era of warning and crisis was indeed well under way.

At this point in the history of climate change knowledge, the field opens and crowds. We could highlight any number of texts and voices from the 1990s to the present, but perhaps the next signal discursive event belongs to Paul Crutzen and Eugene Stoermer. In an issue of the newsletter of the International Geosphere-Biosphere Program released in 2000, the two atmospheric chemists test a new term. In the brief two-page essay, the authors list some of the ways mankind has become a "geological force": fossil fuels that took millions of years to form are rapidly depleting; species have become extinct; and much of the ozone layer has been destroyed. They write, "Considering these and many other major and still growing impacts of human activities on earth and atmosphere, and at all, including global, scales, it seems to us more than appropriate to emphasize the central role of mankind in geology and ecology by proposing the use of the term 'anthropocene' for the current geological epoch" (Crutzen and Stoermer 2000: 17).

This announcement would go on to spark a contentious still-unfolding debate among scholars about the Anthropocene's timeline. In the essay, though, they provisionally date it to the late eighteenth century, "when data retrieved from glacial ice cores show the beginning of a growth in the atmospheric concentrations of several 'greenhouse gases'" (17). Incidentally, this beginning also corresponds, they say, with the 1784 invention of Watt's steam engine.

This epochal naming of course did not suddenly change the material conditions of everyday life. What it changed, or has sought to change, is our cosmology, the way we conceive of ourselves as being-in-the-world. That new cosmology has a dually expanding temporality: it retroactively recodes humanity's role on earth since the eighteenth century and demands that we assume our place in the sediments of geological deep history, but it is also generative and outward-oriented, naming an epoch so that we might some-day become more conscious of ourselves and our world and maybe even *do* something about it. What the Anthropocene names is a new order of time consciousness. And what this issue proposes is that this new structure of consciousness has saturated and will continue to saturate the knowledge we produce in the twenty-first century, that this new mode of living and think-ing in the world is, perhaps, inescapable. All the essays in this collection are of this new cosmology of the Anthropocene, each digging into its own (inter) disciplinary tool kit to carve out its own space in that cosmology. Each of these essays is, therefore, in some direct or indirect way an inheritor of the genealogy of climate change knowledge. They participate in the contempo-rary epistemological order, but they have in them traces of how humans for centuries have come to know their warming world.

≡

Embedment, niche construction, ocean deserts, keeling curves, radiative forcing, ecoacoustics, fitness landscapes, orbital wobbles, particles per million, Anthropo-cene epigenetics, deep history, species, geological force, zoecentric, tipping points, feedforward and feedback loops—if Raymond Williams were writing *Keywords* today, these would be among the new and interruptive terms constituting the lexicon of critical knowledge in an age of climate change. They, of course, would not be the only terms. In Williams's (2015) own formulation they would number as a handful of the concepts and figures coconstituting an "emerging" constellation of thought, alongside a set of other still "domi-nant" and lingeringly "residual" epistemological frameworks organizing the landscape of contemporary critical consideration.

But is that actually the case? Certainly, it is true that this brief list rep-resents only a very partial sample of a much larger and constantly expanding catalog of the new keywords of the Anthropocene. But is it the case that the epistemological and ontological dispensation they coarticulate remains ame-nable to Williams's account of the constant, essentially timeless interplay of the dominant, the residual, and the emergent? This time around, is "emer-gence" different? Does the knowledge world of the Anthropocene (and the posthumanist materialism it is rapidly articulating) coexist with prior criti-cal dispensations (including the older humanist materialism Williams is often held to represent), modifying and altering those previous modes of thought, perhaps marking their transition from a once dominant to a now truly residual status, but nevertheless existing alongside them, inviting us to continue to draw something from these other, long-established forms of thought? Or is the epoch of the Anthropocene a true paradigm-shifting moment? As an epoch of thought, is it as radical in its break from the past as the geological leap from the Holocene?

And if so, how so?

In one or another form, that question runs throughout this collection of essays, not only as a challenge to fashion new forms of thought adequate to the moment but as a question of what to do with our prior modes of thinking, of what to preserve, or abandon, from the projects of critical knowledge before the moment (or, more precisely, before the moment of *awareness*) of climate change.

By one way of answer we turn to one of these new keywords: *feedback* (and, as Tomlinson's essay reminds us, we must also attend to its paired word *feedforward*). Whatever else it is, the epoch of the Anthropocene is an epoch of feedback loops: intensified, expanded, cascading. The fundamental story is familiar. The release of CO_2 into the atmosphere enters into a feedback loop with the planet's carbon cycle and the wobbles in the earth's multimillennial calendar of orbits around the sun, intensifying the effects of radiative forcing, warming the planet, and accelerating glacial and arctic melt, sea-level rise, desertification, coral degradation, and species loss, which in turn threaten global food chains, coastal communities around the planet, transcontinental water supplies, and countless else. As human actions become ever more forceful, the feedback loops of anthropogenic climate change threaten the future of human actors. But as demonstrated by this collection of essays, and the broader discourse of which it is a part, *feedback* denotes more than this. It denotes more than tragic irony. It denotes, potentially, a catastrophic flight beyond irony or any other human capacity to find any adequate rhetorical mode of representing "our" relationship to history: as, at the height of "our" planetary agency, "we" vanish as actors altogether— "we" annul "ourselves." This is the point Tomlinson makes in his analysis of the fundamental change in the nature of "niche construction" that has been wrought in the epoch of the Anthropocene. As he powerfully argues, human life has long been wrapped in a network of environmental feedback loops. We have evolved by adapting to environments that have evolved by adapting to human actions. In that way, we have constantly expanded the human niche, to the point of making that niche coterminous with the globe. What is different, now, is that a set of forces (he includes "astronomical dynamics, tectonic shifts, volcanism, [and] climate cycles") that have had a structuring impact on the viability and ordering of life but which we have not previously had the capacity to effect ("feedforward" elements) have now been drawn inside a massively expanded human "niche" and, thus, drawn into the cycle of *feedback* loops. As that occurs, as the full boundary between what is and is not within our feedback loops collapses, so too does the isolable "difference" of the human. We no longer have the capacity to stand in an ironic, tragic, or melancholic reflection on what "we" have wrought. Because "we" have vanished—into "zoe."

Or that is the implication: one which Tomlinson (and multiple other contributors) acknowledges, even while seeking some way of visualizing, or mobilizing, or, in Catherine Malabou's terms, producing "a kind of mental phenomenon" of this experience of becoming-force, being-zoe, living-as-planet-makers in order to act on it.

On this point—on what is apprehensible as a desire, or a will, or an urge toward a perspective on the Anthropocene that is somehow both within it and at some (perhaps purely imaginative) remove from it—the question of what to do with our other knowledge, our other epistemologies, returns to view. As it becomes dominant, what space does the knowledge-world of the Anthropocene have for other knowledge forms? Not just residual forms. Not only prior forms. But forms yet to be imagined, forms yet to emerge. Or is even asking that question the symptom of an illusion we can no longer afford? Is knowledge in the age of climate change a total and unitary field?

On those questions the notions of "feedback" and "feedforward" take on a second significance, one of deep importance to the contemporary organization of knowledge. As we gestured to earlier, James Chandler (2009) has observed that the nature of "interdisciplinary" knowledge (particularly in the humanities) has been in the midst of a major transformation in recent years. Key to that change, he has suggested, is a gradual outward expansion of conversations among the disciplines, as exchanges among relatively proximate fields (philosophy, psychology, and linguistics, to take one influential trio) have extended to conversations among the more distant disciplines: literature, geology, and evolutionary biology, to take examples from this collection. This is the transformation we earlier had in mind in referring to our moment as the moment of "interdisciplinarity 2.0." What we now want to ask concerns the nature of the feedback loops not just among "single" disciplines but among the broadly defined and long-standing container categories of the human, social, and natural sciences (what Castree calls the "three cultures") during this epoch of critical time. Tomlinson's account of "niche construction" is again helpful here, particularly if we begin with the fields of knowledge generally grouped under the human or humanistic sciences. From that perspective, Chandler's discussion of the transformation in the humanities can be seen as a process of gradually expanding niche construction by the humanities disciplines, as they enter into a set of ever-wider feedback loops not only with the relatively proximate interpretive social sciences but with quantitative disciplines and the sciences of living systems. At that point of the human sciences' massively expanded niche, what, though, happens to interdiscursive, transdisciplinary feedback loops? Do they persist, such that each field (literature, religion, evolutionary biology, philosophy, geology, music, ecology, etc.) continues to modify and coevolve the others even as each field is itself modifying and coevolving? Or is this a moment for *all* the sciences (even as we underline the question for the human sciences), one that is structurally analogous to the moment of the "human" as *it* is caught up in the intensifying loops of anthropogenic climate change? Have we, in a word, reached a tipping point in these exchanges after which the human sciences, like the human, vanish—to be replaced, suddenly but definitively, by the zoe-sciences? Is that the moment we are in?

Perhaps, and as the essays collected here variously stress, wrestling with that question is one of the primary challenges of grappling with the problem of knowledge in the time of climate change. As is another. If we *have* crossed that event horizon—that tipping point in which climate change has radically altered not only the planet, and life on it, but the order of knowledge itself—have we also finally come to the end of feedforward loops? Or is it possible to imagine a reinvention of feedforward possibilities, a reimagination and a new fabrication of some point of feedforward vitality from the conjoined perspectives of the human, social, and natural sciences? Can we fashion a perspective on the Anthropocene that is somehow both within it and at some (seeming) critical distance from it, a perspective through which we *can* "mobilize" our knowledge of having come to this point in the history of knowledge and, so, also mobilize the form that knowledge and the imagination can now take for the future of the planet?

═══

There is one last piece to this shifting epistemological architecture with which we want to conclude, one that nearly every essay in this collection addresses, however implicitly. It is one thing to *know* the kind of world climate change promises, but it is quite another to *feel* that promise, to viscerally experience it, to inhabit it psychologically. Slavoj Žižek (2010: 328) frames this paradox as a chasm "between knowledge and belief": "We *know* the (ecological) catastrophe is possible, probable even, yet we do not *believe* it will really happen." It is the difference between awareness (of facticity), on the one hand, and the *absorption* of that awareness, on the other, where that absorption manifests as a lived, felt, affective response. For Chakrabarty (2009: 221), this gap comes from our incapacity to "experience ourselves as a geological agent": the ungraspability of the modes of deep time and species thinking that this newfound "agency" demands. Our experience, the reasoning goes, refuses phenomenalization. We have arrived at an impasse of non-feeling and nonreflexivity, rendering us "structurally alien" to "our own apocalypse," as Malabou incisively puts it in this issue.

But despite this apparent foreclosure of affect, the question of feeling persists throughout this collection. What animates many of these essays are the ways in which climate change discourse has not simply reshaped the order of knowledge, but how it has done so in the service of this elusive figure of "feeling." The presumption being that "believing" or "feeling" is a necessary precursor to mass mobilization, to bringing on the radical shifts in habit, lifestyle, and worldview that could potentially limit the effects of climate change. Many of these articles reveal a certain desire to narrow this seemingly unthinkable gap between knowing and feeling or, at least, to begin to work through what makes it unthinkable. Malabou, for one, through her neurohistorical optic, makes an appeal for what she calls "new addictions," mental structures different from the ones that brought about this crisis in the first place. Willis Jenkins's proposal for alternative social practices of eating—new modes of commensality with landscapes and nonhumans—also seems in search of experience and feeling. And there is a related sense in Matthew Burtner's suggestion that ecoacoustic music might potentially allow us to "feel place" differently, where "songs of loss" would enable us to experience changing landscapes in novel ways. Yet another strand comes from the cluster of essays in this collection concerned with how best to represent and communicate the science of climate change to the public and to scholars in the human and social sciences. For several contributors, medium is pivotal to narrowing that gap: for Segal, it is long-form science-driven narrative; for David Buckland, Olivia Gray, and Lucy Wood of Cape Farewell, it's aesthetic experience; for Tomlinson, it's modeling and visualization. Finally, moving through all these considerations is how these essays rhetorically and formally *perform* this desire to make us feel, how they enact in language and form this attempt to convince us, as readers, to believe. Here Burtner's field journal excerpts stand out, as does Bently Spang's evocative personal account of textures, colors, places, and histories. Notable, too, are the invigorating formal experimentations in Cohen and Colebrook's essay. As they use the figure of the vortex to theorize a notion of the "critical" as a kind of infinitely valent politics in the time of climate change, Colebrook and Cohen enact that vortex in form and language, their prose gradually accelerating and surging toward a culmination of ecstatic Benjaminian wreckage, leaving the reader reeling, and, indeed, feeling. In all manner of ways, the essays here call on us to push against the numbness that is said to define us as a geological force, insisting that our experience can and must be phenomenalized, that we must search for the hidden movements and mutations that our being-in-this-warming-world comprises.

Like this quest for feeling and belief, this collection can only be a gesture toward the continually receding horizon of our changing world. The essays that follow represent an initial foray into the nexus of knowledge and climate change, just as the keywords, genealogies, and intellectual landscapes outlined here are the initial strokes in a vastly larger and evolving picture. However, these essays do, we think, point toward the coming expansiveness of knowledge production. The exigency of our melting, rising, and vanishing world will only continue to seep into intellectual and artistic disciplines, to deepen the interconnections among the human, social, and natural sciences, to create new vocabularies and languages, to instigate new modes of representation and dissemination. We will also likely witness a recoding in hindsight of past knowledges, those that came before the awareness of climate change, pulling them into the fray of the interdisciplinary feedbacks that will continue to define future knowledge production. Ever-expanding fields of knowledge, coevolving, overlapping, merging, and switching courses, feeding back and forth and back and forth. In this epoch when the human is everything and nothing, unique and precariously ordinary, we might wait and see if knowledge becomes a singular system in perpetual expansion, with infinite epistemological monads shooting from one disparate node to another within a larger constellation we might call, for now at least, the zoe-sciences and geoethics of the earth.

References

Abarbanel, Albert, and Thorp McClusky. 1950. "Is the World Getting Warmer?" *Saturday Evening Post*, July 1.

Adams, John Luther. 2014. *Become Ocean*. Seattle Symphony, conducted by Ludovic Morlot. Cantaloupe CA-21101. Compact disc.

Besel, Richard D. 2013. "Accommodating Climate Change Science: James Hansen and the Rhetorical/Political Emergence of Global Warming." *Science in Context* 26, no. 1: 137–52.

Bonneuil, Christophe, and Jean-Baptist Fressoz. 2016. *The Shock of the Anthropocene: The Earth, History, and Us.* Translated by David Fernbach. London: Verso.

Callendar, Guy. 1939. "The Composition of the Atmosphere through the Ages." *Meteorological Magazine* 74, no. 878: 33–39.

Chakrabarty, Dipesh. 2009. "The Climate of History: Four Theses." *Critical Inquiry* 35, no. 2: 197–222.

Chandler, James. 2009. "Introduction: Doctrines, Disciplines, Discourses, Departments." In "The Fate of Disciplines," edited by James Chandler and Arnold I. Davidson. Special issue, *Critical Inquiry* 35, no. 4: 729–46.

Crutzen, Paul, and Eugene Stoermer. 2000. "The 'Anthropocene.'" *Global Change Newsletter,* no. 41: 17–18.

Fleming, James. 1998. *Historical Perspectives on Climate Change.* New York: Oxford University Press.

Francis. 2015. *Laudato Si'.* w2.vatican.va/content/francesco/en/encyclicals/documents/papa -francesco_20150524_enciclica-laudato-si.html.

Ghosh, Amitav. 2004. *The Hungry Tide.* London: HarperCollins.

IICCS (International Islamic Climate Change Symposium). 2015. "Islamic Declaration on Global Climate Change." islamicclimatedeclaration.org/islamic-declaration-on-global -climate-change.

Klein, Naomi. 2014. *This Changes Everything: Capitalism vs. the Climate.* New York: Simon and Schuster.

Kolbert, Elizabeth. 2014. *The Sixth Extinction: An Unnatural History.* New York: Holt.

Le Guin, Ursula. 1971. *The Lathe of Heaven.* New York: Avon Books.

Marsh, George Perkins. 1847. "Address to the Agricultural Society of Rutland County." cdi.uvm.edu/collections/item/pubagsocaddr (accessed April 27, 2016).

McKibben, Bill. 2005. "What the Warming World Needs Now Is Art, Sweet Art." *Grist,* April 22. grist.org/article/mckibben-imagine.

McKibben, Bill. 2009. "Four Years after My Pleading Essay, Climate Art Is Hot." *Grist,* August 6. grist.org/article/2009-08-05-essay-climate-art-update-bill-mckibben.

Nixon, Rob. 2013. *Slow Violence and the Environmentalism of the Poor.* Cambridge, MA: Harvard University Press.

Okorafor, Nnedi. 2015. *The Book of Phoenix.* New York: DAW Books.

Shabecoff, Philip. 1988. "Global Warming Has Begun, Expert Tells Senate." *New York Times,* June 24. www.nytimes.com/1988/06/24/us/global-warming-has-begun-expert-tells -senate.html.

Star. 1799. "Hornblower v. Boulton and Watt." January 26.

Time. 1939. "Warmer World." January 2.

United Nations. 2015. "Conference of Parties: Twenty-First Session; Adoption of the Paris Agreement." December 12. unfccc.int/resource/docs/2015/cop21/eng/l09r01.pdf.

Weizman, Eyal, and Fazal Sheikh. 2015. *The Conflict Shoreline: Colonialism as Climate Change in the Negev Desert.* Göttingen, Germany: Steidl.

Williams, Raymond. 2015. *Keywords: A Vocabulary of Culture and Society.* New ed. New York: Oxford University Press.

Žižek, Slavoj. 2010. *Living in the End Times.* New York: Verso.

Gary Tomlinson

Two Deep-Historical Models of Climate Crisis

What do humanists have to offer in the ongoing discussion of anthropogenic climate change or the Anthropocene? The science is not ours but viewed at a distance. Meanwhile, pragmatic action is seldom driven by humanist prose, and only in the rarest of cases are humanities professors placed so as to have much impact on climate policy. Our tendency in this situation—it is not the only one where this happens—is to retreat to the humanist comfort zones of cultural theory, critique, or ethical analysis. Even at its best, this represents a move back behind the walls that today separate scholarly humanism from mainstream discourse on important societal issues.

Can we offer more? Dipesh Chakrabarty, a leading humanist participant in the Anthropocene discussion, has pointed to some possibilities. Ethical and critical analysis certainly figures in his work, but it takes a backseat to his central offering: a historiographic meditation with implications for reconceiving our future. The historical perspective is required because, for Chakrabarty, the central problematic of the Anthropocene involves reconciling events that move on vastly different timescales. The Great Acceleration in human population growth and use of fossil fuels

The South Atlantic Quarterly 116:1, January 2017
DOI 10.1215/00382876-3749282   © 2017 Duke University Press

starting after World War II, the Industrial Revolution from the late eighteenth century, five hundred years of Europe-led colonization and globalization, and even recorded human histories of the past several millennia are all dwarfed by the two-hundred-thousand-year career of *Homo sapiens*—itself dwarfed by the histories of the earth's biological and geophysical systems. Chakrabarty describes the rapprochement of these histories as a task of *visualization*, the achievement of a dual-focus view that could at once take in a recent foreground and a deep background. Across the past decade he has employed different conceptual tools to describe this visualization.

In "The Climate of History: Four Theses," an essay that became an instant classic, Chakrabarty (2009) laid down the challenge of the Anthropocene to conventional historical methods that have taken the human alone for their concern. How will an expanded historical project located at the divide between natural and human histories revise our narratives of the recent human developments—the explosive expansion of the technosphere, its turn to fossil fuels, and the burgeoning of global capital—that have made us into geological agents? How will deep histories of universal human experience manage to discern the fine grain of local issues, especially the inequalities of distribution and use of resources so much magnified by industrial modernity? Local, political histories of human difference "as an effect of power" are inadequate to answer these questions (221), and a broad "species thinking" broaching the "boundary parameters of human existence" seems to be the only avenue along which we can take full measure of the peril posed by climate change (217–18). We are left with the concept of *species* itself, always fluid and elusive across long historical spans, as "the name of a placeholder for an emergent, new universal history of humans" in the epoch of the Anthropocene (221).

In the second moment I want to single out, "Climate and Capital: On Conjoined Histories," Chakrabarty (2014) examined more closely the terms of this universal history, in particular its "enjambment" of deep and recent chronologies. He conceived this not as an Annales-like conjuncture—Braudelian *longues durées* rarely come close to species thinking—but instead as a set of supplementary aporias. He specified three conceptual rifts that open as we ponder the intersection of human and transhuman timescales. We face, first, the incapacity of the familiar probabilistic tools of global capital (such as actuarial tables or cost-benefit analyses) to measure uncertainties of climate change of the sort now evidenced in the deep-historical record, which include abrupt, nonlinear shifts at thresholds, irreversibilities beyond them, and runaway feedback. Second, our customary anthropocentrism is incommensurable to a nonhuman-centered thought that could awaken us to "the rude shock of the planet's otherness" (23) (a thought that may be unthinkable, Chakrabarty concedes). And, third, we confront the gulf between the commonalities of our planetary existence and the everyday experience of human difference and division. This gulf was neatly captured in the crux of the 1997 Kyoto Protocol, with its acknowledgment that responsibilities for climate change today are "common but differentiated" across humanity.

The third moment of Chakrabarty's meditation (forthcoming) came in his Tanner Lectures at Yale University, where he described what the human commonality signaled in the Kyoto crux might look like in the Anthropocene. In the event, it looks not so different from the "epochal consciousness" that Karl Jaspers described in the 1950s in the face of the threat of nuclear annihilation. Epochal consciousness is a kind of undivided, non-"departmental" awareness that points toward our shared dwelling, our *common*, even as it flies high over local concerns and actions. Epochal consciousness is not political consciousness, then, but something broader and deeper. In the Anthropocene, Chakrabarty argues, it functions to frame dichotomies universally posed by the new danger. It connects our species to all others in a "zoecentric" view of the planet's capacity to sustain life, opposing more familiar "homocentric" narratives of the past half millennium of globalization and technologization. Within the sphere of the human, it challenges our view of the *homo-* named in that familiar centrism with an *anthropos* that configures the totality of our impact, "collective and unintended," on the planetary system.

It is finally the tension of this epochal consciousness that rivets Chakrabarty and culminates his historiographic meditation. The Tanner Lectures do not resolve the tension so much as carry it down to the level of the individual's Anthropocenic experience. Here Chakrabarty points to a Heideggerian *thrownness*, an experience of our dwelling in the world that can bring us to "fall into deep history," sensing the divergent historical scales brought to consciousness by our present-day conditions. For Martin Heidegger a foundational mood or attunement (*Grundstimmung*) reveals our being in the world more fundamentally than conceptual thought; for Chakrabarty it is a new such attunement that our climate crisis enables us to experience and share. The task had all along been, Chakrabarty (forthcoming) writes, that of "making available to human experience a cascade of events that unfold on multiple scales, many of them *in*human." He urges us to appreciate that "the crisis of climate change, by throwing us into the inhuman timelines of life and geology, also takes us away from the homocentrism that divides us." The inhuman scale of the crisis stimulates a dawning of species and even transspecies thinking.

≡

I have scarcely done justice to the richness of Chakrabarty's historiographic meditation, but I have needed to outline it because I want to build on it using a set of tools different from his. How might we advance his conviction that a certain exercise of historical thought can bring home an experience of the deep history behind anthropogenic climate change? We require conceptual tools that can help to *mobilize* this experience, but for this the usual historical means of the literature on the Anthropocene seem unhelpful, even working against mobility. The cautionary comparisons ("Millions of years ago the planet Venus underwent a runaway greenhouse event, and today temperatures on the surface melt lead"); the statistical alarms ("The rate of species extinction today is estimated to be x; this rivals the rate at the K-T extinction event that killed off the dinosaurs"); the implicit assimilations of human to natural lethality ("The climate changes brought about by the Toba super-eruption seventy-five thousand years ago decreased the population of *Homo sapiens* to a few thousand mating pairs")—these kinds of historical pictures sit rooted on the nonhuman side of the old divide of natural and human history. They are spectacular, *sublime* indexes, but they do little to narrow the distance by which they outreach human measures and which defines their sublimity. Such indexes are today a favorite gambit of "big" history, promulgated so characteristically by it that it is tempting to give them a name: Big-History Sublime. In this, big history contrasts with "deep" history, intent on discerning more local, if still large, continuities (cf. Christian 2004 and Smail 2008). Sublime indexes stand apart from experience—awesome, static, and direly fascinating, like mortality statistics from a distant disaster ("ten thousand dead") or measurements of a supernova ("a billion times brighter than our sun").

To mobilize experience we need instead tools that reveal the *movement* of the processes by which we have come to our present peril and that display it in a way that connects deep to short-range histories. Here scientific models can help, and I will employ two derived from evolutionary biology. I have refashioned these so that they incorporate humanist, historical understandings of the actions and capacities of human sociality and culture. In their customary scientific, quantitative forms the models are hemmed in by the limiting assumptions necessary to bring them within the range of computational capacity, which is almost always constrained by a "dimensionality," a range of factors and functions, lower than that of the systems represented. In nudging the models away from neopositivist scientific explanation and toward historical understanding, I have loosened them in the direction of qualitative description. The sacrifice of precision aids the work of visualization by rendering more clearly the processual change they represent.

=====

The first model I offer represents the machinic processes of evolution, specifically the processes of "niche construction" basic to today's conceptions of the interactions of organisms in ecosystems. By extrapolating these interactions across evolutionary timescales, as many scientists have done, and then understanding the special functioning in them of prehuman and ultimately human cultures (fewer have tried this), we can configure them as a deep human history. The abstract nature of this model spotlights both the long continuities of that history and the turn it has recently, abruptly taken *within* those continuities.

In gauging the evolutionary fitness of organisms, it does not suffice to consider them against a static environment, as if varying life-forms were supplicants knocking at the ecological gates for admittance or extinction. The changeable nature of the selective environment also needs to be taken into account. Moreover, this environmental alterability needs to be understood in part as a function of changes brought about by the evolving organisms themselves. In other words: organisms occupy an ecological niche, but in doing so they alter their niche in ways that in turn alter the selective situation in which their fitness will be determined. This is the fundamental feedback cycle of niche construction, and we can assume that it operates in the evolution of all organisms (Odling-Smee, Laland, and Feldman 2003).

In the niche construction of a given organism or group of organisms, we can assume also that some of its traits determine more powerfully than others its alterations of its environment. The earliest photosynthetic bacteria, for example, lived in an atmosphere with no persisting free oxygen. Their niche-construction no doubt comprised many aspects of their lifeways, but their production of oxygen became its most telling aspect more than two billion years ago and, in the so-called Great Oxygenation Event, brought the composition of the earth's atmosphere close to the one that sustains most life today.

A second example involves *cultural* animals, that is, animals that learn behaviors through social interaction and pass them on to subsequent generations. This is a broad and nonanthropocentric definition of culture, and using it we can think of many mammals and birds, and perhaps even species from other groups, as cultural. For all of them, culture becomes a force in niche construction, but it looms largest among hominins—the group including modern humans and their closest extinct relatives. Early tool-making cultures among hominins no doubt enabled them to change their environments in novel ways. Much later, humans' hunting to extinction of Upper Pleistocene megafauna, from Australia to the Americas, was one outcome of this technocultural niche construction.

In each of these examples the changing nature of the environment exerted changing feedback effects. An atmosphere with growing oxygen levels eventually transformed through selective processes the bacteria that created it as well as other organisms. The lives of ancient humans, similarly, needed to adapt to new patterns once megafauna grew scarce, and these new patterns had long-term selective effects and evolutionary consequences. The second of these examples is systematically identical to the first except in its inclusion of culture in the dynamic of niche construction. It instances not biological evolution but *biocultural* evolution, the tangling of biology and culture in the selective histories of all cultural animals (Boyd and Richerson 1985; Richerson and Boyd 2005).

However widely we extend our definition of culture, it is clear that already by two million years ago the hominin lineage had outstripped all other animals in the complexity of the bodies of cultural materials transmitted across generations (Sterelny 2012). Because of that, our lineage has been unique in the power its cultures have exerted to point the direction of niche construction. As this power increased, the scope of the aspects of the environment affected by hominin niche construction expanded. Early humans using stone-tipped spears to kill mammoths one at a time altered their niche to one degree; later humans using fire to drive herds of mammoths over cliffs enlarged their environmental impact through culture.

Across millions of years of biocultural evolution and the expanding role of culture, certain systems remained *outside* the feedback cycles of hominin niche construction. Astronomical dynamics, tectonic shifts, volcanism, climate cycles, and other such forces were in essence untouched by human culture and behavior (or if touched, touched in a vanishingly small degree). In the language of systems theory, all these forces were in effect *feedforward* elements: external controls that "set" the feedback cycles from without, affecting the elements within them while remaining unaffected by the feedback themselves. Sudden fluctuations in Upper Pleistocene global temperatures, for example, changed human niches but were effectively untouched by humans' changed behaviors in response to them. The climate changes stood outside the mutual alterations brought about more locally by the interactions of humans with their niches.

As the scope of human niche construction expanded, the pace of anthropogenic change eventually accelerated. The newest evidence suggests few revolutionary demarcations in this process. The genetic engineering of many different plants through thousands of years of cultivation was not begun from scratch at the advent of the Holocene, but reaches back to countless less systematic behaviors in the late Pleistocene (Klein 2009; Shryock and Smail 2011). The harvesting of fish and shellfish grew more organized and effective across the late Upper Paleolithic period, but it looks far back into the Middle Paleolithic, well over one hundred thousand years, and such examples of the gradual emergence of humans' modern niche-constructing behaviors could be multiplied (McBrearty and Brooks 2000). Even if gradual, however, the expansion of the scope and speeding up of the pace of human niche construction ultimately had dramatic effects. The clear-cutting of most of the forests of Europe over the past millennium, for example, exerted a collective effect on the biosphere larger than any regional population of Paleolithic peoples could have brought about. And the Anthropocene is the current endpoint of this expansion, the newest upturn in the scope and pace of human niche construction.

The Anthropocene is the point at which human ingenuity and impact have enlarged our niche construction not merely to have a global reach but to encompass planetary systems themselves. But while this is true, oft remarked, and in itself dramatic, focusing on it can obscure a deeper truth brought home by the niche-construction model. The Anthropocene marks the surpassing of a threshold in the mechanisms of niche construction. It registers a rearrangement in which *systems that had always acted as feedforward elements from outside human niche construction have been converted into feedback elements within it.* This is what it means to think of humans as a geological force; it is what brings us face-to-face with Chakrabarty's "boundary parameters of human existence." There is nothing new in the machinic nature of the constructive interactions by which humans inhabit their environments, which connect us not merely to our hominin ancestors but to ancient photosynthetic bacteria and all the life-forms in between. The novelty lies in a new combination of an encompassing *scope* attained by these interactions and a resulting *shift* in their systemic relations.

This approximate visualization of our niche-constructive history refutes the arguments of those who regard present-day climate change as no different from the many climate fluctuations in our deep past. Such claims are at once exactly right and perniciously wrong. Earlier climate changes exerted feedforward impacts; human niches were altered, humans usually struggled to cope with the changes, but the system causing the changes was untouched by their struggles. Now we have incorporated that system into the evolutionary dynamic *we* make. If the niche-constructive model helps us to connect to our deep history, at the same time it offers this connection as an experience of something more than small-increment change and qualitative sameness. The experience encounters disruptions at the heart of long continuities: punctuations that mark qualitative differences within the sameness and that reveal, in the new systemic arrangement of the Anthropocene, a difference of the difference.

Is the evolutionary fitness of *Homo sapiens* changing in the Anthropocene? To pose the question is to make a deep-historical and zoecentric move, for it asks us to widen our focus to take in our species' history and recognize the kinship between our adaptive dynamics and those of all the other organisms with which we share the planet. We can visualize this move using the second model I want to describe.

Since the 1930s, which saw the advent of the so-called "modern synthesis" of evolutionary theory and population genetics, ecologists and evolutionary biologists have often pictured fitness by means of a model known as a "fitness landscape" or "adaptive landscape." The model has taken many forms; one of the commonest is a three-dimensional graph of the sort pictured in figure 1. Here the x and y axes along the base plot the frequency of two variants in a population of organisms; they can be genes, differing versions of the same gene (*alleles*), phenotypic traits, or even more general patterns of behavior. The vertical z axis plots increasing fitness. The resulting contours, forming the "landscape" in question, do not represent any real, physical terrain—it is important to avoid this easy confusion—but plot the peaks and valleys of changing fitness against changing features of the organisms in question.

Some limitations of adaptive landscape modeling are clear enough even from this example (for a general review, see Pigliucci and Kaplan 2006). In the first place it involves a drastic simplification of the relation between fitness and genotype or phenotype—this is the problem of low dimensionality mentioned before. The simplification is necessary to make the model tractable, but it means that the complexity of real situations of adaptive fitness, in real ecosystems, is bound to escape. A second shortcom-

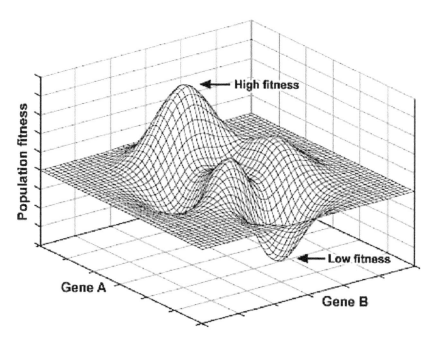

Figure 1. A two-gene fitness landscape, with gene frequencies plotted on the horizontal (*x* and *y*) axes, resulting fitness on the vertical (*z*) axis. Credit: University of California Museum of Paleontology's Understanding Evolution (evolution.berkeley.edu/)

ing is especially relevant here: most adaptive landscape modeling has no way of incorporating the alterability of selective environments (as opposed to organisms in them), even if its *x* and *y* axes plot change against time. That is a big limitation, since all environments for life are systems in flux. It is particularly debilitating in the face of niche construction and its environment-changing feedback circuits.

In spite of such limitations, adaptive landscape modeling has remained popular and has been revised and rehabilitated time and again (Kauffman 1993; Gavrilets 2004, 2010; McGhee 2007). Its appeal is not surprising, since even some of the most mathematically inclined of evolutionary biologists concede that it facilitates an "intuitive metaphorical visualizing" of evolutionary dynamics (Gavrilets 2010: 46). In this catalyzing of intuition, adaptive landscape modeling is an opportune place to seek another scientifically grounded visualization of our deep history and its culmination in our present crisis.

The peaks of figure 1 represent high points of fitness, its valleys low points; the steepness of the inclines represents the abruptness of fitness change as a function of the traits plotted on the x and y axes. Imagine that the x axis plots the size of webs spun by a group of closely related spiders, and y the toxicity of the poisons they use to subdue prey caught in them. What emerges is a snapshot of fitness as it relates to these two phenotypic traits. We might foresee that it would show the landscape sloping up toward the corner of the cube representing spiders with both large webs and high toxicity, but it could also register more complex patterns. The cost to the spiders of spinning larger webs, for example, might introduce a less steep gradient or even open a valley as web size moved beyond some cost/benefit tipping point.

Imagine now graphing cultural traits of ancient hominins. For our distant ancestors, let x represent the overall complexity of the tool technologies they practiced, y the effectiveness of their social skills in transmitting these technologies. These aspects are necessarily measured more approximately than frequencies of genes or even the average size of spiderwebs in an ecosystem. Nevertheless, data for such measurements have been amassed by archaeologists (Klein 2009; Mellars et al. 2007). And narratives of the change in these aspects of hominin cultures have been constructed by deep historians (Gamble 1999, 2007). These suggest a general increase, at a coarse enough scale, across tens or hundreds of millennia, in both the complexity of tools and effectiveness of pedagogy; so increase along the x and y axes loosely tracks change in time also. We have in effect introduced deep history to the graph. We can picture the fitness slope turning upward across time, and were we to extend the x and y axes to the present (i.e., toward the greatest tool complexity and greatest effectiveness of transmission of techniques), the accelerating pace of technocultural achievement would result in a very steep slope.

Exercising now some multidimensional imagination and moving beyond the pictorial limitations of figure 1, think of superimposing this technocultural, historical graph on a map of the ecosystems inhabited by humans. This introduces real environments to the graph, and it now simultaneously moves through millennia (with increasing x and y values) and advances across the world (with human expansion into new territories). What might emerge is a new contour registering the growing power of our technoculture to override the disadvantages inhospitable habitats might otherwise pose to our biological makeup. It would take the shape of a broad fitness *plateau* rather than a peak, representing the universally high level of fitness that complex culture has granted our species, irrespective of habitat.

What we have graphed, in our imaginary, hyperdimensional model, is *Homo sapiens*'s increasing technofitness through time against our expanding niche—with the niche coming, finally, to comprise the whole of the earth's land mass, excepting Antarctica. But there is a problem: we have not yet corrected for a fundamental limitation of the graph, its omission of the changes inevitable in any environment, whether by niche construction or other forces. Return for a moment to the simpler example of spiders, and suppose that some bird or bat population, newly introduced to the local ecosystem, depleted the population of flying insects; or suppose that a new fungal invader killed off the species of plants from which the spiders suspended their webs. The fitness won across evolutionary time through selection for webs and poison would be compromised; the adaptive landscape would be altered, its peak losing height. In a severe, abrupt alteration of the niche, fitness might collapse altogether and, in the graph, the peak disappear. The peak would have become, in a changing niche, a "fitness trap." The trapped spiders, maladapted to the new environment, would colonize another nearby niche or face extinction.

Now return to our human graph. The panhuman fitness plateau we have imagined was achieved long ago, in general outline; the record of human occupation of the six habitable continents precedes the Holocene, reaching back tens of thousands of years. The plateau is not perfectly flat but has its own smaller fitness peaks rising up from it. They reflect the homocentric inequalities in the distribution of technological benefits—the "differentiated"-ness underscored in the Kyoto Protocol—and they are particularly prominent in the most recent portion of the graph. In general the plateau, subpeaks and all, is supported by a niche. This is changeable, like all niches, but shows two special features: its global reach and the fact that it has been constructed to a far greater extent than most others by a single species.

And here, finally, the graph portrays the crisis we face. Today the very technological forces that once steepened the sides of the plateau and flattened its top are quickly undermining the niche that supports it. The plateau we have achieved shows signs of turning into our own fitness trap. It is a part of Chakrabarty's argument that we cannot gain a full view of this process, but partial measures of it are all around us (Kolbert 2014). And, despite the niche-*re*constructive fantasies of geoengineers, it seems unlikely that the broad extent of its tableland, once undermined, will be humanly or humanely restored. Much more likely will be a patchwork of new fitness peaks and valleys representing exacerbated inequities and the fragmentation of the global niche. And what of the possibility of an even more catastrophic collapse of the plateau—for instance a quicker runaway greenhouse effect than current means enable us to predict? Inhabiting a niche that is coterminous with the planet, where will we web makers move?

The model here of the fitness our technoculture has granted us is ambivalent, like the niche-construction model. It portrays a punctuation in a continuity, an anomaly that has emerged from ubiquitous processes with long, continuous histories. The *continuity*, the zoecentric congruency of our role with those of other life-forms, is easy enough to exemplify. (The Great Oxygenation Event beginning more than two billion years ago is also known as the Oxygen Catastrophe, since the atmospheric change brought about by photosynthetic bacteria is thought to have led to a mass extinction of the anaerobic organisms that had evolved up to that time.) The *anomaly* consists in the fact that ours is the first catastrophe brought about by cultural niche construction—a construction, that is, that could have known better.

Chakrabarty's advocacy of species thinking and a zoecentric perspective in approaching climate change has had its critics. The usual charge is that opening the focus so wide renders invisible the urgent politics of inequity among humans. There is no doubt of the inequities, on the one hand, or of the urgent need for greater balance in the distribution of resources, on the other; no doubt, further, that the politics of global capital is a place to pursue that need. Yet it seems ever clearer that this is a different conversation than the one we are called upon to join in the face of Anthropocenic perils. Here humanistic debate over the critique of capital can seem a misdirected activism, the equivalent of rearranging the chairs on deck in the hope that doing so will resteer the ship and so avoid collision.

Such a gesture speaks to the difficulty of imagining the problem, with its vastly disparate scales: shallow and deep histories, human life and all life, local ecologies and planetary dynamics. The rough-and-ready models I have described are no answer to this challenge, but they do point toward the kinds of measures that can reshape our educative mission so that it can expand our imaginative reach. And if the expansion of the human imagination—now faced with the imperative to encompass transhuman and inhuman dimensions—is not a productive activism for humanist scholars, it is unclear to me what can be.

Note

I am grateful to Juliet Fleming and Dipesh Chakrabarty for their reading of and advice on this essay and to Ian Baucom for his invitation to participate in this issue.

References

Boyd, Robert, and Peter J. Richerson. 1985. *Culture and the Evolutionary Process*. Chicago: University of Chicago Press.

Chakrabarty, Dipesh. 2009. "The Climate of History: Four Theses." *Critical Inquiry* 35, no. 2: 197–222.

Chakrabarty, Dipesh. 2014. "Climate and Capital: On Conjoined Histories." *Critical Inquiry* 41, no. 1: 1–23.

Chakrabarty, Dipesh. Forthcoming. "The Human Condition of the Anthropocene." In *Tanner Lectures on Human Values, Yale University*. Salt Lake City: University of Utah Press. tannerlectures.utah.edu/lecture-library.php.

Christian, David. 2004. *Maps of Time: An Introduction to Big History*. Berkeley: University of California Press.

Gamble, Clive. 1999. *The Palaeolithic Societies of Europe*. Cambridge: Cambridge University Press.

Gamble, Clive. 2007. *Origins and Revolutions: Human Identity in Earliest Prehistory*. Cambridge: Cambridge University Press.

Gavrilets, Sergey. 2004. *Fitness Landscapes and the Origin of Species*. Princeton, NJ: Princeton University Press.

Gavrilets, Sergey. 2010. "High-Dimensional Fitness Landscapes and Speciation." In *Evolution: The Extended Synthesis*, edited by Massimo Pigliucci and Gerd B. Müller, 45–80. Cambridge, MA: MIT Press.

Kauffman, Stuart A. 1993. *The Origins of Order: Self-Organization and Selection in Evolution*. New York: Oxford University Press.

Klein, Richard G. 2009. *The Human Career: Human Biological and Cultural Origins*. Chicago: University of Chicago Press.

Kolbert, Elizabeth. 2014. *The Sixth Extinction: An Unnatural History*. New York: Holt.

McBrearty, Sally, and Alison S. Brooks. 2000. "The Revolution That Wasn't: A New Interpretation of the Origin of Modern Human Behavior." *Journal of Human Evolution* 39, no. 5: 453–563.

McGhee, George. 2007. *The Geometry of Evolution: Adaptive Landscapes and Theoretical Morphospaces*. Cambridge: Cambridge University Press.

Mellars, Paul, et al., eds. 2007. *Rethinking the Human Revolution: New Behavioural and Biological Perspectives on the Origin and Dispersal of Modern Humans*. Cambridge, UK: McDonald Institute for Archaeological Research.

Odling-Smee, F. John, Kevin N. Laland, and Marcus W. Feldman. 2003. *Niche Construction: The Neglected Process in Evolution*. Princeton, NJ: Princeton University Press.

Pigliucci, Massimo, and Jonathan Kaplan. 2006. *Making Sense of Evolution: The Conceptual Foundations of Evolutionary Biology*. Chicago: University of Chicago Press.

Richerson, Peter J., and Robert Boyd. 2005. *Not by Genes Alone: How Culture Transformed Human Evolution*. Chicago: University of Chicago Press.

Shryock, Andrew, and Daniel Lord Smail. 2011. *Deep History: The Architecture of Past and Present*. Berkeley: University of California Press.

Smail, Daniel Lord. 2008. *On Deep History and the Brain*. Berkeley: University of California Press.

Sterelny, Kim. 2012. *The Evolved Apprentice: How Evolution Made Humans Unique*. Cambridge, MA: MIT Press.

Bently Spang

On Fire

December 18, 2012, 4:32 p.m., eastern side of
the Northern Cheyenne Reservation five miles
northwest of Ashland, Montana. It's been almost
six months since the 250,000-acre Ash Creek fire,
born on our reservation, roared across this land
like Manifest Destiny. The changing climate all
around us in the months leading up to the fire
warned of its coming. Too wet the year before
and too dry this year, it was a formula for disaster
in any part of the world. I see the memory of it
all around me in the burnt stubble and charred
stands of trees. On June 25, a day or so after the
fire started and the day it blew up, it consumed my
parents' thirty-five-year-old ranch house, sparing
their lives and the lives of my brother, his wife, my
great niece and nephew, my son, and a thousand
or so others in the area—but just barely. I know
fire renews and rejuvenates, but I learned with this
fire that, if we are unprepared, it can also take
much more than it gives.

I'm on the Ashland Flats just above Stebbins Creek. I'm surrounded by big, wide-open
space and am driving on a dirt road across the
flats on my dad's land that he leases from the
tribe. I'm by myself, in my dad's red ranch truck,
a 1990-something Chevy pickup that will last

The South Atlantic Quarterly 116:1, January 2017
DOI 10.1215/00382876-3749293   © 2017 Duke University Press

forever. To my left, eight miles away, is the Divide, a forty-five-mile-long high ridge that splits my reservation in half. To my right, five miles away, is the Tongue River, the eastern boundary of the reservation. It's late afternoon on this chilly winter's day, and I just came from feeding thirty horses at our burned-out ranch five miles northeast of here. It's been my daily routine for a couple of months and will continue until the spring grass comes. Our horses survived the fire, but the grass didn't, so we're feeding them every day, struggling to buy hay and keep them alive just like everyone else with animals and no grass here in southeastern Montana.

I stop on the edge of the flat above Stebbins Creek. There's a stand of young, burnt Ponderosa pine trees one hundred yards below me. They'll do just fine. We call these young trees Jack pines, and they fill a small draw on the edge of the flats that spills into the mile-wide Stebbins Creek drainage below it. I get out of the truck, go around to the passenger side, and open the door. On the seat is my camera rig, a homemade chest cam setup involving a high definition action cam jerry-rigged to several nylon straps taken from a couple of old duffle bags. I strap the makeshift unit on my chest over my winter coat and center the camera over my sternum. I grab my 10" x 14$^1/_8$" pad of heavyweight watercolor paper, close the door, turn the camera on, and head down the hill toward the stand of young trees. On the way, I'm planning my approach. This piece has grown out of my experience with the fire and its aftermath. It's been trapped in my head for some time now, and it's time to let it out. As I've thought about this for the last several months, my plan has become simply to facilitate the voice of the trees—to help them tell their story of the fire.

I walk in among the stand of young, burnt trees, and I'm immersed in tangled black and orange. The dead, orange needles of the young Ponderosa pine cling to the tips of some of the branches but mostly litter the ground. A complex carpet of orange on black over flat ground reaches from burnt tree to burnt tree, with no evidence of the plants my people have come to know so well. Nowhere to be seen are the medicinal, edible, or spiritual plants I've been taught to look for every year by my elders: Bill Tallbull, my uncle Leo, and my grandma Jenny, to name but a few. It's an eerie landscape, stark, unsettling, and melancholy. With few needles left, the trees make almost no noise as the wind pushes through them.

I choose a tree that feels right, whose proportions somehow match my own. The tree I pick is about twenty feet tall with a ten-inch-wide trunk. I get up close and examine the tree. The burnt bark of the tree is thick and bumpy but also shiny and jewel-like, and I can see traces of the jigsaw-puzzle-like characteristic of the un-burnt Ponderosa bark still present. I open my draw-

Figure 1. *On Fire, Tree Study #4,* 2014, Bently Spang, drawing and single-channel video installation, drawing 10" x 14 ^{1}/$_8$"

ing pad, flip to a blank page, and check to make sure my chest cam is on. Grabbing the sketchbook, I place one hand on either side of it as if it were a steering wheel, at 9 o'clock and 3 o'clock, and face the blank page away from me toward the tree. I tentatively push the paper against the burnt trunk of the tree, moving it slowly sideways several times at an angle as I get my bearings. The paper glides smoothly over the trunk. Since it's my first attempt, I can't resist examining the drawing early. This is the only time I will review the drawing mid-performance (and mid-video documentation). From here on I will give myself over to the action completely and view the drawing only when it's finished. I turn the drawing pad over to look at the result and I'm stunned. With just a few movements I can already see the tree's story of the fire, see the flames swirling, and feel the heat. The marks are sublime (see, e.g., figure 1). Immediately, I see that their power emanates from my powerlessness, exponentially. The more I facilitate and the less I orchestrate, the truer the story will be.

I press paper to tree again and continue. I work hard to clear my mind and let the tree control the marks. I focus on what's in my zone of access, what I can physically reach. I become conscious of my movements, the rhythm they produce, and slowly understand that we're locked in a dance

Figure 2. *On Fire*, video still not in installation, 2014, Bently Spang, drawing and single-channel video installation

and the tree is leading. My guiding mantra evolves into "follow the tree's contours just as they are and for as long as physically possible, and then the action will be done." I circle the tree, rubbing the paper on every available surface. Ash is in my mouth and eyes, and the branches of neighboring trees scratch at my face and arms as I push the drawing pad over the surface of the tree. My arms ache, fingers are cold and numb, and my glasses have fogged up. I shut off the chest cam and it's done. I examine the final drawing. The finished story is evident and clear: complete. I'm spent but elated. I tear this drawing from the spiral keeper of the drawing pad and drop it on the ground face up. It almost disappears as it hits the ground. I look at the drawing turning my head slightly, and I see that the heavyweight watercolor paper was the right choice. In this angle of the light I can see deep, embossed scratches in the paper. A lesser paper would have been destroyed from contact with the sharp edges of broken branches. I place a medium-sized rock on the page to stop the wind from taking this one back.

I create three more drawings in that first outing and finish just before the sun goes down. Rocks hold down all the drawings (see figure 2). I photograph the grouping and stand back to consider them. Each one is different, but all use the same language. These are young trees I would have come to know eventually, like the mature trees with thick trunks and gnarled branches that I've come to love. They live alongside the animal trails I've ridden horseback on and walked for my whole life in this place. These are the trails my relatives walked along with dog travois and rode horses on for thousands of years; it's where they learned to maintain the balance of this place. We call ourselves Tsitsistas/Suhtaio, though others have named us Northern Cheyenne, and we belong to this land.

These old trees know us. They've watched us for many years. They love us—all of us—and our history is in them. I see our history in these drawings and in the drawings and video to come over the next year. It's there, right alongside the trees' story of the fire.

Catherine Malabou

The Brain of History, or,
The Mentality of the Anthropocene

This essay is a response to the highly challenging topic on which Ian Baucom and Matthew
Omelsky asked me to elaborate: "For your contribution," they wrote, "we would be particularly interested in an essay that investigates the intersection
of philosophy and neuroscience as it relates to climate change" (pers. comm., October 10, 2015).
After some time, I decided to explore the link
between the current constitution of the brain as
the new subject of history and the type of awareness demanded by the Anthropocene.

An immediate answer to Baucom and Omelsky's challenge would have been an exploration of
the relationship between the brain and the "environment." It is, of course, a widespread idea in
global change literature that "the Anthropocene
idea abolishes the break between nature and culture, between human history and the history of life
and Earth," as well as between "environment and
society" (Bonneuil and Fressoz 2016: 19, 37). The
blurring of these frontiers, of course, necessitates a
study of the profound interaction between the soci-
ological and the ecological, understanding them as
parts of the same metabolism. I believe that this
notion of "interaction" requires closer analysis,

The South Atlantic Quarterly 116:1, January 2017
DOI 10.1215/00382876-3749304 © 2017 Duke University Press

though, and renders necessary a preliminary study of the specific concept of history in which it currently takes place.

If the Anthropocene acquires the status of a true geological epoch, it is obvious that such an epoch will determine the historical representation as well as the social and political meaning of the events occurring in it. In other words, this new geological era will not and cannot have the neutrality and a-subjectivity characteristic of geological eras in general. The Anthropocene situates the human being itself between nature and history. On the one hand, it is still of course the subject of its own history, responsible, and conscious. Consciousness of history, or "historicity," is not separable from history itself. It entails memory, capacity to change, and, precisely, responsibility. On the other hand, though, the human of the Anthropocene, defined as a geological force, must be seen as neutral and indifferent, as a geological reality itself. The two sides of this new identity cannot mirror each other, causing a break in reflexivity.

The awareness of the Anthropocene, then, originates through an interruption of consciousness. Such is the problem. I intend to ask whether such an interruption opens the space for a substitution of the brain for consciousness. I proceed to a confrontation between two different points of view on this question. According to the first, the Anthropocene forces us to consider the human as a *geological* agent pure and simple. Such is Dipesh Chakrabarty's position. I refer to his two now famous articles (Chakrabarty 2009, 2012). According to the second, understanding the Anthropocene necessarily privileges the role of the brain and thus biology. This is the approach Daniel Lord Smail takes in his *On Deep History and the Brain* (2008). I show how their two approaches may be seen as complementing each other and introduce in the debate, as a medium term and under a new form, some important and unjustly forgotten elements brought to light by some prominent French historians from the École des Annales—like those of "mentality" and "slow" or "long term" temporality.

Chakrabarty denies any metaphorical understanding of the "geological." If the human has become a geological form, there has to exist somewhere, at a certain level, an isomorphy, or structural sameness, between humanity and geology. This isomorphy is what emerges—at least in the form of a question—when consciousness, precisely, gets interrupted by this very fact. Human subjectivity, as geologized, so to speak, is broken into at least two parts, revealing the split between an agent endowed with free will and the capacity to self-reflect and a neutral inorganic power, which paralyzes the energy of the former. Once again, we are not facing the dichotomy between the historical and the biological; we are not dealing with the relationship between man understood as a living being and man understood as a subject.

Man cannot *appear* to itself as a geological force, because being a geological force is a mode of disappearance. Therefore, the becoming force of the human is beyond any phenomenology and has no ontological status. Human subjectivity is in a sense reduced to atoms without any atomic intention and has become structurally alien, by want of reflexivity, to its own apocalypse.

A major common point between Chakrabarty and Smail is the necessity to consider that history does not start with recorded history, but has to be envisaged as deep history. As Chakrabarty (2009: 213) suggests, "Species thinking . . . is connected to the enterprise of deep history." Let's recall the definition of *deep history* proposed by Edward Wilson (1996: ix–x), to whom both Chakrabarty and Smail refer: "Human behavior is seen as the product not just of recorded history, ten thousand years recent, but of deep history, the combined genetic and cultural changes that created humanity over hundreds of [thousands of] years."

According to Chakrabarty, however, biological "deep past" is certainly not deep enough. In that sense, therefore, a "neurohistorical" approach to the Anthropocene remains insufficient. Neurocentrism is just another version of anthropocentrism. Focusing on the biological only, Smail would miss the geological dimension of the human: "Smail's book pursues possible connections between biology and culture—between the history of the human brain and cultural history, in particular—while being always sensitive to the limits of biological reasoning. But it is the history of human biology and not any recent theses about the newly acquired geological agency of humans that concerns Smail" (Chakrabarty 2009: 206). The human's recent status as geological agent paradoxically draws the historian back to a very ancient past, a time when the human itself did not exist—a time that thus exceeds "prehistory."

One will immediately argue that Smail, in his book, is precisely undertaking a deconstruction of the concept of prehistory. Clearly, the notion of deep history represents for him the result of such a deconstruction. Deep history, then, substitutes itself for prehistory. According to the usual view, history starts with the rise of civilization and departs from a "buffer zone" between biological evolution and history proper—such a buffer zone is what precisely is called prehistory. If history must be understood, as Wilson suggests, as the originary intimate interaction between the genetic and the cultural, it starts with the beginning of hominization and does not require the "pre" (Smail 2008).

Smail's approach is clearly an epigenetic one, which forbids the assimilation of "hominization" with the history of consciousness. Epigenetics is a branch of molecular biology that studies the mechanisms that modify the function of genes by activating or deactivating them without altering the DNA sequence in the formation of the phenotype. Epigenetic modifications depend on two types of causes: *internal* and *structural*, on the one hand, and *environmental*, on the other. In the first case, it is a matter of the physical and chemical mechanisms (RNA, nucleosome, methylation). In the second, epigenetics supplies genetic material with a means of reacting to the evolution of environmental conditions. The definition of phenotypical malleability proposed by the American biologist Mary Jane West-Eberhard (2003: 34) is eloquent in this respect: it is a matter of the "ability of an organism to react to an environmental input with a change in form, state, movement, or rate of activity." Contemporary epigenetics reintroduces the development of the individual into the heart of evolution, opening a new theoretical space called "evolutionary developmental biology," or "evo-devo."

Lambros Malafouris, in his book *How Things Shape the Mind: A Theory of Material Engagement*, shows how epigenetics has modified the usual view of cognitive development, thus constituting cognitive archeology a major field in historical studies. "Cognitive development," he writes,

> is explained as the emergent product . . . of these constraints [from genes and the individual cell to the physical and social environment]. In this context, the view of brain and cognitive development known as *probabilistic epigenesis* . . . which emphasizes the interactions between experience and gene expression . . . is of special interest. The unidirectional formula (prevalent in molecular biology) by which genes drive and determine behavior is replaced with a new scheme that explicitly recognizes the bidirectionality of influences between the genetic, behavioral, environmental, and socio-cultural levels of analysis." (Malafouris 2013: 40)

This new scheme requires, as Malafouris brilliantly shows, a materialist approach of the interaction between the biological and the cultural. Hence the subtitle of the book: *A Theory of Material Engagement*. The epigenetic crossing and interaction in question take place *through things, through matter*, which is also to say, *through the inorganic*. It is a "nonrepresentative" vision of interaction, which requires no subject-object relationship, no mind seeing in advance what has to be made or fabricated. Mind, brain, behavior, and the created object happen together; all are part of the same process. "The cognitive life of things is not exhausted by their possible causal role in shaping some aspect of human intelligent behavior; the cognitive life of things also embodies a crucial enactive and constitutive role" (Malafouris 2013: 44). Therefore, to explore the relationships between the brain and its "environment" is a much wider and deeper task than to study the role of the "human" in its "milieu," precisely because it lays the foundation, for an essential part, on a nonhuman materiality and cannot be limited to a biological form of inquiry. In that sense, ecology to come acquires a new meaning: "This new ecology cannot be reduced to any of its constitutive elements (biological or artificial) and thus cannot be accounted for by looking at the isolated properties of persons or things. The challenge for archaeology, in this respect, is to reveal and articulate the variety of forms that cognitive extension can take and the diversity of feedback relationships between objects and the embodied brain as they become realized in different periods and cultural settings" (82). Malafouris then argues that this ecology should be understood as a result of the "embedment" of the human brain. "The term 'embedment,'" Malafouris (2010: 52) writes, "derives from the fusion of the terms 'embodiment'—referring to the intrinsic relationship between brain and body—and 'embeddedness'—describing the intrinsic relationship between brain/body and environment."

To conclude on that point and go back to our initial discussion, we can see that Smail's and Malafouris's approaches to the brain/environment relationship are not "strictly" biological but include, as a central element, the inorganic materiality of things. As Smail (2008: 48) declares: "The great historical disciplines, including geology, evolutionary biology and ethology, archeology, historical linguistics, and cosmology, all rely on evidence that has been extracted from things. Lumps of rocks, fossils, mitochondrial DNA, isotopes, behavioral patterns, potsherds, phonemes: all these things encode information about the past." "History is something," he continues, "that *happens* to people, things, organisms, and is not *made* by them" (57). Deep history, conjoined with archeology of the mind, or "neuroarcheology," would then extend the limits of the "brain" well beyond reflexivity and consciousness, well beyond "historicity" as well. As archeological, the brain/ environment relationship is already also geological. It remains clear, though, that Chakrabarty would not be entirely convinced by such an argument. Even if nonanthropocentric, even if thing- and inorganic-matter-oriented, even if including at its core a neutral, a-reflexive, nonrepresentative type of interaction as well as cognitive assemblages, the conjoined point of view of deep history and archeology of the mind still takes the "human" as a point of departure. The process of hominization is of course inseparable from an evolutionary perspective. Chakrabarty's perspective is very close to that of French philosopher Quentin Meillassoux in his book *After Finitude*. Meillassoux argues for a "noncorrelationist" approach to the "real," which would not lay foundation on the subject-object relationship at all and would totally elude the presence of the human on earth as a point of departure. There exists a mode of exploration of deep past (of the extremely deep past) that does not even consider the emergence of life in general as a "beginning." Deep past, then, becomes an "ancestrality" devoid of any "ancestors": "I will call 'ancestral,'" Meillassoux (2008: 10) writes, "any reality anterior to the emergence of the human species—or even anterior to every recognized form of life on earth." The archive, here, is not the object, not even the thing, not even the fossil, but what Meillassoux calls the *arche-fossil*:

> I will call "arche-fossil" or "fossil-matter" not just materials indicating the traces of past life, according to the familiar sense of the term "fossil," but materials indicating the existence of an ancestral reality or event; one that is anterior to terrestrial life. An arche-fossil thus designates the material support on the basis of which the experiments that yield estimates of ancestral phenomena proceed—for example, an isotope whose rate of radioactive decay we know, or the luminous emission of a star that informs us as to the date of its formation. (10)

For Meillassoux, the earth is entirely indifferent to our existence, anterior to any form of human presence—be it neural, be it neutral.

Again, these affirmations resonate with Chakrabarty's claim that the notion of the "geological," in the term *geological agent*, forever remains outside human experience. "How does a social historian go about writing a *human* history of an uninhabited and uninhabitable vast expanse of snow and ice?" he asks when talking about the Antarctic (Chakrabarty 2012: 11). A decorrelated subject cannot access itself as decorrelated. "We cannot ever experience ourselves as a geophysical force—though we now *know* that this is one of the modes of our collective existence" (12). Chakrabarty's analysis adds an important element to Meillassoux's thesis when it takes into account the experience of the impossibility to experience decorrelationism. We can conceptualize it but not experience it.

> Who is the we? We humans never experience ourselves as a species. We can only intellectually comprehend or infer the existence of the human species but never experience it as such. There could be no phenomenology of us as

a species. Even if we were to emotionally identify with a word like *mankind*, we would not know what being a species is, for, in species history, humans are only an instance of the concept species as indeed would be any other life form. But one never experiences being a concept. (Chakrabarty 2009: 220)

At this point, a major issue appears, relaunching the discussion and a return to Smail's analysis. First, we do not see what a species can be outside the biological point of view. Why keep that term? Second, I do not understand why the fact of becoming a geological form would have to remain entirely conceptual, without producing a kind of *mental phenomenon.* "Climate scientists' history reminds us . . . that we now also have a mode of existence in which *we*—collectively and as a geophysical force and in ways we cannot experience ourselves—are 'indifferent' or 'neutral' (*I do not mean these as mental or experienced states*) to questions of intrahuman justice" (Chakrabarty 2012: 14; emphasis mine). Before coming to the political consequences of such a statement, I would like to ask why precisely we could not be susceptible to experience mentally and psychically the indifference and neutrality that have become part of our nature. Deprived of any empiricality, mental or psychic effects, the assumption of the human as a geological force remains a pure abstract argument, and, in that sense, it appears as an ontological or metaphysical structure. Just like Meillassoux, Chakrabarty ends up failing to empiricize the very structure that is supposed to detranscendentalize, so to speak, the empirical. Why should there be any intermediary locus of experience between consciousness and the suspension of consciousness?

This is where the brain demands recognition! Is not the brain, on which Chakrabarty remains silent, an essential intermediary between the historical, the biological, and the geological? That site of experience we are looking for?

≡

This brings us back to Smail and to one of the most important and interesting aspects of his analysis, the *theory of addiction.* Smail insists that the constant interaction between the brain and the environment is essentially based on brain-body state alterations. The brain maintains itself in its changing environment by becoming addicted to it, understanding "addiction" in the proper sense as a "psychotropy," a significant transformation or alteration of the psyche. These altering effects result from the action of neurotransmitters "such as testosterone and other androgens, estrogen, serotonin, dopamine, endorphins, oxytocin, prolactin, vasopressin, epinephrine, and so on.

Produced in glands and synapses throughout the body, these chemicals facilitate or block the signals passing along neural pathways" (Smail 2008: 113). Such chemicals, which determine emotions, feelings, and affects in general, can be modulated according to the demands of the behavioral adaptation they make possible. Adaptation, here, is two-sided. It is of course adaptation to the external world, but it is also the adaptation of the brain to its own modifications.

All important changes in deep history, like the passage of one age to another, have always produced new addictive processes and chemical bodily state modulations:

> A neurohistorical model offers an equally grand explanatory paradigm, proposing that some of the direction we detect in recent history has been created by ongoing experiments with new psychotropic mechanisms that themselves evolved against the evolutionary backdrop of human neurophysiology. The Neolithic revolution between 10,000 and 5,000 years ago transformed human ecology and led to fundamental and irreversible changes in demographics, politics, society, and economies. In this changing ecology, new mechanisms for modulating body states emerged through processes of undirected cultural evolution. (187)

We have to understand that

> the expansion in calories available for human consumption, the domestication of animals useful as sources of energy, the practice of sedentism, the growing density of human settlements—such were the changes characteristic of the Neolithic revolution in all parts of the world where agriculture was independently invented: Mesopotamia, Africa, China, Mesoamerica, and other sites. All these changes created, in effect, a new neurophysiological ecosystem, a field of evolutionary adaptation in which the sorts of customs and habits that generate new neural configurations or alter brain-body states could evolve in unpredictable ways. (155)

From this, Smail concludes, "Civilization did not bring an end to biology" (155). Again, deep history reveals the profound interaction of nature and history through the mediation of the brain as both a biological and cultural adaptor. Human practices alter or affect brain-body chemistry, and, in return, brain-body chemistry alters or affects human practices. Brain epigenetic power acts as a medium between its deep past and the environment.

"The mood-altering practices, behaviors, and institutions generated by human culture are what I refer to, collectively, as *psychotropic mechanisms*,"

Smail explains. "*Psychotropic* is a strong word but not wholly inapt, for these mechanisms have neurochemical effects that are not all that dissimilar from those produced by the drugs normally called psychotropic or psychoactive" (161). Further, "Psychotropy comes in different forms: things we do that shape the moods of others; things we do to ourselves; things we ingest" (164).

We can distinguish here between autotropic and allotropic psychotropic, that is, addictive substances and practices acting on the self, and addictive practices acting on the other political addictive practices. Among the former are "coffee, sugar, chocolate, and tobacco" (179), which first began circulating in Europe in the seventeenth and eighteenth centuries. "All of these products have mildly addictive or mood-altering properties" (179). To these alcohol and drugs will later be added.

Smail recalls that the current meaning of the term *addiction* emerged in the late seventeenth century. "Earlier, the word had implied the state of being bound or indebted to a person—to a lord, for example, or perhaps to the devil" (183). This old meaning helps us understand what constitutes allotropy. Psychotropic addictive chemical mechanisms can also be induced in subjects out of power excess and abuse of domination. Stress and more general affective states of dependence, what Baruch Spinoza calls "sad passions," are essential aspects of psychotropy, caused in contexts of dominance. The crossing point between modularity and change coincides precisely with the crossing point between biology and politics: "Humans possess relatively plastic or manipulable neural states and brain-body chemistries," such that "moods, emotions, and predispositions inherited from the ancestral past" can be "violated, manipulated, or modulated" (Smail 2008: 117).

According to Smail, autotropic and allotropic addictive processes automatically mark the point of indiscernibility between biology (chemical substances and mechanisms) and culture (being-in-the-world). We find again the idea that the brain is the mediator between the two dimensions of (deep) history: the natural and the historical.

How can we extend these remarks to the current situation? First, they lead us to admit that only new addictions will help us to lessen the effects of climate change (eating differently, traveling differently, dressing differently, etc.). Addictive processes have in large part caused the Anthropocene, and only new addictions will be able to partly counter them. Second, they force us to elaborate a renewed concept of the addicted subject, of suspended consciousness and intermittent freedom. Third, they allow us to argue that the neutrality Chakrabarty speaks of is not conceivable outside of a new psychotropy, a mental and psychic experience of the disaffection of experience. Such a psychotropy would precisely fill the gap between the transcendental structure of the geological dimension of the human and the practical disaffection of historical reflexivity. The subject of the Anthropocene cannot but become addicted to its own indifference—addicted to the concept it has become. And that happens in the brain.

The motif of a narcolepsy of consciousness, as both cause and effect of the technological destruction of nature, had already been interestingly and importantly suggested by Marshall McLuhan. His analysis seems to fit the framework of the current ecological crisis perfectly. Technological development coincides for him with an extension of the nervous system to the very limits of the world: "After three thousand years of explosion, by means of fragmentary and mechanical technologies," he writes, "the Western world is imploding. During the mechanical ages we had extended our bodies in space. Today, after more than a century of electric technology, we have extended our central nervous system itself in a global embrace, abolishing both space and time as far as our planet is concerned" (McLuhan [1964] 1990: 52). The extension of the nervous system to the world has a double contradictory effect, acting as a pain killer (a "counter-irritant") to the extent that it suppresses all alterity and, at the same time and for the same reason, acting as a destructive power. Such is the structure of our "narcotic culture." Every technological device is a prolongation of the brain and the organism, and McLuhan characterizes this prolongation as a process of "auto-amputation" that helps lower the pressure and creates anxiety, thus putting at work an economy of pleasure as "numbness."

One might argue that the world about which McLuhan talks, the world to which the nervous system extends its frontiers is an image, a reflecting surface, whereas the split Chakrabarty analyzes as the separation between the human as a historical agent and the human as a geological force confronts two heterogeneous entities that cannot reflect each other at all. Nevertheless, if we look closely at what McLuhan says about mirroring, narcissism, and the projection of one's own image, we see that reflection is for him immediately suspended by a spontaneous petrification, a geologization of both the gaze and the image. On the myth of Narcissus, McLuhan writes ([1964] 1990: 53): "As counter-irritant, the image produces a generalized numbness or shock that declines recognition. Self-amputation forbids self-recognition." Indifference and neutrality, once again, can be mental phenomena, even when their manifestations may seem totally alien to any mental or internalizing structure. Again, I do not think that the neutralization of consciousness due to its "geologization" can happen without the intermediary of brain processes resulting from its interaction with the world. Indeed, I have tried to show elsewhere that indifference has become the global current *Stimmung,* that is, atunement or affect (Malabou 2012).

Such an indifference, this interruption of consciousness or awareness, directly challenges the concept of responsibility, which is of course central in our debate. How can we feel genuinely responsible for what we have done to the earth if such a deed is the result of an addicted and addictive slumber of responsibility itself? It seems impossible to produce a genuine awareness of addiction (awareness of addiction is always an addicted form of awareness). Only the setting of new addictions can help in breaking old ones. Ecology has to become a new libidinal economy.

These are some of the issues that political discourses on climate change, as demonstrated at conferences like the recent twenty-first session of the Conference of the Parties (COP21) to the United Nations Framework Convention on Climate Change in Paris, do not genuinely take into account. Most of the time, the official ecological discourse is still only a discourse on awareness and responsibility. That of course does not mean that the human is not responsible for global warming. Nevertheless, the type of responsibility requested by the Anthropocene is extremely paradoxical and difficult to the extent that it implies the acknowledgment of an essential paralysis of responsibility.

Chakrabarty would no doubt argue that these last developments remain caught in the correlationist frame. They would still be human, all too human. Do they not let aside the issue of nature as such to only take into account humanity's technoscientific power and its psychotropic causes and consequences?

The traditional concept of history, Chakrabarty writes, implies a disavowal of the fact that nature can have a history. It presupposes a strict border between pure contingent facts (natural ones) and events understood as acts of agents. Benedetto Croce, for example, claims that "there is no world but the human world" (Chakrabarty 2009: 203). French historian Fernand Braudel, in his book *The Mediterranean and the Ancient World* (2001), of course rebelled against such a vision by taking into account the specific temporality of the Mediterranean natural environment, the soil, the biosphere, and so on. Nevertheless, this time of nature is still seen as purely repetitive and mechanical, deprived of any agency or eventual power; it "is a history of constant repetition, ever-recurring cycles" (Chakrabarty 2009: 204). Such a contention is not sustainable any longer, because the age of the Anthropocene teaches something already widespread in the "literature of global warming": "The overall environment can sometimes reach a tipping point at which this slow and apparently timeless backdrop for human actions transforms itself with a speed that can only spell disaster for human beings" (Chakrabarty 2009: 205).

How do we respond to this? It is obvious that Braudel has not thematized or even perceived the historicity of nature, its mutability and ability to transform itself. In *The Mediterranean and the Ancient World* (Braudel 2001), the analysis of climate is definitely poor, as Braudel does not say a word, or at least nothing significant, about ecology. In that sense, Chakrabarty is right to challenge the cyclical vision of natural time that still governs Braudel's notion of nature's time and space. It seems to me, though, that Chakrabarty does not see how helpful Braudel nevertheless can be for our discussion. It is true that what Braudel calls the "geohistorical time," the archaic natural time, does not change. The "very long term" time, made of thousands of years, geological time proper, seems to be deprived of any capacity to transform itself. But it is striking to note that the two other levels Braudel distinguishes, that of economic and social time (middle term duration) and that of the event (short term temporality), are also contaminated by the first level's immobility. And here is the interesting point. Braudel has perhaps failed to take into account the historical force of nature, but he certainly very early and accurately perceived the irrevocable naturalization of human history, that is, of economic, political, and social time. He described better than anyone else the narcolepsy of historical temporality, to such a point that he was accused of depoliticizing it.

Deconstructing the privilege of the event, Braudel showed that a geological principle, that of a blind slowing force, was operating at all layers of time. In that sense, he anticipated something from the current situation, to the extent that he announced that historical consciousness had to acknowledge its own naturalization and suspension by entering the reign of immobility. In that sense, what Chakrabarty sees as a consequence (the human transformed into a geological force because of climate change and the entry into the Anthropocene), Braudel saw as a beginning (history has always already slowed down, thus preparing itself for its own neutralization by nature). What Braudel said about capitalism is extremely interesting in this respect. He argued that material life progresses by means of "slow evolutions." Advances occur "very slowly over long periods by the initiative of groups of men, not individuals . . . , and in countless varied and obscure ways" (Braudel 1973: 258). Great technical revolutions infiltrate society "slowly and with difficulty . . . to speak of revolution here is to use a figure of speech. Nothing took place at break-neck speed" (442).

One might object again that long term temporality presupposes an essential passivity and unchangeability of nature, that it cannot account for a sudden constitution of nature itself as a historical acting agent, like the one we are currently witnessing with the Anthropocene. That is true. But the problem, as we have seen all along, is that approaching the historical force of nature paradoxically leads us to slow down, to face the suspension of consciousness, the numbness and slumber of our responsibility. It is in a certain sense like exchanging roles, nature becoming historical and the anthropos becoming natural. This exchange constitutes a new form of human experience, and this Braudel helps us to conceptualize.

The third generation of the Annales School in France—Marc Ferro, Jacques Le Goff, and Emmanuel Le Roy Ladurie—still increased the part played by the very long term temporality. As one of them declares: "Time is fully human, and yet, it is as motionless as geographic evolution" (Dosse quoting Aries 1987: 165).[1] Braudel's work found itself extended and prolongated by the introduction of an important concept that emerged at that time in historical science, that of "mentality," closer to the psychological than to the intellectual. The acknowledgment of slow time, or long term time, gave way to a "history of mentalities" (*histoire des mentalités*). Based on "material culture," that is, on the similarities between the mind's rhythms and natural cycles, history of mentalities provided its readers with descriptions and analyses of uses, repetitions, habits, and representations. Philippe Aries (1981) declared that the history of mentalities situated itself "at the crossing point between the biological and the social" (quoted in Dosse 1987: 198).

As we already noticed, this crossing point between the biological and the social does not mean that the biological must be taken as a point of departure or that the human as a living being should become the origin of historical research. The history of mentality also includes, as one of essential dimension, the materiality of inorganic nature, the soil, the rocks, the mountains, the rivers, the earth. A mentality is a hybrid concept that comprehends not only the psychic and the social but also the originary likeliness of the mind and the fossil, the inscription of naturality in thought and behavior. Mentality, in that sense, is rooted in the brain and not in consciousness. "The human reduced to its 'mental' is the object rather than the subject of its own history" ("L'homme réduit à son mental est objet de son histoire plutôt que sujet") (Dosse 1987: 206). Jean Delumeau (1990), author of the important *La peur en Occident, XIVe–XVIIIe siècles: Une cité assiégée* (*Sin and Fear: The Emergence of a Western Guilt Culture, Thirteenth to Eighteenth Centuries*), writes, while playing with the multiple sense of the term *natural:* "Fear is natural" (quoted in Dosse 1987: 206). As a consequence of all previous analyses, we may consider history of mentalities to be the first form of environmental studies in France. Could it be that new histories of mentalities, which would bring together the geological, biological, and cultural current dimensions of historical (non) awareness, may open a new chapter of Anthropocenic study?

═══

What seems to me challengeable in Chakrabarty's work is the claim of an impossibility to phenomenalize the geological becoming of the human. This "species" the human remains a pure void concept until it can be filled with intuition, that is, with empirical and sensuous content, if not with awareness. A renewed and reelaborated concept of mentality might precisely help provide the missing content of this form. There necessarily exists a mental effect of the numbness and paralysis of consciousness, a mental effect of the new narcoleptic structure of humanity's (impossible) reflection on itself. We have seen, with Smail and McLuhan, that this mental effect was a neural one in the first place. Again, it is not a matter of thinking the brain "in" its environment; it's a matter of seeing the brain *as* an environment, *as* a metabolic place. Therefore, I prefer using the term *mental* rather than *neural*, because *mental* immediately evokes the merging and mingling of different registers of materialities. In that sense, getting accustomed to the new condition of the human as a geological agent will of course require a new mentality, that is, new addictions, new bodily adaptations to an inorganic and earthly corporeity, a new natural history. A history, still, nevertheless.

Reading Braudel and his followers helps us perceive that the narcolepsy of consciousness constitutes an irreducible dimension of history. Long term temporality, immobility, and very slow evolution show that deep history has always been inscribed at the heart of history, as this numbness of time and action that submits cultural evolution to a geophysical rhythm. Braudel is perhaps not a thinker of climate change, but he is a great theoretician of a new form of Marxism that binds the critique of capital to a study of the irreducible naturality, neutrality, and passivity of time. The critique addressed to the historians of long term duration and mentalities was the same as the ones currently addressed to Chakrabarty, all pointing, in both cases, at a supposed depoliticization of history. François Dosse (1987: 258) wrote that with the École des Annales, in the end, "history ha[d] negated itself." He wished that "the event" might come back in order to wake up time from its geological slumber. . . . He could not foresee that with the Anthropocene, long term temporality would precisely acquire the status of an event—which would free the attempt at thinking ecology and politics differently.

Note

1   Unless otherwise indicated, all translations are mine.

References

Aries, Philippe. 1981. *The Hour of Our Death: The Classic History of Western Attitudes toward Death over the Last One Thousand Years*. Translated by Helen Weaver. New York: Vintage Books.

Bonneuil, Christophe, and Jean-Baptiste Fressoz. 2016. *The Shock of the Anthropocene: The Earth, History, and Us*. Translated by David Fernbach. London: Verso.

Braudel, Fernand. 1973. *Capitalism and Material Life, 1400–1800*. Translated by Miriam Kochan. New York: Harper and Row.

Braudel, Fernand. 2001. *The Mediterranean and the Ancient World*. Translated by Siân Reynolds. London: Penguin Books.

Chakrabarty, Dipesh. 2009. "The Climate of History: Four Theses." *Critical Inquiry* 35, no. 2: 197–222.

Chakrabarty, Dipesh. 2012. "Postcolonial Studies and the Challenge of Climate Change." *New Literary History* 43, no. 1: 1–18.

Delumeau, Jean. 1990. *Sin and Fear: The Emergence of a Western Guilt Culture, Thirteenth to Eighteenth Centuries*. Translated by Eric Nicholson. Chicago: University of Chicago Press.

Dosse, François. 1987. *L'histoire en miettes: Des Annales à la "nouvelle histoire"* (*Fragmented History: From the Annales School to "New History"*). Paris: La Découverte.

Malabou, Catherine. 2012. *The New Wounded: From Neurosis to Brain Damage*. Translated by Steven Miller. New York: Fordham University Press.

Malafouris, Lambros. 2010. "Metaplasticity and the Human Becoming: Principles of Neuroarcheology." *Journal of Anthropological Sciences* 88: 49–72.

Malafouris, Lambros. 2013. *How Things Shape the Mind: A Theory of Material Engagement*. Cambridge, MA: MIT Press.

McLuhan, Marshall. (1964) 1990. *Understanding Media: The Extensions of Man*. New York: St. Martin's.

Meillassoux, Quentin. 2008. *After Finitude: An Essay on the Necessity of Contingency*. Translated by Ray Brassier. London: Continuum.

Smail, Daniel Lord. 2008. *On Deep History and the Brain*. Berkeley: University of California Press.

West-Eberhard, Mary Jane. 2003. *Developmental Plasticity and Evolution*. New York: Oxford University Press.

Wilson, Edward. 1996. *In Search of Nature*. Washington, DC: Island.

Noel Castree

Global Change Research and the "People Disciplines": Toward a New Dispensation

Climate scientists today enjoy an extraordinary epistemological privilege. They make claims about the global atmosphere that are simultaneously claims upon the totality of humanity. Summarized as average temperature targets, shrinking carbon budgets, and parts per million concentrations of greenhouse gases, these scientists' findings and predictions are provocative. They invite us to identify and eliminate the root causes of atmospheric change that will soon rewrite the global geography of ecosystems, coastlines, ice sheets, and much else besides. Relatedly, they invite us to ask deep questions about how we should live on our one and only planet. But these scientists are not alone. In recent years their warnings about "dangerous climate change" have been folded into a set of much grander scientific pronouncements. Teams of environmental researchers across several disciplines have together sounded the alarm about the unprecedented scale, scope, and magnitude of the human impact on earth. Proclamations about the end of the Holocene (Steffen et al. 2011), the prospect of biophysical tipping points (Barnosky et al. 2012), and the imminent transgression of "planetary boundaries" (Rockström et al. 2009) all position anthropogenic climate

The South Atlantic Quarterly 116:1, January 2017
DOI 10.1215/00382876-3749315 © 2017 Duke University Press

change as one aspect of a much larger problem: namely, an entire "earth system" perturbed by peoples' collective activities over several decades. Today humans are not merely climate changers: we are, so many scientists tell us, akin to a geological force capable of altering the cryosphere, biosphere, hydrosphere, lithosphere, and atmosphere simultaneously.

In this article I consider how the epochal claims emanating from a range of geoscience disciplines—including but going beyond climate science—relate to the social sciences and humanities (the "people's disciplines," hereafter SSH). If these disciplines speak of an earth in crisis, then the environmentally inflected parts of the SSH have an equally weighty responsibility and opportunity. At the level of both the "is" and the "ought," they get to speak for some or all of the 7 billion *Homo sapiens* implicated in the drama of global environmental change. They have a chance to significantly shape public understanding of what an anthropogenic earth means for us and nonhumans; they could, directly or otherwise, influence decision making in politics, business, and the third sector. In addition, they might feasibly "speak back" to the geoscientific research that is already inspiring a lot of activity in the SSH. This is because the "social heart of global environmental change" (Hackmann, Moser, and St. Clair 2014) might require a different sort of geoscience in order to beat strongly in the future.

I use the conditional terms *could* and *might* because the SSH are not yet changing the broader intellectual climate within or outside universities to any notable degree. Currently, the discourse about global environmental change is dominated by natural scientists—in academia and the wider world. The pope's 2015 encyclical, *Laudato Si'*, is one of the exceptions that prove the rule; others are the best-selling books authored by a few prominent, environmentally minded commentators such as Bill McKibben, Tim Flannery, and Mark Lynas. The balance needs to shift toward the broader SSH so that human causes, consequences, and responses are understood with all the richness they deserve. It is not that the so-called human dimensions have been ignored; on the contrary, they have been examined vigorously in parts of the SSH (such as environmental economics) for many years. The challenge is to widen, diversify, and effectively communicate our understanding of these dimensions so that geoscientists and everyone else can better understand what our planetary malaise could and should mean for us and for our descendants.

Looking at the current relationship between the geosciences and the environmentally inflected regions of the "people disciplines," my argument is simple enough. I suggest that a combination of ignorance, timidity, and distance conspire to make the geoscience-SSH relationship an anemic one in respect to the causes, symptoms, and effects of global environmental change. For now, at least, the radical implications of global geoscience are not shaking up the conduct of inquiry in the SSH in ways that might rebound formatively on geoscience itself or the wider society. Looking ahead, that needs to change.

Changes to Global Change Science

Climate science is arguably the most globally prominent part of global change science. Since the first United Nations Earth Summit in 1992, its findings about global warming have been the focus of concern, debate, and challenge in government, commerce, and civil society. The Intergovernmental Panel on Climate Change (IPCC), of course, has been central to this effort. Forming a bridge between environmental research and public policy, it has allowed climate scientists to speak in a common voice after careful weighing of voluminous and growing bodies of evidence. But whereas the IPCC is given to communicating in measured language, individual climate scientists are not so constrained. A few, such as James Hansen (2009) and Michael Mann (2014), have spoken out passionately about the dangers posed by runaway greenhouse gas emissions. As Naomi Klein (2014) interprets it, the implications of anthropogenic climate change stand to change everything if taken seriously by those beyond the scientific community.

However, that makes it sound as if speaking truth to power defines the professional role of "concerned climate scientists" without remainder. In other areas of global change science this presumption has been challenged. Though conducting and communicating fundamental research into the functioning of the changing earth system is necessary, some have asked if more can be done. As Nathan Sayre et al. (2013: 339) put it, "Changing the *role* of [global change] science is necessary but not sufficient to meet the challenges before us—the *practices* of [the] science must also change" (emphasis added). There are three aspects to this change in practices, all predicated on the fact that the end of the Holocene, the risk of crossing critical thresholds, and the transgression of planetary boundaries are (like climate change) all ultimately human questions as much as physical questions.

First, several commentators have noted that for matters of fact about the earth to become facts that matter for people outside geoscience, more careful attention has to be paid to "messaging." An example is the *Scientific Consensus Statement on Maintaining Humanity's Life Support Systems in the*

Twenty-First Century, authored by biologist Anthony Barnosky and colleagues (see Barnosky et al. 2014a). Released in May 2013, it was targeted at policy makers—with current California governor Jerry Brown a willing intermediary to get the statement taken seriously elsewhere in the world of government. Unlike the tomes produced by the IPCC working groups and the lengthy summaries for policy makers they yield, the consensus statement is an attempt to describe earth system change in a clear, succinct way that decision makers can understand. The authors then reflected on the success of the statement in order to distill lessons for other global change scientists in the future (Barnosky et al. 2014b). Relatedly, Adam Corner and Chris Groves (2014) argue that new intermediate institutions between geoscience and society are needed to translate factual matters into the value-based beliefs that motivate people to act (or not, as the case may be).

Second, because environmental change has human causes and consequences, it has been argued that interdisciplinary science is called for that can incorporate "human dimensions." In effect, this means understanding contemporary humans as *part of* the cryosphere, biosphere, hydrosphere, lithosphere, and atmosphere, not external to them. It entails a recognition that environmental issues are also issues of human well-being, and vice versa. Several geoscientists have called for more and better research into peoples' thoughts, emotions, and actions so that "coupled" understanding eventuates, leading to better predictions about risks and remedies. An example comes from the pages of *Nature*. There Paul Palmer and Matt Smith (2014) argued for expanded computer models of climate that build in realistic information about human perceptions and responses as the climate changes and as people, in turn, continue to affect (and adapt to) the climate. This argument for change implies more and better interactions between geoscientists and specialists studying psychology, economics, and so on.

Third, several leading geoscientists have called for a turn toward "decision-relevant" or "actionable" research that can be of use by politicians, business leaders, and communities. For instance, Ruth DeFries, Paul Crutzen, and colleagues envisage research that focuses "proactively on solutions that are tractable and specific to particular circumstances" (DeFries et al. 2012: 604). Meanwhile, Margaret Palmer (2012) of the National Socio-Environmental Synthesis Center in Maryland calls on researchers to move outside their comfort zones and coproduce applied knowledge with real-world stakeholders. Again, these calls for change implicate the people disciplines because an understanding of society, economy, culture, and politics is directly relevant to knowing what kind of practical solutions (e.g., technology-led adaptation policies) are likely to "work" on the ground.

Though lack of space prevents me from citing more examples, the calls for a new modus operandi defined by these three changes are fairly widespread (for a more detailed account, see Castree 2016). In sum, global change science is set to morph, with geoscientists among its number realizing that they need to more fully embed their research in the human dimensions of a planet under pressure. All this has an institutional dimension that should, in time, prove consequential. The new Future Earth initiative (www .futureearth.org/) assimilates three of the four long-standing global change research programs.[1] It has high-level support globally.[2] Its architects hope to engender "a new type of science that links disciplines, knowledge systems and societal partners to support a more agile global innovation system" (Future Earth 2014: 2). Two of its three overarching research themes are "global development" and "transformations toward sustainability." The transformations theme evidences a particular wish to make at least some global change researchers agents of significant change outside the universities and institutes they call home. It is very likely that Future Earth will set the tone for many national-level environmental change programs in the immediate future.

Global Change Research, the Social Sciences, and the Humanities

The incipient changes to global change research create clear possibilities for two things to happen. The first is more and broader interaction between geoscience and the environmentally inflected parts of the SSH. The second is greater visibility of these parts outside universities—the sort of visibility that climate science has enjoyed for over twenty years. With both things in mind, I consider below how SSH practitioners have recently responded not only to climate science but also to the epochal claims made by geoscientists located in several specialist fields.

One response has been to consider the significant implications for the established identities and practices of the SSH. Dipesh Chakrabarty's much-cited *Critical Inquiry* essay "The Climate of History: Four Theses" (2009) provides a fairly well-known example. Reflecting on the discipline of history, he argues that the onset of the Anthropocene unsettles its ontological predicates (such as human history being distinct from earth history). The upshot, he argues, is that studies of the past must be rethought—for instance, histories of human emancipation from poverty and disease since the 1850s must now also be histories of planetary degradation because fossil fuels have been so central to human "development." Another example is Timothy Clark's book *Ecocriticism on the Edge* (2015). Ecocriticism involves interpreting creative works (e.g., novels) that call into question or valorize certain human perceptions and uses of the nonhuman world. Clark argues that the Holocene's eclipse disrupts the normative reference points of the field. This is because ecocritics can no longer presume that what appears environmentally progressive at one spatiotemporal scale will not have regressive impacts at other scales—such are the complex, ramified teleconnections of an earth system undergoing anthropogenic forcing.

A second response has been to advertise the value of SSH fields that have hitherto not been central to the study of "human dimensions." Consider these two examples that take the form of disciplinary manifestos. Susan Clayton et al. (2015: 644) argue that psychology is "uniquely placed to understand individual- and household-level factors in socio-ecological systems." They highlight three areas where the discipline can enrich understanding and management of human behavior as climate change escalates. Likewise, Jessica Barnes et al. (2013: 541) note anthropology's marginal role in climate change debates and highlight the value of its "in-depth fieldwork methodology . . . and broad, holistic view of society." In both examples the authors make the case in a publication outlet read by many geoscientists, the journal *Nature Climate Change*.

A third response has been to continue research into human dimensions that has long been central to the enterprise and also visible to geoscientists, politicians, and others. Environmental economics remains preeminent here. It has been the one area of the SSH that has most shaped societal understandings of the causes of environmental change and feasible solutions. For instance, in two recently published books the British brace of Sir Nicholas Stern (2015) and Dieter Helm (2015) put private property rights, prices, and economic reason at the heart of any "solution" to anthropogenic climate change. In so doing, they extend a stream of thought whose tributaries coalesced back in the early 1980s and animated several carbon trading schemes up to the present. Broadening that stream beyond climate economics, the recent worldwide move toward "payments for ecosystem services" shows that the wider biogeographical domain is now also being routinely subject to economic reasoning. That said, ecological economics is beginning to exert a greater influence in some policy arenas. For example, it is leaving an intellectual imprint on the new Intergovernmental Platform on Biodiversity and Ecosystem Services (which is a sort of twin to the IPCC; see Díaz et al. 2015). Despite being criticized for losing some of its "alternative" credentials (e.g., by Spash 2012), ecological economics' influence suggests that new bodies of thought can sometimes jostle with established approaches to "human dimensions."

A fourth response has been to explore established themes and questions in the wider SSH in light of the "runaway" human impact on earth. A number of rather "academic" publications within the SSH evidence this response as scholars internalize the "shock of the Anthropocene" (to reference Bonneuil and Fressoz 2016). For instance, writings by literary critic Timothy Morton (2010), geographer Kathryn Yusoff (2015), and sociologist Nigel Clark (2011) explore the implications of the Anthropocene for the cognitive, affective, and moral norms that for decades have governed our self-understanding as Westerners. Each author challenges the descriptive, explanatory, and evaluative repertoire of his or her discipline and points readers toward new intellectual horizons. Meanwhile, Jason Moore (2015) reframes the human dimensions of the Anthropocene as the latest and grandest instance of a long-running phenomenon: capitalism's war on the earth. Unlike many environmental historians, though, he tries to dispense with the nature-society dualism in his reconstruction of world ecological history since 1500.

A fifth response, not a common one to be sure, is to question the science that is sounding the environmental alarm. Where the previous four responses treat the science uncritically, some in the SSH see it as implicated in the major problems of society, economy, politics, and culture that its findings otherwise place in the spotlight. Take Eileen Crist (2013), writing in the journal *Environmental Humanities*. Far from being objective, she sees the science behind the Anthropocene proposition as suffused with contestable value judgments that scientists are trying to naturalize (wittingly or otherwise). For instance, Will Steffen and colleagues have talked several times about the need for planetary stewardship (see, e.g., Steffen et al. 2011), an "ought" that for them flows from the "fact" of humans' planetary impact. However, for Crist (2013: 133) they thereby "veer away from environmentalism's dark idiom of destruction, depredation, rape, loss, devastation . . . and so forth into . . . [a] tame vocabulary that humans are changing [the earth]." As Crist sees it, this bespeaks a short-circuiting of the is-ought link so as to narrow normative reasoning and human response.

The Role of the People Disciplines in Understanding and Affecting the "Age of Humans"

What can we infer from these reactions to climate change science in particular and geoscience more generally? First, it's clear that certain approaches to understanding people are easier to "sell" as relevant to tackling global environmental change. It is symptomatic that Barnes et al. (2013) advertise a discipline as diverse as anthropology as if it's an analytical social science that produces actionable data about people as social animals. Its "soft," interpretive aspects are underplayed and so too are its idiographic traditions and associated ideas of cultural diversity (even incommensurability). Similarly, the sort of critical scholarship Marxists produce on the human "drivers" of global change (e.g., Moore 2015) is generally invisible to global change scientists and those outside academia. The continued prominence of environmental economics, the confident advocacy of behavioral science by Clayton et al. (2015), and the rarity of alternative approaches (like ecological economics) in the policy and public mainstream speak to how narrowly human dimensions are framed.

Second, and relatedly, humanists and critical social scientists often remain content to respond to geoscience at a distance within their established disciplinary domains—be it affirmatively (like Chakrabarty, T. Clark, Morton, Yusoff, N. Clark, and Moore) or critically (like Crist). This distance allows them to be intellectually creative about the "natural," the "social," and the "human"; equally, it allows them to venture robust judgments of the science when necessary. But it also ensures that society, policy, and the underpinning science remain unaffected by alternative framings of what global environmental change is caused by, does (to humans and nonhumans), and should lead to (in terms of suitable responses). Any citation analysis quickly reveals that climate scientists, geoscientists, and science-minded members of the people disciplines (like Stern) scarcely consider critical social science or the environmental humanities as relevant. Likewise, one rarely sees a critical social science or humanities "twin" to the likes of Hansen or Mann in wider debates about the earth and its future. Someone like Australian philosopher Clive Hamilton (2013) is a rarity in this respect.

The upshot is that the relationship between scientists studying a fast-changing planet and social scientists and humanists concerned with the same thing is both narrow (where potentially strong) and weak (in those places where breadth would enrich both science and wider understandings of global change). Why is this? I can think of two reasons, one of which is fairly obvious. Despite the intellectual differences among the various branches of geoscience behind a concept like the Anthropocene, there is nonetheless a prevalent assumption that societies can be analyzed and managed in ways not dissimilar to environmental systems. The earlier mentioned article by Palmer and Smith (2014) is one example of this approach, but there are many others. For instance, in a manifesto arguing for geoscience "with" society rather than simply "about" it, Romain Seidl et al. (2013) identify the people disciplines salient to that endeavor. "The essential natural and social science disciplines," they assert, are "(economic) geography, industrial and regional economics, business and management sciences, industrial ecology, environmental sciences, and regional and economic development planning" (8). Apparently, the humanities are irrelevant. Meanwhile, only those disciplines that presume there is a single reality out there awaiting analysis with the "right" questions, concepts, and methods to hand are cited. As the *Nature* editorial "Time for the Social Sciences" (2015) revealed, the watchword is *integration*: add in explanations and evidence about humans to paint a more complete picture of a world where society and environment bleed into each other ever more. Epistemic unity is here vouchsafed by a presumptive ontological monism.

This sounds as if I am berating geoscientists and a narrow band of environmental social scientists for restricting our understanding of human dimensions. But it is not so simple. On those rare occasions when critical social scientists and humanists have tried to speak about the earth across the "three cultures" divide, they have not been terribly successful so far. Consider the Swedish environmental historian Sverker Sörlin. In 2012 he published a brief manifesto for the environmental humanities in a journal—*BioScience*—largely read by life scientists. That is all to the good . . . and yet: despite arguing for a rich understanding of people's behavior, he fails—ironically—to define what is specific about the environmental humanities. Meanwhile, when the respected former climate scientist Mike Hulme (2014c) pointed to the limits of physical science on the online news site The Conversation, he made it seem as if "human dimensions" are external to the facts and predictions emanating from satellite observation systems and climate models. Though this argument usefully challenges the "one world" presumption that supports the idea of seamless epistemic integration, it also inadvertently perpetuates the myth of value-free science that Crist rightly challenges. Hulme locates the all-important value-based discussions about the world we want inside "society" as if science *itself* is not a thoroughly social enterprise that's hardwired (in changing and contingent ways) to specific value-based ways of thinking and acting.

Of course, when challenging the image of science as a truth-seeking enterprise that stands above politics, morality, and so on—as Sheila Jasanoff (2014) has done in other contexts—the risk is that scientists switch off. What's more, it does not help if one makes the case in places or in ways that geoscientists do not register. Take Hulme's stirring case for the insertion of "virtue" into the conduct of science and any resulting applications, such as geotechnologies. Rather than appearing in a little-read online journal (*Humanities* [Hulme 2014b]) or as a Polity Press book (Hulme 2014a), this case really needs to be made in a prominent outlet like *Science* and in ways that detail why geoscience should productively utilize its own political dimensions (not shy away from them). Otherwise, it risks being ignored or else misunderstood as an illicit attempt to distort science for extrascientific reasons (recalling the "science wars" in the United States in the 1990s).

The Need for a New Dispensation

I have argued that global change scientists "interpellate" social scientists in specific and circumscribed ways, while assuming that the humanities are largely irrelevant to their research into a changing earth system. I have also argued that critical social scientists and environmental humanists have thus far done a poor job of reaching out to geoscientists or to people outside universities. The result is that the wider debate about the planet and its future remains dominated by a particular set of concepts, metaphors, and values. These reflect a belief, rooted in science, that objectively measurable "problems" can yield appropriate "solutions" once sufficiently "joined-up" research and thorough stakeholder consultation have occurred, allied with cooperation among nations.

There are, in my view, three serious problems with this state of affairs. First, the is-ought relationship is underdetermined. Far from assuming that the earth's environment can be managed wisely by reforming the current political economy, geoscientists like Rockström and Crutzen could just as well recognize the more radical normative implications of their own science. Presently, the "transformations" theme flagged in the new Future Earth initiative is belied by the political gradualism of global change science. There is a clear reticence to harness science to more revolutionary ends (as, for example, in the 1930s when there was much talk in the West of "socialist science"; see Castree 2015).

Second, and relatedly, when geoscience turns to the quantitative, analytical, and nomothetic parts of social science for help, it actively promotes a specific set of judgments about how we should live on earth as if they are somehow set in stone. For instance, the "market failure" and "tragedy of the commons" arguments of environmental economists focus collective attention on property rights, contracts, and monetary exchanges. Modeling a coupled earth system using this approach to human behavior is all well and good in the eyes of some . . . but only if you don't want to tackle the deep-seated cultural beliefs and fundamental social relations that, as Klein (2014) argues, enable rampant environmental degradation across the globe.

Third, while scientific facts, predictions, and inventions can speak to more than one political-moral agenda, it's important to recognize that objectivity is a stubborn and unhelpful myth. Geoscientists and science-minded social researchers fool themselves and sell the rest of us short when they pretend otherwise, ignoring decades of empirical work by historians and sociologists of science. What counts as "evidence" and what passes for "relevant knowledge" are necessarily *relative* to the diverse and debatable values and goals that different societies hold dear. These essential "human dimensions" are not merely outside geoscience, something to be studied by SSH specialists on the other side of campus. These dimensions are both inside and directly germane to the conduct of scientific inquiry into a fast-changing earth. The upshot is that geoscience-SSH engagements need to push beyond cognitive issues to encompass ethical and even aesthetic ones (in overt and reflexive ways). Only then will academic knowledge of our planet's present and future be sufficiently plural and value-laden to create real options for public debate and human decision making.

I have had to simplify what is, in fact, a complex story. As I showed earlier, global change science is undergoing change in three respects. Meanwhile, the SSH are responding to the insights of geoscientists in a variety of ways. But, fundamentally, this response amounts to stasis in the guise of a change to professional practices. What is now required is a new means of combining expertise across the "three cultures" divide. Epistemic communities need do so not merely to collaborate but to *unsettle each other* so that a new modus operandi emerges. A more inclusive, more multidisciplinary, more dialogical global change research deserves to become influential worldwide. The stakes are high and time is scarce. However, if current arrangements prevail, then an all-too-familiar future awaits us, one in which only knowledge that favors dominant interests gets to shape human self-understanding.

Notes

1   These programs are the International Geosphere-Biosphere Program, launched in 1987, which followed the World Climate Research Program, created in 1980; the International Human Dimensions Program, formed in 1990; and Diversitas, launched in 1991 and focusing on global biodiversity and biogeography. After the Amsterdam Declaration by participating members in 2001, the programs were connected through the so-called Earth System Science Partnership (which ended in 2013), and a set of joint projects ensued (see Ignaciuk et al. 2012). Some of the projects roll forward under a Future Earth umbrella, but new ones referenced to the second and third Future Earth themes will start up in the next few years.

2   Future Earth is sponsored by the Science and Technology Alliance for Global Sustainability; the International Council of Science (ICSU); the International Social Science Council (ISSC); the Belmont Forum of national funding agencies; the new Sustainable Development Solutions Network; the United Nations Educational, Scientific, and Cultural Organization; the United Nations Environment Program; the United Nations University; and the World Meteorological Organization. Future Earth emerged out of a visioning process sponsored by the ICSU (2010) and the ISSC. It was initiated in 2009 with a "task team" that comprised Johan Rockström, Walter Reid, Heide Hackmann, Khotso Mokhele, Elinor Ostrom, Kari Raivio, Hans Schellnhuber, and Anne Whyte.

References

Barnes, Jessica, et al. 2013. "Contribution of Anthropology to the Study of Climate Change." *Nature Climate Change* 3, no. 6: 541–44.

Barnosky, Anthony, et al. 2012. "Approaching a State Shift in Earth's Biosphere." *Nature* 486, no. 7401: 52–58.

Barnosky, Anthony, et al. 2014a. "Introducing the *Scientific Consensus Statement on Maintaining Humanity's Life Support Systems in the Twenty-First Century*." *Anthropocene Review* 1, no. 1: 78–109.

Barnosky, Anthony, et al. 2014b. "Translating Science for Decision Makers to Help Navigate the Anthropocene." *Anthropocene Review* 1, no. 2: 160–70.

Bonneuil, Christophe, and Jean-Baptiste Fressoz. 2016. *The Shock of the Anthropocene: The Earth, History, and Us.* Translated by David Fernbach. London: Verso.

Castree, Noel. 2015. "Unfree Radicals?" *Antipode.* Early view publication: doi:10.1111/anti.12187.

Castree, Noel. 2016. "Geography and the New Social Contract for Global Change Research." *Transactions of the Institute of British Geographers* 41, no. 3: 328–47.

Chakrabarty, Dipesh. 2009. "The Climate of History: Four Theses." *Critical Inquiry* 35, no. 2: 197–222.

Clark, Nigel. 2011. *Inhuman Nature: Sociable Life on a Dynamic Planet.* London: Sage.

Clark, Timothy. 2015. *Ecocriticism on the Edge: The Anthropocene as a Threshold Concept.* London: Bloomsbury.

Clayton, Susan, et al. 2015. "Psychological Research and Global Climate Change." *Nature Climate Change* 5, no. 7: 640–46.

Corner, Adam, and Chris Groves. 2014. "Breaking the Climate Change Communication Deadlock." *Nature Climate Change* 4, no. 9: 743–45.

Crist, Eileen. 2013. "On the Poverty of Our Nomenclature." *Environmental Humanities* 3: 129–47.

DeFries, Ruth, et al. 2012. "Planetary Opportunities: A Social Contract for Global Change Science to Contribute to a Sustainable Future." *BioScience* 62, no. 6: 603–6.

Díaz, Sandra, et al. 2015. "The IPBES Conceptual Framework—Connecting Nature and People." *Current Opinion in Environmental Sustainability* 14, no. 1: 1–16.

Future Earth. 2014. *Strategic Research Agenda 2014.* Paris: International Council for Science.

Hackmann, Heide, Susanne C. Moser, and Asuncion Lera St. Clair. 2014. "The Social Heart of Global Environmental Change." *Nature Climate Change* 4, no. 8: 653–55.

Hamilton, Clive. 2013. *Earthmasters: The Dawn of the Age of Climate Engineering.* New Haven, CT: Yale University Press.

Hansen, James. 2009. *Storms of My Grandchildren: The Truth about the Coming Climate Catastrophe and Our Last Chance to Save Humanity.* London: Bloomsbury.

Helm, Dieter. 2015. *Natural Capital: Valuing the Planet.* New Haven, CT: Yale University Press.

Hulme, Mike. 2014a. *Can Science Fix Climate Change?* Cambridge, UK: Polity.

Hulme, Mike. 2014b. "Climate Change and Virtue: An Apologetic." *Humanities* 3, no. 3: 299–312.

Hulme, Mike. 2014c. "Science Can't Settle What Should Be Done about Climate Change." The Conversation, February 4. theconversation.com/science-cant-settle-what-should-be-done-about-climate-change-22727.

Ignaciuk, Ada, et al. 2012. "Responding to Complex Societal Challenges: A Decade of Earth System Science Partnership (ESSP) Interdisciplinary Research." *Current Opinion in Environmental Sustainability* 4, no. 1: 147–58.

Jasanoff, Sheila. 2014. *Science and Public Reason.* London: Earthscan.

Klein, Naomi. 2014. *This Changes Everything: Capitalism vs. the Climate.* New York: Simon and Shuster.

Mann, Michael. 2014. "If You See Something, Say Something." *New York Times,* January 17.

Moore, Jason. 2015. *Capitalism in the Web of Life.* London: Verso.

Morton, Timothy. 2010. *The Ecological Thought.* Cambridge, MA: Harvard University Press.

Nature. 2015. "Time for the Social Sciences." 517, no. 7532: 5.

Palmer, Margaret. 2012. "Socio-environmental Sustainability and Actionable Science." *BioScience* 62, no. 1: 5–6.

Palmer, Paul, and Matt Smith. 2014. "Model Human Adaptation to Climate Change." *Nature* 512, no. 7515: 365–66.

Rockström, Johan, et al. 2009. "A Safe Operating Space for Humanity." *Nature* 461, no. 7263: 472–75.

Sayre, Nathan, et al. 2013. "Invitation to Earth Stewardship." *Frontiers in Ecology and the Environment* 11, no. 7: 339.

Seidl, Romain, et al. 2013. "Science with Society in the Anthropocene." *Ambio* 42, no. 1: 5–12.

Sörlin, Sverker. 2012. "Environmental Humanities: Why Should Biologists Take Them Seriously?" *BioScience* 62, no. 9: 788–89.

Spash, Clive. 2012. "New Foundations for Ecological Economics." *Ecological Economics* 77, no. 1: 36–47.

Steffen, Will, et al. 2011. "The Anthropocene: From Global Change to Planetary Stewardship." *Ambio* 40, no. 7: 739–61.

Stern, Nicholas. 2015. *Why Are We Waiting? The Logic, Urgency, and Promise of Tackling Climate Change.* Cambridge, MA: MIT Press.

Yusoff, Kathryn. 2015. "Geologic Subjects: Nonhuman Origins, Geomorphic Aesthetics, and the Art of Becoming Inhuman." *Cultural Geographies* 22, no. 3: 383–407.

Willis Jenkins

Feasts of the Anthropocene:
Beyond Climate Change as Special Object
in the Study of Religion

In his history of the feast, the archaeologist Martin Jones (2007) develops a religious hypothesis about the origins of modern monocultures. Why did wheat take over the continent of Europe fifteen hundred years ago? Not because it was easier to grow or because it produced more calories; rye, barley, and other grains were better adapted to local soils and could deliver more nutrition. Jones thinks that wheat won because devotion to light bread followed the growth of Christianity.

At the center of the Christian rite was an airy bread that needed to be made from wheat. The dark breads made with local grains became associated with paganism and were abandoned as territories came under control of Christendom. Historical patterns of cereal agriculture, argues Jones, follow the shifting boundary between pagan and Christian Europe. Under the culinary sign of the Eucharist, wheat bread came to symbolize civilization. The association endured through the Protestant Reformation—which reconsidered other dimensions of Communion bread, but not wheat. With the North American dust bowl as his example, Jones suggests that when Europeans set off to colonize new worlds they carried with them a

The South Atlantic Quarterly 116:1, January 2017
DOI 10.1215/00382876-3749326   © 2017 Duke University Press

shared devotion to wheat that was as violent to native soils as zeal for Christianity was to native cultures.

If Jones is even partially correct, his account shows how a religious feast shaped one pathway by which humans are now changing the climate. With the bread of daily tables following cultural preferences developed in the symbolic world of the Communion table, wheat agriculture now terraforms earth's surface, which in turn influences how the planet regulates thermal energy. Those connections do not mean that climate change is a direct consequence of religion, any more than it is of eating wheat. They just illustrate that, insofar as Christian ritual food influenced a culinary aesthetic that in turn shaped paths of agricultural production, a religious feast has become materially entangled with climate.

The entanglement of ritual eating with a planetary system exemplifies how climate change is shifting conditions for the disciplinary study of religion. For example, anthropological and ritual-theory research can ask whether and how experiences of ritual eating become inflected by species-level metabolism of the planet as participants come to understand the connections. Theological debates over the metaphysics of the sacrament acquire an unanticipated biophysical referent as competing notions of "nature and grace" leave material traces in the atmosphere. Perhaps those debates have always been influenced by climate; research correlating the Little Ice Age to cultural stress driving (among other things) conflict between Protestants and Catholics reveals climate as actant in religious affairs (see Parker 2013).[1] Historical research on developments and fragmentations of the Communion feast may then consider how climate changes may have shaped theological conflicts and liturgical innovations.

So far within religious studies, however, climate change typically appears as a special object of study rather than as labile pressure across an entire field of inquiry.[2] Research tends toward two treatments of climate: as special object of religious politics or as special object of religious interpretation. The first is usually motivated by interest in how religion influences views of political responsibility for climate change. Results so far seem less clear than one might think. When the American Academy of Religion commissioned a study of the question, the results showed that when religion is defined in terms of identity and climate in terms of politics, the two may not bear significant relation to each other; political affiliation, ethnicity, and global geography are all more significant (Jones, Cox, and Navarro-Rivera 2014). Undeterred, when the *Journal of the American Academy of Religion* devoted a focus issue on climate change the following year, in 2015, it framed the domain of inquiry as a political object in urgent need of religious attention.

The second, and more interesting, treatment studies "how climate change comes to matter" within a particular community or its vernaculars (see Callison 2014). This may include constructive accounts of how climate appears by the light of some tradition, as, famously, in Pope Francis's *Laudato Si'*, and the criticism around such accounts. This treatment also includes more ethnographic accounts of how religious inheritances are involved in contextual interpretations of climate change, such as how Bhutan deploys classical Buddhist inheritances to articulate its position on climate change (Branch 2014), or ways that devotion to the Ganges river adapts to retreat of its glacial source, or renegotiations of indigenous cultural identities in the midst of global environmental shifts (see Crate 2011). Sometimes climate change is treated in terms of pressure on religious traditions to invent new interpretive possibilities (Jenkins 2013). Still, even there, climate remains a special object of religious interpretation.

Religious interpretations of climate change undoubtedly remain a critical part of social responses to climate change. However, if treated only as a special object, as another peculiar phenomenon for the study of religion to curate, then the discipline misses how climate change drives more subtle and fundamental shifts as it exerts a kind of tectonic stress across multiple cultural domains. Oblique and pervasive, the stress does not always present as "climate change," yet it is already affecting a wide range of phenomena studied by religionists.

This essay focuses on how that stress shows up in one particular domain: food. I argue that as various movements work with food to develop possibilities of political and cultural imagination that confront some of the stresses associated with pervasive anthropogenic stress, they carry implicitly religious dimensions, or are at least apt for the analyses of religious studies. This essay therefore tacks against the view that, to reckon with climate change, the discipline of religious studies must turn toward the sky; here climatogenic influences on religious systems show up within the field's widely remarked "quotidian turn."

Three Gastronomic Theses about the Climate of Religion

"As the flows of energy and matter around the world are altered, and a new geological epoch emerges," asks Bronislaw Szerszynski (2015), "what will become of the sacred?" In a departure that would have outraged American environmental writers of the twentieth century, the icon of specialness in environmental thought seems to have shifted from wilderness toward food. The shift is evident in academic journals, where interest in food and agriculture is displacing theories of nature's value, and in the public visibility of food movements, which seem to attract the young activists that in a previous generation would have been fighting to conserve wild lands. In *After Nature*, the legal scholar Jedediah Purdy (2015) suggests that thinking through food allows environmental thought to reckon with key uncertainties of life in the Anthropocene. Food opens moral and political functions of nature necessary to interpret conditions of pervasive anthropogenic influence, which are no longer as available through the idea of wilderness.

The idea of the Anthropocene seems like an astonishing gift to the humanities generally and religious studies in particular: a physical scientist (the atmospheric chemist Paul Crutzen) has proposed to return the human to the center of knowledge and with it the role of humanistic methods and fundamental questions of meaning and purpose. It is, however, a perilous gift, bearing potential to bind its recipients to new circulations of naturalized power. Without directly entering debates about whether it naturalizes dominations of humans over earth or of North Atlantic technocracy over all else, I here offer three theses about how religious engagement with food can take up some of the critical stresses borne by the Anthropocene idea.

Postnatural Ecological Politics

What made nature sacred to a wilderness thinker like John Muir was its utter difference from humanity. "The next politics of nature," writes Purdy (2015: 21), "will be something different and more intense: an effort at active responsibility for the world we make and for the ways of life that world fosters or destroys." As climate forces disciplines to confront hybrid environments on a planetary scale, food offers a synecdoche of the intellectual challenge—responsibility for a human-made world on which we remain utterly dependent. It also offers a site for experimenting with vocabularies of nature in which it can be both special and produced. As the hybrid product of a biocultural assemblage, food requires its interpreters to think without foundational reference to "pure nature."

In an explosively influential essay, Dipesh Chakrabarty (2009) writes that climate change undermines a fundamental assumption of his discipline of history: no longer is nature the context for history, for it has become participant in history. "In a purblindness that has marked all of human history before today," agrees Purdy (2015: 21), "nature has been the thing without politics." Purdy and Chakrabarty overstate the punctuality of rupture, but they are nonetheless right to see that every discipline in the modern humanities is liable to epistemological trouble caused by pervasive anthropogenic influence. For religious studies, insofar as religion is entangled with the ways that cultures make environments, no longer can objects like nitrogen cycles be safely excluded from the worlds studied by religionists (as if creeping "dead zones" did not already beg for religious interpretation). Insofar as a modern disciplinary assumption of the study of religion has been that nature is the thing without religion, "nature" in that sense no longer exists, and earth is now (again?) actant in religious productions.

Anthropogenic influence over the sky disturbs cultural assumptions about the range of human agency. In many traditions the sky is symbolically associated with the superhuman. Whether the domain of gods or stochastic systems (or both), the sky has been the province of forces beyond the human (Donner 2007). Now human action is so entangled in the domain of gods and forces that climate engineering is a plausible undertaking. We cultivate land (agriculture) and sea (aquaculture), argues the climate scientist Mike Hulme (2015); so now we must recognize that humans cultivate the sky ("weatherculture").

The metaphor of "cultivation," argues Hulme, opens an uncomfortable but appropriate way of thinking about the human relationship with the sky. As with agriculture, the question is not *if* humans should be involved but what are the criteria for good involvements. The sort of criteria needed to make sense of climate engineering, Hulme suggests, have less to do with temperature outcomes than with the kind of human-sky relationship to which we aspire. Agrarian models of relation, in which criteria are shaped through collaborations of humans and others, seem especially apt. Perhaps one reason why neo-agrarian writers like Wendell Berry have captured the interest of so many is that they make good farming into an emblem of an appropriate pattern of collaboration with other creatures and ecological systems. In the biocultural collaborations through which we make food, thinks Berry, we become violent or caring, exploitative or just in our relations with one another. Hulme extends that thought to making climate. "Rather than putting science, economics, politics or the planet at the centre of the story of climate change," he writes, "I am suggesting that we put the humanities— our self-understanding of human purpose and virtue—at the centre" (Hulme 2014: 308). As the sky becomes an arena of practical action it becomes a domain whose relations shape our personhood, for better or worse.

Food offers a site to develop a postnatural ecological politics in which humans have responsibility and nonhumans have agency. Food thus opens a scene of biocultural relations through which to develop new vocabularies of ethical life with nature. In contemporary agrarian, culinary, and alimentary writing, various connections of aesthetics and morality attempt to connect human self-understanding and human enfleshment in a living world. If the shift from wilderness to food in environmental thought tracks a larger intellectual shift needed to make moral sense of the Anthropocene, then contemporary gastronomic fascinations do not always represent a bourgeois evasion of politics by decadence; it may represent the beginning of new political orderings. Patricia Storace (2014), observing the surge of recent books on food, writes that "what makes the new range and possibility of writing about food . . . exciting is that we are witnessing a rare tectonic shifting of a deeply rooted aesthetic and moral hierarchy." Food practices may seek to shift the politics of nature they carry.

Storace remembers that Confucius cultivated manners of eating as a philosophy of life because, for him, the practice of eating was a microcosm of how humans should govern themselves and their world. A similar claim could be made for eating in many other traditions, which explains why intentional departures from conventional table manners, culinary arts, or agricultural habits can disrupt entire cultural regimes; manners of eating often connect cultivation of self with governance of nature. Food movements intending to reshape the way nature is governed may develop biocultural practices that have self-formational functions conventionally associated with religious practices. At least, the terms of religious studies might help interpret contemporary connections of ways of eating with ways of life.

Identity and Commensality

David Freidenreich's *Foreigners and Their Food* (2011) may be the finest comparative study available of religious food practices. Freidenreich examines how Jewish, Christian, and Islamic authorities articulated food restrictions in order to transmit community identity and regulate cross-tradition relations. Arguments over what to eat and how it could be prepared, shows Freidenreich, were fundamentally about *who* was eating; food rules maintained a symbolic order of difference and identity.

Identity is a major organizing category for religious studies and especially for religious ethics, which conventionally organizes inquiry around traditions and typically thinks of traditions in correspondence to identities maintained by religious memberships. Work in the field generally supposes that each tradition has its own history and internal criteria, usually generated by arguments over the identities transmitted by that tradition. Comparative or connective conversations must be undertaken with great caution, which means that they always reproduce the methodological significance of identity.

Chakrabarty observes that in his discipline of history, freedom typically organizes research, as historians often suppose that the significance of their project derives from its relevance to struggles for freedom. Freedom informs what a historian seeks to know. But, he now notices, the growth of modern ideas of freedom correlates with growing use of fossil fuels. His much-quoted line: "The mansion of modern freedoms stands on an ever-expanding base of fossil-fuel use" (Chakrabarty 2009: 208). An organizing category for human history is involved in history in a geological register. Analogous implications reverberate across the humanities: What happens to the concepts that organize research in religious studies when we reckon with their emergence in conditions of geological power?

Human action at the planetary scale is an aggregate force, indifferent to the identities of the many agents contributing to its cumulative effect. *To what extent are the inquiries in religious ethics organized by a figure of the human who belongs to a previous epoch—one in which humans did not understand themselves as bound together in an accidental empire, a common geological action?* Whatever knowledge religionists create about some particular religious world, the ways in which a world produces its difference from other worlds, we must now recognize, is involved in earth-scaled, intergenerational productions. The point here is not simply that many cultural worlds share one planet but that formations of identity and difference condition how they produce a planetary effect. In turn, the planetary effect, signaled most clearly in climate change, may in turn begin to bear on senses of identity and difference. Geological agency certainly does not signal the end of formations of religious difference, but it does pressure those formations to recognize that the identities they sustain are also participants in a common species history. As climate acts on persons, it draws them into an identity-opening relation.

Awareness of global ecological change is already altering how some Jewish, Christian, and Muslim communities practice their (different) food rules. Eco-halal, for example, incorporates ecological concerns into traditional food rules. It is not yet clear what such variations mean for the way those food rules transmit symbolic orders of religious identity. Kecia Ali (2015: 282), in the course of making an argument that Muslims should become vegetarian, argues that eco-halal concern for animals and ecology appropriately diminishes the priority of performing authentic identity while nonetheless elevating interest in how food practices construct "a habitually virtuous self." Islamic difference is not sublimated to the planetary because, for Ali, the tradition contextualizes the development of globally concerned food practices within habits of self-scrutiny, hospitality, and moderation. So here the particular moral practices that produce an Islamic self incorporate a planetary relation. Moreover, claims Ali, the tradition's context for developing a virtuous person guards against some liabilities of food movements. Self-scrutiny, hospitality, and moderation, for example, might help prevent vegetarianism from becoming a mere consumer identity or grounds for total judgment of nonvegetarians.

Ali brings into view what the identity-focused inquiry of Freidenreich's project can occlude: that global environmental relations exert pressure on the maintenance of particular identities, which may give rise to notions of virtue inflected by cross-border ecological relations. Nonetheless, Freidenreich's book also implies the possibility of another way of organizing research. The three traditions had such nuanced food rules precisely because they all knew the power of the table; commensality creates community. That power suggests that contemporary tables of all sorts could be considered sites of religious production, insofar as they generate possibilities of character and community.

Courtney Bender (2003), drawing on her fieldwork at an organization that prepared and delivered gourmet food to people with AIDS, calls for the study of religion to look beyond officially religious settings toward ways that people create shared meaning without shared identity. Observing how volunteers from different worlds generated a shared sense of how to confront the suffering of others through the practice of offering food, Bender came to think that preparation of food for the sick functioned as a religion-like practice in that it forged shared senses of self.

Bender's fieldwork lines up with what Thomas Tweed (2015) calls "the quotidian turn" in the study of religion. Research focusing on "everyday" or "lived" religion departs from conventional disciplinary attention to the formal literature of elite communities to consider meanings carried by everyday practices. The quotidian, here, encompasses both the vernacular pieties of religious believers and religious dimensions of practices not connected to inherited devotional commitments of faith identities. That latter sense could include the way that modern food movements involve searches for meaning and practices of moral formation that seem religious in some sense. In fact, religion scholars have begun to observe culinary conversion narratives among vegans and locavores and to inquire into the relation of foodways and moral cosmology (Zeller 2015).

In conditions where climate exerts oblique pressure across quotidian life, food movements that (in various ways) renegotiate human relations to earth may function as a kind of table. Vegetarianism, locavorism, and food sovereignty may allow participants to collaboratively reshape biocultural practices of self formation. Food movements sometimes create the sort of commensality that religious traditions often attempt to regulate because it so powerfully shapes senses of community and self.

They may even understand themselves to collaborate with the nonhuman world as they do. Jane Bennett (2010: 51) describes the slow food movement as artful renegotiation that recognizes "food as itself an actant in an agentic assemblage that includes among its members my metabolism, cognition, and moral responsibility." The implied solidarity of commensality may therefore extend beyond the human world. Graham Harvey, in *Food, Sex, and Strangers* (2014), agrees with others in the quotidian turn that religious studies has been overly fascinated by the cognitive beliefs held by elites. Religion, argues Harvey, is about how people negotiate what to eat, with whom to have sex, how to treat strangers—and maybe about patterns that connect those negotiations. In fact, Harvey speculates that the first everyday problem religion met was the awkward need of some beings to eat other beings; religion arose, he suggests, as a cross-species etiquette of eating—a way of negotiating the taking of life. If so, then exploring food practices as religious practices may develop ways to recover the action of nonhumans in shaping human engagements with the world. Ritual acknowledgments of the creatures who have become food may give them a place at the table (not just on the table but sometimes "at the table" through being "on the table"). It is possible to consider locavorism and animal-friendly food in this posthumanist way: as commensality with landscapes or other sentients.

Moral Agency in a Double Register

The intimacy of the table seems distant from the abstract scope of climate, which involves relations at a scale that no person directly experiences. "Humanity" causes radiative forcing in the atmosphere, but no one in particular does that. Rather, climate change is a supervening causal description of phenomena caught up in systemic shifts that, although happening at unprecedented speed, are perceptible only through narrative connections of probabilities unfolding at a geological scale. The rise of humanity as a planetary force seems to overwhelm human meaning at the ordinary scale, in quotidian life.

Persons find themselves acted upon by systems circulating aggregate human agency through planetary relations that threaten a sense of meaningful moral agency. "People are not equipped with the mental and emotional repertoire to deal with such a vast scale of events," writes Bruno Latour (2014: 1); "they have difficulty submitting to such a rapid acceleration for which, in addition, they are supposed to feel responsible while, in the meantime, this call for action has none of the traits of their older revolutionary dreams." In the very historical moment that humans learn they are responsible for the sky, they find themselves overwhelmed by the scales of agency involved and thus incompetent to bear responsibility.

Friction between registers of agency is part of what makes climate change a "wicked problem"—a problem that resists formulation in part because of complex scales and puzzles over how to define it. The scientist Will Steffen (2011: 31) calls climate change a "diabolical problem," in part because responding to the basic threat it poses involves renegotiating "the fundamental relationship of humanity with the rest of nature." Even worse, it may overwhelm the concepts we have to interpret that relationship. Dale Jamieson (2014) argues that received concepts of responsibility fail in the odd registers and complex systems involved in climate change, making it clear that humanity is in trouble but unclear whether anyone in particular is responsible for it. Moral agency seems overwhelmed by (structural) wickedness.

With Anthropocene wickedness in mind, consider now how Tweed (2006: 54), current president of the American Academy of Religion, defines our disciplinary object: "Religions are confluences of organic-cultural flows that intensify joy and confront suffering by drawing on human and suprahuman forces to make homes and cross boundaries." In conditions of climate change, an odd twist becomes possible: humanity has become one of the suprahuman forces, as the ways by which we make homes and cross boundaries set in motion biocultural flows that change the skies. What does that mean for joy and suffering? As the discipline interprets climate flows as a religious object, it alienates ordinary experience. Climatic agencies threaten the quotidian.

Precisely because food is so basic and everyday, intimately involved in making homes and boundaries, it serves as an arena in which to enact agency and interpret complex systems. While the ability to act meaningfully seems undermined by global structures and planetary systems, food choices remain a site of relative agency. Ordinary persons may sense in a food choice the opportunity to choose between biocultural systems of sustenance or, in a food movement, the chance to help create an alternative system. The political theorists David Schlosberg and Roman Coles (2015) argue that food movements represent a direct materialist form of politics; by seeking different material circulations, they enact different possibilities of human-earth relations. Such "prefigurative politics" practice disbelief in the main channels of circulation by organizing alternatives and so thereby apply critical pressure on the biggest geopolitical structures organizing human life. Food generates ways to think about general relations of humanity and nature—which is one of the alienating features of climate change.

The deep cultural potential of food movements suggests why they can generate serious conflicts. Any food movement with political or cultural ambitions beyond informing consumer choice depends on the idea that food practices carry structures of meaning—culturally formed senses of self and world that function as moral cosmologies. What permits that assumption? The anthropologist Joel Robbins (2007) thinks that his discipline has emphasized structure in order to denaturalize cultural perceptions of freedom, and he observes how anthropologists of morality have recently been working to recover a sphere of freedom in order to bring into view forms of action undertaken as self-conscious moral commitments. Robbins wants anthropology to hold on to the way that practices carry cultural structures while integrating the ways in which agents self-consciously exercise freedom. In stable times, a bounded arena for choice (e.g., whom to marry) has little influence on the structure of relation between domains (e.g., marriage choices typically cannot influence patterns of relation between family life and professional life). However, argues Robbins, in periods of cultural stress, individuals may find that their choices bear the conflict between domains, such that by deciding on how to act within one domain, they are evaluating how domains should relate to another.

That helps explain why food movements may have deeper influence than the mere market signals of shifting consumer preferences. Through the self-conscious enactments of moral agency that they cultivate, food movements may attempt to unsettle and renegotiate the values organizing broad cultural structures of relation. They may even draw interpretive attention to fundamental relations of humanity and earth. As they do, they involve individual moral agency in interpretations of how the species should act and, more importantly, connect those interpretations to moral meaning. Working from a quotidian arena of personal agency, food movements can open symbolic conflicts over how earth should be inhabited and how humans should understand themselves within their inhabitation. Insofar as they do, food practices sustain a religious possibility, for they enact interpretive gestures of how to become human in the Anthropocene.

Conclusion

I have argued that climate change should be approached not only as a special object of study but also as a pervasive stress on conditions of cultural experience and especially on those formations approached by the study of religion. If there is anything productive to that argument, it suggests that the *Journal of the American Academy of Religion*'s 1995 focus issue on food might be as important for interpreting Anthropocene relations as its focus issue on climate change. For the feasts that emerge from biocultural flows and suprahuman forces to make our world also hold keys to interpreting it and the possibilities of bearing responsibility for it.

Notes

1 *Actant* refers to Bruno Latour's (1999: 75) use of the term.
2 With *special object* I pick up a key concept from Ann Taves (2011) without substantively engaging her broader approach to the study of religion.

References

Ali, Kecia. 2015. "Muslims and Meat-Eating: Vegetarianism, Gender, and Identity." *Journal of Religious Ethics* 43, no. 2: 268–88.

Bender, Courtney. 2003. *Heaven's Kitchen: Living Religion at God's Love We Deliver.* Chicago: University of Chicago Press.

Bennett, Jane. 2010. *Vibrant Matter: A Political Ecology of Things.* Durham, NC: Duke University Press.

Branch, Matt. 2014. "Climate Change Projects in the Land of Gross National Happiness: Does Religion Play a Role in Environmental Policy in Bhutan?" In *How the World's Religions Are Responding to Climate Change: Social Scientific Investigations,* edited by Robin Globus Veldman, Andrew Szasz, and Randolph Haluza-DeLay, 47–61. London: Routledge.

Callison, Candis. 2014. *How Climate Change Comes to Matter: The Communal Facts of Life.* Durham, NC: Duke University Press.

Chakrabarty, Dipesh. 2009. "The Climate of History: Four Theses." *Critical Inquiry* 35, no. 2: 197–222.

Crate, Susan. 2011. "Climate and Culture: Anthropology in the Era of Contemporary Climate Change." *Annual Review of Anthropology* 40: 175–94.

Donner, Simon D. 2007. "Domain of the Gods: An Editorial Essay." *Climatic Change* 85, no. 3: 231–36.

Freidenreich, David. 2011. *Foreigners and Their Food: Constructing Otherness in Jewish, Christian, and Islamic Law*. Berkeley: University of California Press.

Harvey, Graham. 2014. *Food, Sex, and Strangers: Understanding Religion as Everyday Life*. New York: Routledge.

Hulme, Mike. 2014. "Climate Change and Virtue: An Apologetic." *Humanities* 3: 299–312.

Hulme, Mike. 2015. "Better Weather? The Cultivation of the Sky." *Cultural Anthropology* 30, no. 2: 236–44.

Jamieson, Dale. 2014. *Reason in a Dark Time: Why the Struggle against Climate Change Failed—and What It Means for Our Future*. New York: Oxford University Press.

Jenkins, Willis. 2013. *The Future of Ethics: Sustainability, Social Justice, and Religious Creativity*. Washington, DC: Georgetown University Press.

Jones, Martin. 2007. *Feast: Why Humans Share Food*. New York: Oxford University Press.

Jones, Robert P., Daniel Cox, and Juhem Navarro-Rivera. 2014. *Believers, Sympathizers, and Skeptics: Why Americans Are Conflicted about Climate Change, Environmental Policy, and Science*. Washington, DC: Public Religion Research Institute.

Latour, Bruno. 1999. *The Politics of Nature: How to Bring the Sciences into Democracy*. Translated by Catherine Porter. Cambridge, MA: Harvard University Press.

Latour, Bruno. 2014. "Agency at the Time of the Anthropocene." *New Literary History* 45, no. 1: 1–18.

Parker, Geoffrey. 2013. *Global Crisis: War, Climate Change, and Catastrophe in the Seventeenth Century*. New Haven, CT: Yale University Press.

Purdy, Jedediah. 2015. *After Nature: A Politics for the Anthropocene*. Cambridge, MA: Harvard University Press.

Robbins, Joel. 2007. "Between Reproduction and Freedom: Morality, Value, and Radical Cultural Change." *Ethnos: Journal of Anthropology* 72, no. 3: 293–314.

Schlosberg, David, and Roman Coles. 2015. "The New Environmentalism of Everyday Life: Sustainability, Material Flows, and Movements." *Contemporary Political Theory* 15, no. 2: 160–81.

Steffen, Will. 2011. "A Truly Complex and Diabolical Policy Problem." In *The Oxford Handbook of Climate Change and Society*, edited by John Dryzek, Richard Norgaard, and David Schlosberg, 21–37. New York: Oxford University Press.

Storace, Patricia. 2014. "Seduced by the Food on Your Plate." *New York Review of Books*, December 18. www.nybooks.com/articles/2014/12/18/seduced-food-your-plate/.

Szerszynski, Bronislaw. 2015. "Gods of the Anthropocene." Paper presented at the conference "Unexpected Encounters with Deep Time: Enchantment," University of Edinburgh, November 25–26.

Taves, Ann. 2011. *Religious Experience Reconsidered: A Building-Block Approach to the Study of Religion and Other Special Things*. Princeton, NJ: Princeton University Press.

Tweed, Thomas. 2006. *Crossing and Dwelling: A Theory of Religion*. Cambridge, MA: Harvard University Press.

Tweed, Thomas. 2015. "After the Quotidian Turn: Interpretive Categories and Scholarly Trajectories in the Study of Religion since the 1960s." *Journal of Religion* 95, no. 3: 361–85.

Zeller, Benjamin. 2015. "Quasi-Religious American Foodways: The Cases of Vegetarianism and Locavorism." In *Religion, Food, and Eating in North America*, edited by Benjamin Zeller et al., 294–312. New York: Columbia University Press.

Rosi Braidotti

Critical Posthuman Knowledges

The convergence of posthumanism and postan-thropocentrism is currently producing a field of posthuman critical enquiry that is more than the sum of its parts and points to a qualitative leap in new directions (Braidotti 2013). The critique of the humanist ideal of Man as the allegedly universal measure of all things, on the one hand, and the rejection of species hierarchy and human exceptionalism, on the other, are equally interdisciplinary in character, but they refer to different theoretical and disciplinary genealogies. They converge, however, in enabling the emergence of posthuman knowledges.

By way of introduction, let me say that I practice critical thinking by drawing cartographies of the power operational in and immanent to the production of discourses and practices circulating in our sociopolitical order and integral to our subject formation (Foucault 1970). This approach is supported by two main theoretical pillars: the first is feminist epistemology, with its emphasis on the situated and accountable nature of knowledge (Harding 1986; Rich 1987; Haraway 1988; Hill Collins 1991). The second is a monistic neomaterialist philosophy inspired by Gilles Deleuze, which assumes all matter is one and that

The South Atlantic Quarterly 116:1, January 2017
DOI 10.1215/00382876-3749337 © 2017 Duke University Press

it is intelligent and self-organizing (autopoietic). In critical Spinozism (Deleuze 1988, 1990), thinking—in philosophy, art, and science—is the conceptual counterpart of the ability to enter modes of relation, to affect and be affected, sustaining qualitative shifts and creative tensions accordingly (Deleuze and Guattari 1994). Simultaneously critical and creative, posthuman thought pursues the actualization of intensive or virtual relations, inhabited by a vitalist and multidirectional memory that works in terms of transpositions, that is to say, generative cross-pollination (Ansell Pearson 1999) and nomadic interconnections (Braidotti 2006). Thinking is indeed the stuff of the world (Alaimo 2014).

A cartography is consequently a theoretically based and politically informed reading of the present that aims at exposing power both as entrapment (*potestas*) and as empowerment (*potentia*) in the production of knowledge and subjectivity (Braidotti 1994, 2011a, 2011b). In my cartography, the posthuman is less of a concept than a *conceptual* persona, that is to say, a theoretically powered navigational tool that helps us think along and across the complexities of the present. My argument in this essay is consequently that qualitatively new discourses are emerging across a number of fields, which constitute the vitality of contemporary posthuman scholarship.[1] Their relevance is framed by the urgency of the Anthropocene condition, which I read in the light of Félix Guattari's (2000) three ecologies as being environmentally, socioeconomically, and affectively and psychically unprecedented. The combination of fast technological advances on the one hand and the exacerbation of economic and social inequalities on the other makes for a multifaceted and conflict-ridden situation. To discuss the posthuman is also to stare into the abyss of the inhumanity of our times.

Transdisciplinary Knowledges

The exuberant growth of posthuman knowledges tends to concentrate in a number of transdisciplinary fields that do not coincide with the traditional humanities disciplines but are rather hybrid crossover formations. They are generated mostly from critical "studies" areas and produce their own extradisciplinary offsprings. For instance, cultural studies and comparative literature have spawned ecocriticism and animal studies. Science and technology studies has pioneered a number of variations of biotechnological and disability studies. Media studies is a planet of its own, which has led to new media, and more. Environmental studies has always been postanthropocentric and today mutates into a number of neomaterialist variations. I shall return to this.

Feminist theory, notably ecofeminism, has long struck an imaginary alliance with science fiction to support the insurrection of women—as the others of "Man," and of other "others," like nonwhites (postcolonial, black, Jewish, indigenous, and native subjects) with nonhuman agents (animals, insects, plants, tress, viruses, fungi, bacteria, and technological automata). Never quite certain as to the human rights assigned to their sex, LBGT+ seize the opportunity of exiting the binary gender system and taking the posthuman leap. There is no question that contemporary feminist theory is productively posthuman.[2]

The critical studies areas have provided the prototypes of the radical epistemologies that voice the situated knowledges of the structural "others" of humanistic Man. The first generation of these studies shares a number of metamethodological premises. First, it has often criticized the academic humanities on two grounds: structural anthropocentrism, on the one hand, and in-built Eurocentrism and "methodological nationalism" (Beck 2007), which Vandana Shiva (1993) called "monocultures of the mind," on the other. Second, they are firmly grounded in the world, which means that they take real-life events and, by extension, power seriously. They both criticize dominant vision of knowledge production and actualize the virtual insights and competences of marginalized subjects (Braidotti 2002, 2006). The main feature of these studies areas is their relative disengagement from the traditional methods of the academic disciplines. This disidentification, or nomadic exodus from disciplinary homes, fosters accountability for the present, in a mode that Michel Foucault (Foucault and Blanchot 1987) defined as "the philosophy of the outside."

The first generation of critical studies caused both internal fractures and the dislocation of outerdisciplinary boundaries in the humanities, but the studies do not merely oppose humanism. They also create alternative visions of the self, the human, knowledge, and society. Notions such as a female/feminist humanity (Irigaray) and black humanity are part of this tradition of more inclusive humanism (Braidotti 2016).

The posthuman turn is marked by a second generation of studies areas that address more directly the question of anthropocentrism, while remaining committed to social justice and ethical accountability. For instance, consider posthuman/inhuman/nonhuman studies; cultural studies of science and technology; secularism and postsecular studies; posthuman disability, fat, sleep, fashion, and diet studies; critical management studies; and success and celebrity studies. New media proliferated into a whole series of subsections and metafields: software, Internet, game, algorithmic, and critical code studies, and more. Further analyses of the social forms of exclusion and dominations perpetuated by the current world-order of "bio-piracy" (Shiva 1997), necropolitics (Mbembe 2003), and systemic dispossession (Sassen 2014) produce other discourses. These inhuman(e) aspects have been taken up by conflict studies and peace research; post-Soviet/communist studies; human rights studies, humanitarian management; migration studies; mobility studies; human-rights-oriented medicine; trauma, memory, and reconciliation studies; security studies; death studies; suicide studies; queer inhuman studies; and extinction studies, and the list is still growing.

Whereas the multifaceted critiques and revisions of humanism produced by the first generation of studies areas—like women's, feminist, gender, and queer studies, and postcolonial studies—empowered the sexualized and racialized human "others" to emancipate themselves from the dialectics of anthropomorphic oppositional hierarchical relations, the crisis of Anthropos relinquishes the forces of the naturalized others. Now we are "humanimals," and the Earth and its cosmos have become a political arena.

This planetary insight is compounded by another crucial factor: high technological mediation, or digital "second" life. What used to be the continuum of "naturecultures" (Haraway 1997, 2003) has evolved into "medianatures" (Parikka 2015). My monistic—material and vitalist—approach posits a media ecological continuum (Fuller 2005, 2008; Hansen 2006) based on a new understanding of nonhuman life—*zoe*—also as machinic autopoiesis (Guattari 1995; Braidotti 2002, 2006). This general ecology (Hörl 2013) foregrounds not just any form of materiality, but rather a geological (Parikka 2015), transcorporeal (Alaimo 2010), and terrestrial (Protevi 2013) kind of materialism.

Ever mindful of the fact that these developments take place within the axiomatic system (Deleuze and Guattari 1987; Toscano 2005) of so-called cognitive capitalism (Moulier Boutang 2012), I want to stress that what constitutes capital value today is the informational power of living matter itself, its immanent qualities and self-organizing capacity. Advanced capitalism profits from the scientific and economic understanding of all that lives. *Zoe*—vital power—gets transposed into data banks of biogenetic, neural, and mediatic information about individuals, populations, and species. This erases categorical differences between humans and nonhumans when it comes to profiting from them. Data mining includes profiling practices and risk assessments that identify different types or characteristics as strategic targets for knowledge/power practices. There is therefore an opportunistic angle to the posthuman discussion, which requires critical attention.

This fast-growing scholarly landscape indicates that the proper study of the humanities is no longer Man and this generic figure is in trouble, with the blessing of cognitive capitalist economics. Donna Haraway's analysis of the Capitalocene (2015) confirms her earlier analyses, which argued that "Man the taxonomic type [has] become Man the brand" (1997: 74). Massumi (1998) writes about "Ex-Man": "a genetic matrix embedded in the materiality of the human"; Hardt and Negri (2000: 215) see a sort of "anthropological exodus" from the dominant configurations of the human as the king of creation. Panic-stricken social theorists argue about the future of the human, for instance, Habermas (2003), Fukuyama (2002), Sloterdijk (2009), and Derrida (in Borradori 2003). In response to such outpours of anxiety, I want to argue that the evidence provided by the growing posthuman scholarship shows no crisis, but rather a remarkable upsurge of inspiration.

But what does it mean for successive generations of critical studies areas to emerge and proliferate in such a context? I approach the question on the basis of the affirmative ethics drawn from contemporary neo-Spinozism. A neomaterialist vital position offers a viable alternative to the profit-minded knowledge practices of biomediated cognitive capitalism. Taking living matter as *zoe*, a geocentered process that interacts in complex ways with the technosocial, psychic, and natural environments and resists the overcoding by the profit principle (and the structural inequalities it entails), I propose an affirmative plane of composition of transversal subjectivities. Subjectivity can then be redefined as an expanded self, whose relational capacity is not confined within the human species but includes nonanthropomorphic elements. *Zoe*-centered egalitarianism, the nonhuman, vital force of life, is the transversal entity that allows us to think across previously segregated species, categories, and domains. Neomaterialist immanence leads nomadic subjects to posit collective accountability also for the sustainability of our knowledge production and to resist the opportunistic transspecies commodification of life.

The crucial issue is that of the speeds of de/reterritorialization and the toxic saturation of the present by cognitive capitalism, to the detriment of the actualization of the virtual, and the extent to which they affect knowledge practices in the contemporary university and scientific community. How to tell the difference between affirmative and reactive modes of knowledge production is the fundamental question. Because power, in my scheme of thought, is a multilayered and dynamic entity, and because as embedded and embodied, relational, and affective subjects, we are immanent to the very conditions we are trying to change, we need to make the careful ethical distinction between different speeds of both knowledge production—with the predictable margins of institutional capitalization—and the construction of alternative knowing subject formations.

Let me apply these insights to the last phase of my cartography, namely, how the studies areas, which historically have been the motor of both critique and creativity, are currently crossbreeding and nomadically generating posthuman knowledges, which I call the *critical posthumanities.*

The Critical Posthumanities

Today the critical posthumanities are emerging as postdisciplinary discursive fronts not only around the edges of the classical disciplines but also as offshoots of the established studies areas. The terminological exuberance of the field is significant: the digital and the environmental humanities are but the tip of the Anthropocenic iceberg of the "emerging humanities."[3] In my assessment the emerging humanities represent both an alternative to the neoliberal governance of academic knowledge, dominated by STEM fetishism, and a renegotiation of its terms. As Deleuze and Guattari (1994) argue, deepening Foucault's insight about the multilayered structure of power (as both *potestas* and *potentia*): it is not a question of either/or, but of "and . . . and." Let me explain.

We could take the critical posthumanities as expressing an increase of metadiscursive energy on the part of the disciplines of the humanities, so as to reassert their institutional power while making a shift toward extradisciplinary encounters in the world. But we could also see these developments as a rhizomatic political economy of endless expansion of multiple studies and sprawling posthumanities as heterogeneous assemblages (Deleuze and Guattari 1994). This is a postdisciplinary (Lykke 2011) approach, fueled by the active desire to actualize unprecedented modes of epistemic relations. Nomadic subjects produce nomadic humanities (Stimpson 2016).

Whichever approach we may prefer (and it *is* a matter of "and . . . and," not either/or), the defining feature of the posthumanities—which makes them critical in the intensive or qualitative sense of the term—is their supradisciplinary character. In other words, the field is taken as a constitutive block, composed of the classical disciplines plus the transdisciplinary studies areas, plus the overcoding flows of cognitive capitalism, plus our desire for adequate knowledges, and so on. In any case, the driving force for knowledge production is not disciplinary purity, but rather the modes of relation these discourses are able and willing to engage in. The point of encounter or assemblage for the critical posthumanities is the acknowledgment of the porous nature not only of their institutional boundaries, but also of their epistemic core, which gets redefined in terms of relational capacity. The supradisciplinary sensibility allows for movement to be set in action within the different fields of knowledge production.

Thus, if we take the environmental, we can see it both as a majoritarian formation, contiguous with neoliberal economics, stemming from both comparative literature and environmental studies and consolidating them both. Power being productive as well as prohibitive, this results in a quantitative proliferation of studies of nonhuman objects and themes. This quantitative accumulation, joining forces with multidisciplinary components from outside the humanities (mostly social sciences, anthropology, and geology and environmental sciences), gets to recode its field of activity as the environmental humanities. The field is so dynamic, it has produced several specialized scholarly journals[4] and counts as an established academic field.

Similarly, the digital humanities can be framed by a majoritarian narrative that traces a straight line from media studies, via the application of computing methods to humanities. This posits human-technological relations as a major research theme and establishes a field that is so advanced that it publishes specialized journals and curricula and international institutional networks.

But this majoritarian metapattern—both driven by the speed of reterritorialization of neoliberal economics and limited by it—is not all there is to posthuman knowledges. A minor metapattern is also at work here, indexed on the becoming-minoritarian of knowledge production practices. I could express it with a provocative question: What does it say about the contemporary posthumanities that so few institutions have embraced feminist/queer/migrant/poor/decolonial/diasporic/disabled/diseased humanities? The speed of deterritorialization of these "minor" subjects of knowledge, or "missing peoples," is of an altogether different order from the majority-driven values. Cognitive capitalism cannot or does not want to overcode these minoritarian subjects to the same extent as it territorializes other established discourses. This is the opening we need in which to compose a different plane of encounters. Granting to minoritarian subjects the political potential of carrying alternative modes of becoming, I want to propose a different metapattern that actualizes the "missing peoples."

This second option rests on a crucial distinction between quantitative or extensive and qualitative or intensive states, which Deleuze (1988) adapts from Spinoza's ethical system. My cartography so far shows a quantitative proliferation of discourses, fields, and themes generated from posthuman locations. Many of these objects of study have already been itemized and quantified for the academic market inquiry. A focus on nonhuman objects/things (Deleuze and Guattari 1987) and a quantitative proliferation of discourses without qualitative shifts is an insufficient condition for the production of new concepts and conceptual practices. In order to set up credible and rigorous critical posthumanities, we need a qualitative shift.

The qualitative criteria I want to suggest are (1) supradisciplinarity, (2) metadiscursivity, (3) material grounding, and (4) nomadic generative force or affirmative ethics. These general principles get operationalized in a series of methodological guidelines, which include cartographic accuracy, with the corollary of ethical accountability, and the combination of critique with creativity, including a flair for paradoxes and the recognition of the specificity of art practices. Other criteria are nonlinearity, the powers of memory and the imagination, and the strategy of defamiliarization (Braidotti 2013). I regret that I cannot expand on them here.

To apply these qualitative distinctions to the point I made earlier about different speeds of de/reterritorialization of contemporary knowledge practices, I need to argue two potentially contradictory cases at the same time. This is not irrationality but complexity. On the one hand, it is clear that the critical posthumanities are caught in the instrumental spin of neoliberal logic of capitalizing on life itself. They are developing faster than the academic institutions can keep up with, and they are growing either from the transdisciplinary studies or among the university, social movements, and corporate interests. On the other hand, they pursue and even radicalize the aims and affects of the studies (notably the second generation). This means that the posthumanities coexist but do not coincide with the profit-oriented reacquisitions of life as capital—both financial and cognitive—that is the core of advanced capitalism. The distinction I seek is ethical; it is about what kind of affirmative assemblages we are capable of sustaining, knowing that their political force lies in actualizing "collective imaginings" (Gatens and Lloyd 1999) or virtual futures (Braidotti 2006).

Complexity becomes the operative word and, applied to the analysis of posthuman knowledges, it produces the useful distinction Deleuze makes between royal and minor science/knowledge. Royal science is institutionally implemented and well funded, being compatible with the economic imperatives of advanced capitalism and its cognitive excursions into living matter (Bonta and Protevi 2004). Minor science, on the other hand, is underfunded and marginalized, while acting as an ethically transformative and politically empowering event. The monistic, ecosophical, and geocentered turn that sustains the critical posthumanities gains strength from this distinction between actualized states of "royal science" and the virtual becoming of "minor science" (DeLanda 2002). The emphasis on matter as autopoetic supports a call for a retuning of the scientific laws according to a view of the subject of knowledge as a complex singularity, an affective assemblage, and a relational vitalist entity. All this marks a qualitative and methodological shift that goes beyond mere quantitative proliferations of objects of study.

The combination of the high degree of supradisciplinary hybridization I analyzed above and the monistic idea of vital geocentrism—the love of *zoe*—as a qualitative criterion frames an ethics of affirmation that casts the method of defamiliarizing our habits of thought in a new direction. We are now encouraged to build on the postcolonial injunction of "unlearning our privilege as our loss" (Spivak 1990: 9) toward a qualitative assessment of our relational deficits and injuries, notably toward nonhuman others. The question is: what is an embrained body and embodied brain capable of becoming? The frame of reference becomes the world, in all its open-ended, interrelational, transnational, multisexed, and transspecies flows of becoming (Braidotti 2006, 2013).

In other words, affirmative ethics, grounded in the politics of immanence (Deleuze 2003), opens up margins of differentiation and negotiations within the reterritorializations of cognitive capitalism. The overflowing codes of capital never fully saturate the processes of becoming, and therefore the minor discourses always contain margins of disenfranchisement from royal science, because power is not a single entity but a multilayered, dynamic, and strategic situation. The task of posthuman critical knowledge is in activating subjects to enter into new affective assemblages, to cocreate alternative ethical forces and political codes—in other words, to instill processes of becoming for the multiple missing people.

Given that rhizomic multidirectionality is the rule for both royal and minor science and related knowledge production systems, let me conclude by pointing to some planes of organization of knowledge that are taking place within the critical posthumanities. Considering the high degrees of specialization required by the generations of transdisciplinary studies areas and the fact that each transdisciplinary plateau is framed by specific affective assemblages and relations, it follows that no two planes of composition are the same. The current recomposition of posthuman knowledges shows patterns of organization but also of resegregation of discourses. Feminist, queer, migrant, poor, decolonial, diasporic, disabled, and diseased perspectives do not enjoy the benefits of royal representation in the contemporary posthuman landscape. As I argued earlier, their speed of deterritorialization is other than that of royal science.

This is where the emphasis on rhizomatic energy of the field allows me to identify the forces that overflow and overturn majoritarian knowledge production. The strength of minoritarian subjects consists in their capacity to carry alternative modes of becoming that break up segregational majoritarian patterns. New border crossings are being set up that aim at actualizing these missing peoples.

For instance, significant new links are being set between postcolonial theories, the environmental humanities, and indigenous epistemologies, resulting in growing convergence between them (Nixon 2011). This results in the production of new areas of studies that cross over the complex postanthropocentric axes: postcolonial environmental humanities come to the fore. Similar developments are filling in missing links in the digital humanities. Postcolonial digital humanities is now an emerging field, digital media providing the most comprehensive platform to rethink transnational spaces and contexts (Nakamura 2002; Ponzanesi and Leurs 2014). These new assemblages pursue the aims of classical postcolonial studies, across the reterritorialized digital humanities platform, into the complexity of minor science. And so are the decolonial digital humanities, for example the Hastac Scholars Forum,[5] explicitly inspired by Walter Mignolo's (2011) work. This results in new alliances between environmentalists and legal specialists, indigenous and non-Western epistemologies, First Nation peoples, new media activists, IT engineers, and antiglobalization forces, which constitute a significant example of new political assemblages.[6]

These multiple hybrid connections of the minor sciences that sustain these new epistemological openings are not the effect of spontaneous generation, but rather the result of the hard work of communities of thinkers and activists—alternative collective assemblages—that reconstitute not only the missing links in academic practices, but also and especially the missing people. The struggle for their visibility and emergence drives the radical politics of immanence, aimed at actualizing minority-driven knowledges through transversal alliances. The people who were missing—even from minor science—get constituted as political subjects of knowledge through such alliances.

Within a neomonistic Spinozist frame, the political—that is to say, the actualization of the virtual—is driven by the ethics of affirmation. This entails the overthrowing of negativity through the recasting of the oppositional, resisting self ("I would prefer not to") into a collective assemblage ("we"). This transversal alliance today is technologically mediated, and it always involves nonhuman agents (land, water, plastic, wires, information highways, algorithms, etc.). It is a praxis that involves the formation of a new alliance, a new people. The activating factor in the politics of immanence is a plane of transposition of forces—in both spatial and temporal terms—from past to future and from the virtual to the actual. It is the actualization of a virtuality.

The point of this actualization is to provide an adequate expression of what bodies can do and think and enact. The degree of adequacy is estimated in terms of one's intensity, that is, one's ability to process pain and negativity, to turn the painful experience of inexistence into relational encounters and knowledge production. This is liberation through the understanding of our bondage, as Spinoza teaches us (Lloyd 1994, 1996). The politics of immanence composes planes of becoming for a missing people that was never fully part of the "human," and therefore was able to trigger a becoming-minor of the human as a vector of composition of a new people and a new earth.

Instead of taking a flight into an abstract idea of a new pan-human, bonded in negative passions like fear of extinction, I want to make a plea for monistic affirmative politics grounded on immanent interconnections: a transversal composition of multiple assemblages of active minoritarian subjects. This framework provides theoretical grounding for the emergence of the critical posthumanities as a supradisciplinary, rhizomic field of contemporary posthuman knowledges that are contiguous with, but not identical to, cognitive capitalism, being driven by radically different ethical affects.

The critical posthumanities design a horizon of becoming for an academic minor science that the contemporary university would do well to heed. It involves multidirectional openings toward social and cultural movements, new kinds of economically productive practices in a market economy liberated from capitalist axioms, and multiple curiosity-driven knowledge practices that do not coincide with the profit motive of cognitive capitalism.

The task of critical subjects of knowledge is to pursue the posthuman, all-too-human praxis of speaking truth to power and working toward the composition of planes of immanence for missing peoples, respecting the complex singularities that constitute our respective locations. "We" is the product of a praxis, not a given. The dwellers of this planet at this point in time are interconnected but also internally fractured by the classical axes of negative differentiation: class, race, gender and sexual orientations, and age and ablebodiedness continue to index access to normal humanity. This rhizomic field of posthuman knowledges does not aspire to a consensus about a new humanity but labors to produce a workable frame for the actualization of the many missing people, whose "minor" or nomadic knowledge is the breeding ground for possible futures.

Notes

1   For an overview, see Braidotti and Hlavajova, forthcoming.
2   For an overview, see Braidotti 2015 and forthcoming.
3   A brief overview of new developments would have to include the following fields: medical humanities; bio-humanities; energy humanities; digital humanities; public humanities; civic humanities; community humanities; global humanities; ecological humanities; environmental humanities; sustainable humanities; interactive humanities; organic humanities; neural-evolutionary humanities; entrepreneurial humanities; translational humanities; greater humanities; and resilient humanities.
4   The two major journals in the field are *Environmental Humanities* (www.dukeupress .edu/environmental-humanities) and *Resilience: A Journal of the Environmental Humanities* (www.resiliencejournal.org).
5   See HASTAC Scholars Program 2015. With thanks to Matthew Fuller.
6   See, for instance, the land/media/indigenous project based in British Columbia: Bleck, Dodds, and Williams 2013.

References

Alaimo, Stacy. 2010. *Bodily Natures: Science, Environment, and the Material Self.* Bloomington: Indiana University Press.

Alaimo, Stacy. 2014. "Thinking as the Stuff of the World." *O-Zone: A Journal of Object-Oriented Studies* 1. O-zone-journal.org/.

Ansell Pearson, Keith. 1999. *Germinal Life: The Difference and Repetition of Deleuze.* London: Routledge.

Beck, Ulrich. 2007. "The Cosmopolitan Condition: Why Methodological Nationalism Fails." *Theory, Culture and Society* 24, no. 7–8: 286–90.

Bleck, Nancy, Katherine Dodds, and Bill Chief Williams. 2013. *Picturing Transformations.* Vancouver: Figure 1.

Bonta, Mark, and John Protevi. 2004. *Deleuze and Geophilosophy: A Guide and Glossary.* Edinburgh: Edinburgh University Press.

Borradori, Giovanna. 2003. *Philosophy in a Time of Terror.* Chicago: University of Chicago Press.

Braidotti, Rosi. 1994. *Nomadic Subjects: Embodiment and Sexual Difference in Contemporary Feminist Theory.* 1st ed. New York: Columbia University Press.

Braidotti, Rosi. 2002. *Metamorphoses: Towards a Materialist Theory of Becoming.* Cambridge: Polity.

Braidotti, Rosi. 2006. *Transpositions: On Nomadic Ethics.* Cambridge: Polity.

Braidotti, Rosi. 2011a. *Nomadic Subjects: Embodiment and Sexual Difference in Contemporary Feminist Theory.* New York: Columbia University Press.

Braidotti, Rosi. 2011b. *Nomadic Theory: The Portable Rosi Braidotti.* New York: Columbia University Press.

Braidotti, Rosi. 2013. *The Posthuman.* Cambridge: Polity.

Braidotti, Rosi. 2015. "The Posthuman in Feminist Theory." In *The Oxford Handbook of Feminist Theory*, edited by Lisa Disch and Mary Hawkesworth, 673–98. Oxford: Oxford University Press.

Braidotti, Rosi. 2016. "The Contested Posthumanities." In *Conflicting Humanities*, edited by Rosi Braidotti and Paul Gilroy, 9–46. London: Bloomsbury Academic.

Braidotti, Rosi. Forthcoming. "Four Theses on Posthuman Feminism." In *Anthropocene Feminism*, edited by Richard Grusin. Minneapolis: Minnesota University Press.

Braidotti, Rosi, and Maria Hlavajova. Forthcoming. *Posthuman Glossary*. London: Bloomsbury Academic.

DeLanda, Manuel. 2002. *Intensive Science and Virtual Philosophy*. London: Bloomsbury.

Deleuze, Gilles. 1988. *Spinoza: Practical Philosophy*. San Francisco, CA: City Lights Books.

Deleuze, Gilles. 1990. *Expressionism in Philosophy: Spinoza*. New York: Zone Books.

Deleuze, Gilles. 2003. *Pure Immanence: Essays on a Life*. New York: Zone Books.

Deleuze, Gilles, and Félix Guattari. 1987. *A Thousand Plateaus: Capitalism and Schizophrenia*. Minneapolis: University of Minnesota Press.

Deleuze, Gilles, and Félix Guattari. 1994. *What Is Philosophy?* New York: Columbia University Press.

Foucault, Michel. 1970. *The Order of Things: An Archaeology of the Human Sciences*. New York: Pantheon.

Foucault, Michel, and Maurice Blanchot. 1987. *Foucault/Blanchot*. New York: Zone Books.

Fukuyama, Francis. 2002. *Our Posthuman Future: Consequences of the Biotechnological Revolution*. London: Profile Books.

Fuller, Matthew. 2005. *Media Ecologies: Materialist Energies in Art and Technoculture*. Cambridge, MA: MIT Press.

Fuller, Matthew. 2008. *Software Studies: A Lexicon*. Cambridge, MA: MIT Press.

Gatens, Moira, and Genevieve Lloyd. 1999. *Collective Imaginings*. New York: Routledge.

Guattari, Félix. 1995. *Chaosmosis: An Ethico-Aesthetic Paradigm*. Sydney: Power Publications.

Guattari, Félix. 2000. *The Three Ecologies*. London: Athlone Press.

Habermas, Jürgen. 2003. *The Future of Human Nature*. Cambridge: Polity.

Hansen, Mark. 2006. *Bodies in Code: Interfaces with Digital Media*. New York: Routledge.

Haraway, Donna. 1988. "Situated Knowledges: The Science Question in Feminism and the Privilege of Partial Perspective." *Feminist Studies* 14, no. 3: 575–99.

Haraway, Donna. 1997. *Modest_Witness@Second_Millennium: FemaleMan©_Meets_ Onco-Mouse™: Feminism and Technoscience*. New York: Routledge.

Haraway, Donna. 2003. *The Companion Species Manifesto: Dogs, People, and Significant Otherness*. Chicago: Prickly Paradigm Press.

Haraway, Donna. 2015. "Anthropocene, Capitalocene, Plantationocene, Cthulucene: Making Kin." *Environmental Humanities* 6, no. 1: 159–65.

Harding, Sandra. 1986. *The Science Question in Feminism*. Ithaca, NY: Cornell University Press.

Hardt, Michael, and Antonio Negri. 2000. *Empire*. Cambridge, MA: Harvard University Press.

HASTAC Scholars Program. 2015. "Decolonizing the Digital." Forum hosted by micha cárdenas, Noha F. Beydoun, and Alainya Kavaloski. May 27. www.hastac.org/initiatives/hastac-scholars/scholars-forums/decolonizing-digital.

Hill Collins, Patricia. 1991. *Black Feminist Thought: Knowledge, Consciousness, and the Politics of Empowerment*. New York: Routledge.

Hörl, Erich. 2013. "A Thousand Ecologies: The Process of Cyberneticization and General Ecology." In *The Whole Earth: California and the Disappearance of the Outside*, edited by Diedrich Diederichsen and Anselm Franke, 121–30. Berlin: Sternberg Press.

Lloyd, Genevieve. 1994. *Part of Nature: Self-Knowledge in Spinoza's "Ethics."* Ithaca, NY: Cornell University Press.

Lloyd, Genevieve. 1996. *Routledge Philosophy Guidebook to Spinoza and the "Ethics."* London: Routledge.

Lykke, Nina. 2011. "This Discipline Which Is Not One: Feminist Studies as a Post-Discipline." *Theories and Methodologies in Postgraduate Feminist Research: Researching Differently*, edited by Rosemarie Buikema, Gabriele Griffin, and Nina Lykke, 137–51. New York: Routledge.

Massumi, Brian. 1998. "Sensing the Virtual, Building the Insensible." *Architectural Design* 68, no. 5–6: 16–24.

Mbembe, Achille. 2003. "Necropolitics." *Public Culture* 15, no. 1: 11–40.

Mignolo, Walter. 2011. *The Darker Side of Western Modernity: Global Futures, Decolonial Options*. Durham, NC: Duke University Press.

Moulier Boutang, Yann. 2012. *Cognitive Capitalism*. Cambridge: Polity.

Nakamura, Lisa. 2002. *Cybertypes: Race, Ethnicity, and Identity on the Internet*. London: Routledge.

Nixon, Rob. 2011. *Slow Violence and the Environmentalism of the Poor*. Cambridge, MA: Harvard University Press.

Parikka, Jussi. 2015. *A Geology of Media*. Minneapolis: University of Minnesota Press.

Ponzanesi, Sandra, and Koen Leurs. 2014. "On Digital Crossings in Europe." *Crossings: Journal of Migration and Culture* 5, no. 1: 3–22.

Protevi, John. 2013. *Life, War, Earth: Deleuze and the Sciences*. Minneapolis: University of Minnesota Press.

Rich, Adrienne. 1987. *Blood, Bread, and Poetry: Selected Prose, 1979–1985*. London: Virago Press.

Sassen, Saskia. 2014. *Expulsions: Brutality and Complexity in the Global Economy*. Cambridge, MA: Belknap Press of Harvard University Press.

Shiva, Vandana. 1993. *Monocultures of the Mind: Perspectives on Biodiversity and Biotechnology*. London: Palgrave.

Shiva, Vandana. 1997. *Biopiracy: The Plunder of Nature and Knowledge*. Boston: South End Press.

Sloterdijk, Peter. 2009. "Rules for the Human Zoo: A Response to the 'Letter on Humanism.'" *Environment and Planning D: Society and Space* 27, no. 1: 12–28.

Spivak, Gayatri C. 1990. "Criticism, Feminism, and the Institution." In *The Postcolonial Critic*, 1–16. London: Routledge.

Stimpson, Catherine R. 2016. "The Nomadic Humanities." *Los Angeles Review of Books*, July.

Toscano, Alberto. 2005. "Axiomatic." *The Deleuze Dictionary*, edited by Adrian Parr, 17–18. Edinburgh: Edinburgh University Press.

David Buckland, Olivia Gray, and Lucy Wood

The Cultural Challenge of Climate Change

In 2000 the Cape Farewell project was born, and over the subsequent fifteen years it has given rise to an outpouring of creative activity that, in varying ways, addresses the scientific reality of climate change through the lens of cultural and civic engagement. The scientists have stated the problem and articulated the challenge; the solution to averting catastrophic climate disruption is embedded in the way we choose to live our civic and urban lives; it is about creating a sustainable global culture.

The original objective of Cape Farewell was to craft a different language with which to understand the science of climate change, one that is more human and palatable for public consumption. Data-heavy and scientific-based communication on climate change has given rise to polarized opinions that are often based more on dogma than on reason.

Climate change demands that civic society changes. Our addiction to fossil fuel for energy is not sustainable, and we have an extremely short window of time to avert major planetary catastrophe. Motivating the necessary engagement and change will require significant behavioral and cultural shifts. How do we therefore communicate this urgency in an effective way? Without

The South Atlantic Quarterly 116:1, January 2017
DOI 10.1215/00382876-3749348 © 2017 Duke University Press

preaching, art is a possible means—it has the ability to reach into peoples' psyches, where reasoned argument can often fail.

Storytellers, C. S. Lewis said, carry meaning in a way that rational truth-tellers cannot. "For me," the novelist wrote, "reason is the natural organ of truth; but imagination is the organ of meaning. Imagination, producing new metaphors or reviving old, is not the cause of truth, but its condition" (Lewis 1939: 157–58).

The Beginnings

Expedition—a journey undertaken by a group of people with a particular purpose, especially that of exploration, research.
—*Oxford Dictionaries Online*

In May 2003, twenty scientists, artists, writers, and filmmakers set sail north from Norway in a hundred-year-old schooner, the *Noorderlicht*, on what was to become the first of eight Cape Farewell expeditions in the High Arctic.

We voyaged into absent and cold places, where one of the most significant events of our time was being played out: the effects of climate change and the birth of the Anthropocene.[1] We have entered a new "age," replacing the twelve thousand years of the Holocene. Our feverish human activity has produced a force equal in power to the natural forces that govern our planetary system. While pretty impressive, this is also deeply troubling—humans are now masters of their own and our planet's fate.

The Cape Farewell expeditionary force had to crew and steer the *Noorderlicht* through very dangerous ice seas, each course plotted to realize a scientific inquiry and creative objective. We used the notion of expedition as a tool of shared interrogation to investigate the future-truth of climate change. We measured at depth the ocean currents and the retreat of the glaciers, studied polar bears, and made time for the creatives to work, have immersive experiences, and evolve the beginnings of creative inquiry. The aim was to interrogate the scientists' work—to discover how our planet is being affected by human activity and consider what the climate challenge will mean to future human civilization.

The expectation placed on the artists was not to make fundamental changes to their art and practice but for them to "lend" their fine-tuned skills to address what has been described as humanity's greatest challenge, ever. The physical and metaphorical notion of "expedition" enabled a shared activity to take place among disparate crews of extraordinary inquisitors, including scientists, creatives, media, and educators.

Initially, the climate scientists thought that the artists and creatives would illustrate their scientific knowledge and concerns, but it quickly became clear that the process of artistic inquiry does not merely illustrate. The creatives learned, absorbed, inhabited the science, the physical harshness of the High Arctic, and through highly developed creative antennae and skills produced entire new ways of seeing and experiencing. They created stories, narratives, artworks that were to become public facing, inspiring, transporting, accurate. Climate science deals in data that are often perceived as abstract and planetary—enormous in scale; what the Cape Farewell residents did was to create something on a human scale—their personal narrative, a physical emotional engagement that told of the future-truth of where humanity is heading.

The Art

I think of art, at its most significant, as a DEW line, a Distant Early Warning system that can always be relied on to tell the old culture what is beginning to happen to it.
—*Marshall McLuhan, DEW-Line Newsletter*, 1964

Poet Nick Drake voyaged to the "Farewell Glacier" in October 2010. As he was about to leave the *Noorderlicht* and the ice of the High Arctic and return to his hometown of London, he crafted these words:

> Will we remember what we wished for?
> Have we come to our senses, like acolytes who have seen the extinction
>   of the future in a bad dream?
> Can we return with a story or a song that will save us just in time?
> And what will we say of this dying monster in its last lair when we are
>   home again?
> Will we understand at last what we have tried and failed to make out,
> In the infinite fractures of its great blind, archaic mirror of lost time,
>   was only ourselves?
> Can we see now we have lived like gods on borrowed time?
> And when we return to the immediate moments of our illuminated
>   cities and warm living rooms,
> How will we recall this frozen auditorium and its oracular silence,
> And the last long performance of its disappearing act? (Drake 2011)
> Artists work and live within the milieu of their times; it seems very
>   obvious that they should wish to engage and be inspired by
>   the massive change implied by human and planetary activity
>   as it enters into the Anthropocene.

The Cape Farewell expeditions were a shared artistic-scientific inquiry, an interrogation of what exactly climate change is and what it will become in the coming decades. Climate scientists were clear in their prognosis, now confirmed by the 2014 Intergovernmental Panel on Climate Change report. The artists-creatives needed to embrace the mathematical climate models that can, with a fair degree of certainty, predict the physical near future of our existence on earth (mankind has never before had access to such a tool) and how to give meaning to what was soon to be identified as the age of the Anthropocene. Climate change will affect the way we live and think about ourselves. It will challenge our notions of self and civic society and how our habitat (the planet) is under threat from our feverish activity.

Booker Prize winner Ian McEwan wrote the following words in 2006, after his expedition to the Arctic with Cape Farewell:

> The pressure of our numbers, the abundance of our inventions, the blind forces of our desires—the hot breath of our civilisation. How can we begin to retrain ourselves? We resemble successful lichen, a ravaging bloom of algae, a mould enveloping a fruit.

> We are fouling our nest, and we know we must act decisively, against our immediate inclinations. But can we agree among ourselves?

> We are a clever but quarrelsome species—in our public debates we can sound like a rookery in full throat. We are superstitious, hierarchical and self-interested, just when the moment requires us to be rational, even-handed and altruistic.

> Pessimism is intellectually delicious, even thrilling, but the matter before us is too serious for mere self-pleasuring. On our side we have our rationality, which finds its highest expression and formalisation in good science. And we have a talent for working together—when it suits us.

> Are we at the beginning of an unprecedented era of international co-operation, or are we living in an Edwardian summer of reckless denial? Is this the beginning, or the beginning of the end? (2006: 10–11)

Looking back over these expeditions and the 200-plus creatives, educationists, and climate scientists who ventured to the High Arctic, and the creative outpouring that they manifested, it is not possible to form a single critique or evaluate the measurability of civic impact. The body of work produced under the Cape Farewell umbrella is substantial, now so numerous and so distinctly focused that it could be argued that a new artistic-cultural movement has been formed. Cape Farewell films have been broadcast on the BBC and Sundance; McEwan wrote the novel *Solar*; the *Burning Ice* exhibition toured the world; in 2009 the *U-n-f-o-l-d* exhibition became the first climate exhibition ever to be shown in Beijing. The 2009–10 *eARTh* exhibition at the Royal Academy of Arts in London showcased the global creative response by artists who have taken on board the challenge that our environment and cultures are facing and envisioned, through art, a new and compelling narrative.

In 2010 the Cape Farewell team, our board, and a selected group of advisers reassessed the future course of the organization. We acted with the knowledge that human-triggered climate change was a given fact and that we needed to continue interrogating the future with the mind's eye focused on solutions. It was important to stay concentrated on our own strengths and our history—we would use the notion of explorer and expedition to work toward visioning and inspiring a necessary and sustainable cultural shift. Climate is culture, and by *culture* we mean *civilization* in its most global and complex sense, including civic society, economics, technology, and energy production. The scientists have told us that we have a problem, but they cannot solve it—that is up to civic choice.

Sea Change

In 2011 Ruth Little (Cape Farewell associate director) set up the Scottish islands four-year program—the Sea Change (Tionndadh na Mara) project. In her essay "The Slow Craft of Contemporary Expedition: Islandings," she states:

> The Sea Change project focuses on Scotland's islands because island communities and ecologies, just like boats, offer both palpable and symbolic evidence of the reality of resource constraint; the relationship between needs and limits that is in the end the stuff of climate change. In urban environments, it's easy to look away. On islands, the costs of obtaining resources and removing waste offer opportunities for radical, small-scale and contained experiment in resource use and energy supply, in projects which strive, at times against all the odds, to develop and maintain community cohesion and economic, social and environmental diversity and resilience. (Little 2012: 18)

Over fifty artists, writers, musicians, and performers have created climate-focused works for exhibitions, theatrical performances, and a Gallic musical festival during the four years of the project, which is still ongoing. At its core is a vocal composition, "Guth na eòin | Voice of the Bird," created for a choir of female singers for performance outdoors on Canna, in the Inner Hebrides

Figure 1. *Voice of the Bird* by Hanna Tuulikki

(see figure 1). The piece reinterprets archival material, fragmenting and rebuilding extracts of Gaelic songs into an extended soundscape that grows out of and responds to the landscape. It explores the relationship between the Scottish Gaelic tradition and bird communities, evoking the sounds, movements, and interactions of several bird species within a Hebridean landscape.

Carbon 14

The Carbon 14 exhibition/festival at the Royal Ontario Museum in Toronto, in 2013–14, became a collective name for artistic engagement that interrogates the near future urban space we humans will inhabit as climate disruption becomes a physical reality. On November 11, 2011, eleven "informers" and twenty-six creatives gathered on the banks of Lake Ontario for a unique expedition (that did not physically move anywhere) designed to facilitate the making of new artworks for the Royal Ontario Museum exhibition in 2013. Creatives gathered from the United States, Canada, the United Kingdom, and Mexico to explore the whole canopy of human endeavor with one single coda: that the feverish human activity that for two hundred years has achieved extraordinary successes has one notable downside—our dangerously overheating habitat.

Deconstructing how our society operates and how it might work if it buys into achieving a stable climate and sustainable future was the challenge given to the informers. The informers were chosen for their commitment to change and for their commitment to climate engagement. Collectively, they mapped the scientific, political, economic, spiritual, technological, and civic space with the twenty-six gathered creatives. Two days of intense sharing and inspiration cumulated in an introduction at the Royal Ontario Museum galleries, which were to become the staging ground of the Carbon 14 festival. Over the next eighteen months the creatives formulated their works, and, curated by David Buckland and Claire Sykes, the Carbon 14 four-month festival took place, centered at the Royal Ontario Museum and spread throughout the city.

The following is a list of works and creatives included in the Carbon 14 festival:

> *The Unsolicited Reply*—Lisa Steel and Kim Tomczak
> **crazyweather*—Sharon Switze
> *A Draught of the Blue*—Minerva Cuevas
> *Global Warming*—Jaco Ishulutaq
> Qapirgajuq, *Inuit Knowledge and Climate Change*—Zacharias Kunuk and
>   Ian Mauro
> *Quniq, Qunbuq, Quabaa*—Don Weber
> *Deep Time*—Melanie Gilligan and Tom Ackers
> *The Potential Project*—Mel Chin
> *The Silver Bullet*—David Buckland and Tom Rand
> *Beekeeping for All*—Myfanwy MacLeod and Janna Levitt
> *The Trial of David Suzuki*—Laurie Brown
> *Post-Normal*—Tanya Tagaq
> *Sea Sick*—Alanna Mitchell
> *This Clement World*—Cynthia Hopkins

The Trial of David Suzuki—Laurie Brown

In November 2013, David Suzuki (see figure 2) was put on trial and charged with seditious libel in a "theatrical" court at the Royal Ontario Museum in front of an audience of four hundred people, and the proceedings were broadcast live on the Internet. In addition to a lay jury of twelve, those present were a judge, a prosecuting council, a defense council, and expert witnesses. Suzuki's crime—seditious libel. He had publicly written and published the Carbon Manifesto, a bold, uncompromising plan that spells out

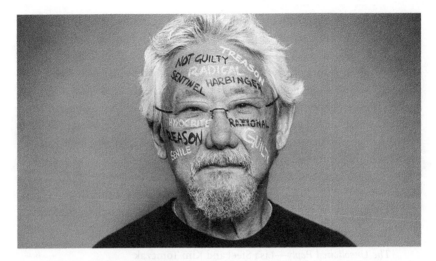

Figure 2. David Suzuki. Photo: ©Raina+Wilson Photography, 2013. Courtesy of Laurie Brown and Cape Farewell Foundation, Toronto

the end of the tar sands and sets a new course for the future of sustainable energy. The manifesto directly charges the Canadian government with complicity in subsidizing the tar sands and threatening the financial security of the country. Suzuki maintains that the manifesto is a truthful document that recommends the overthrow of the Canadian government—at the trial he asserted that the manifesto is not libelous but truthful, the substance of his defense. After a theatrical legal battle played out before the citizens of Toronto, he was found not guilty by the jury.

The Cape Farewell work continues under the project headlines:

The FarmART project examines food security, the macro biome of soil, and farm practices.

The Cape Farewell Lovelock Art Commission. An artist works with the archive of James Lovelock and the Gaia theory, producing a yearly exhibition shown at the Museum of Science and Industry in Manchester.

ArtCOP21. With the historic twenty-first session of the Conference of the Parties (COP21) to the United Nations Framework Convention on Climate Change looming, Cape Farewell and its French partners the Coalition for Art and Sustainable Development (COAL) had the ambition to build a global festival of civic engagement with climate change. ArtCOP21 was launched in September 2015 to act as an inclusive cultural platform for activity that engages wide audiences in the climate challenge in the lead-up to and during the climate summit. We understood that the negotiations of COP21 would take place behind closed doors and in dry, bureaucratic lan-

Figure 3. *Evaporation* by Tania Kovats and a performance of *The Wave* by Jonathan Dove, at the Manchester Museum of Science and Industry, 2015, as part of ArtCOP21

guage. ArtCOP21 took on Cape Farewell's defining principles and sought to engage with hundreds of thousands of members of the public in a more human, visceral way.

Climate change is too often viewed through a policy or scientific lens. ArtCOP21 aimed to challenge this trope, arguing that climate is very much a people problem—not one to be left solely to the politicians. Indeed, it is the biggest "people" problem we've ever faced. But the biggest challenge is to move people to care in the first place, because denial is a powerful thing, particularly when people are faced with what feels like an impossible task.

ArtCOP21 exceeded all of our expectations and built up an enormous cultural momentum—numbering 551 events in fifty-four countries at final count and reaching a live global audience of over 750,000 people. The festival brought a huge and inventive array of exhibitions, concerts, marches, conferences, workshops, public art installations, plays, forums, screenings, and guided walks to the streets of Paris and across the world. From a concert in the Arctic Circle featuring Led Zeppelin's John Paul Jones to a street art exhibition in Benin, Africa, the four corners of the earth were truly involved.

The festival sought out work that was provocative, moving, inspiring—work that uses creativity to reframe the catastrophic, negative language of the climate battle, into an opportunity for positive change (see figure 3). The thousands of voices involved in ArtCOP21 argued that what we need is a major cultural shift in how we produce energy, consume, exchange, work, and, ultimately, define ourselves and our culture. We need to move to a post-carbon culture and economy, and fast.

The Critique

The COP21 agreement was historic insofar as it represented an acknowledgment of the reality of man-made climate change; the global mediators on climate had gathered in Paris and achieved an accord on climate change acceptable to 195 countries. On any measure, it was no mean feat. The accord is an interesting marker but is by no means sufficient to avert destructive climate change.

There are, however, clear targets set out (in part):

Paragraph 17: "to hold the increase in the global average temperature to below 2°C above pre-industrial levels by reducing emissions to 40 gigatonnes or to 1.5°C above pre-industrial levels"

Paragraph 23: "a time frame up to 2025 to communicate by 2020 a new nationally determined contribution and to do so every five years"

Paragraph 115: "a concrete roadmap to achieve the goal of jointly providing USD 100 billion annually by 2020 for mitigation and adaptation." (UNFCCC 2015)

These are real numbers and real-time scales. The ball now moves into the court of those entrusted to ratify and deliver on those targets—basically, our global civic society.

In one sense, the delivery is easy: to decarbonize our energy production. We have the technology, the financing is in place, and we could deliver this transformation within the stated time frame—but we probably can't and won't. The challenge has moved beyond the scientists and is all about our international culture in its broadest sense.

This is only the very beginning of a far longer and harder battle. The real challenge continues. The fossil fuel industries will fight hard to maintain their polluting status quo. In 2007 artist Damien Hirst created *For the Love of God*, a diamond-encrusted skull valued at $50 million. "The skull is out of this world, celestial almost," wrote Rudi Fuchs. "It proclaims victory over decay. At the same time . . . it represents death as something infinitely more relentless" (quoted in Other Criteria 2016). Hirst claimed that he sold the piece for the full asking price, in cash, leaving no paper trail. The consortium that bought the piece included Hirst himself. The duplicity and skullduggery of the artwork is probably the most accurate mirror of our times; it has no moral value, its point is greed, and it reflects the reactive capitalism that governs us.

In contrast, Cape Farewell, COAL, and a consortium of global cultural players created "a global festival of cultural activity on climate change" (see the Artcop21 website landing page 2016). By mid-December, when the COP21 treaty was signed, 560 cultural climate events had been staged in over fifty-four countries. Millions engaged with social media and directly with the events, all reflecting the power of the commons. How do we take back control of the value of art against the forces of a distorted market, and how do we take back control of how we produce energy against the distorted forces of the carbon industries? How do we move forward from just reactive capitalism?

Climate Is Culture

We need a cultural shift in our ambition, behavior, and values to build a sustainable, fossil-free energy future. Cape Farewell aims to change the way we think about climate by engaging our greatest creative and visionary minds to work with scientists, clean-tech entrepreneurs, sociologists, and designers to envision and help create and build the noncarbon civic society we need. The Energy Renaissance project is a key example of the work that we do.

For this project, Cape Farewell has teamed up with Hammerhead VR, a pioneering virtual reality and immersive content studio, and the Environmental Research Group at King's College London to create an immersive virtual reality experience for Utopia 2016, at Somerset House in October 2016.

The final experience will enable audiences to interact virtually with the physical environment of the Strand—the busy area surrounding Somerset House. Through virtual reality and the implementation of behavioral, scientific, and technological changes, individuals will transform their city into a greener, more peaceful neighborhood that no longer poses a threat to health and, by doing so, will address climate challenge.

Across the world, scientists, environmentalists, and entrepreneurs are taking up the challenge of pollution and climate change—the Energy Renaissance project places the individual at the center of urban evolution, where his or her actions form vital steps toward an easily achievable, safer, and healthier post-carbon urban future. The project draws on gaming, immersive theater, and stunning graphics to create a visceral experience, one not set in a fictional future but inspired and informed by present-day reality.

Asking artists and creatives to focus their activity to produce works that are transformative, that is, with an "agenda," is dangerous territory. These creative efforts can easily fall into the trap of activism and propaganda, and the internal debate within Cape Farewell over such efforts is deep and endless. Set against this challenge, the prize is worth striving for. It is very evident that the time frame set by the scientists, and now the COP21 accord, is very short and the demands are very clear. The step change needed is not within the realm of possibility given the powerful and rich opposition to the fundamental shift needed in energy production. Strong laws are needed, but laws mirror and are dependent on the societies that form them. The COP21 treaty cannot be acted upon without the buy in of civic society—our global culture—that is the aim of projects like Energy Renaissance.

Something extraordinary happened in Paris—two small not-for-profits, with a total workforce of six, achieved a global first—a worldwide festival of cultural activity on climate, a festival totally dependent on a cultural awareness of the need to engage and the need to change the direction of our moral and behavioral compass. Our international call had an unprecedented response—it is clear that there is a very real and growing appetite for change, and Cape Farewell is looking to take the ArtCOP21 movement forward into a major global movement in the years to come.

Ultimately, we must remain positive; this challenge is an opportunity for us to build the cleaner, greener, fairer, and more sustainable global society we all aspire to. We have the technology and the capability to redirect financial resources to power this change. The reality is that if we don't act, the outcome could well be catastrophic—indeed, it could signal the end of the human journey or certainly render our earth completely uninhabitable for a significant majority. But, above all, we need to focus on the opportunities of the shift, not the sacrifices. We need to find a new way to narrate and envision this future that is tangible for people.

We must continue this most important of tasks, and we are working with ever greater conviction to help spearhead a major global cultural shift: a new beginning, an energy renaissance.

Note

1   "'Anthropocene' is a term widely used since its coining by Paul Crutzen and Eugene Stoermer in 2000 to denote the present time interval, in which many geologically significant conditions and processes are profoundly altered by human activities" (Subcommission on Quaternary Stratigraphy 2016).

References

Artcop21 website landing page. 2016. www.artcop21.com/ (accessed August 22, 2016).
Drake, Nick. 2011. "'The Farewell Glacier' by Nick Drake." Vimeo video, 6:22. October 25. vimeo.com/31104125.
Lewis, C. S. 1939. "Bluspels and Flalansferes: A Semantic Nightmare." In *Rehabilitations and Other Essays*, 133–58. London: Oxford University Press.

McEwan, Ian. 2006. "The Hot Breath of Our Civilisation." In *Burning Ice: Art and Climate Change*, by David Buckland et al. London: Cape Farewell.

Other Criteria. 2016. "Damien Hirst—For the Love of God—Poster." othercriteria.com/uk /artwork/damien-hirst-for-the-love-of-god-front-skull-poster (accessed April 21, 2016).

Subcommission on Quaternary Stratigraphy. 2016. "Working Group on the 'Anthropocene.'" quaternary.stratigraphy.org/workinggroups/anthropocene (accessed August 22, 2016).

UNFCCC (United Nations Framework Convention on Climate Change). 2015. "Adoption of the Paris Agreement." December 12. unfccc.int/resource/docs/2015/cop21/eng/l09.pdf.

Utopia 2016. "Utopia 2016: A Year of Imagination and Possibility." utopia.somersethouse.org .uk (accessed April 21, 2016).

Little, Ruth. 2012. "The Slow Craft of Contemporary Expedition: Islandings." In *Expedition*, edited by Chris Wainwright and CCW Graduate School, 13–28. London: CCW Graduate School.

Astrid Ulloa

The Geopolitics of Carbonized Nature and the Zero Carbon Citizen

Introduction

Indigenous peoples in Latin America, who have substantial constitutional rights in various countries, are positioned as major political actors with respect to climate change policies. The effects of climate change on territories and resources are effectively refiguring local indigenous dynamics. Included among the many changes in indigenous life, particularly for women, are the ways that transnational forces are commodifying the climate and incorporating indigenous territories into green markets through programs such as the initiative Reducing Emissions from Deforestation and Forest Degradation (REDD). From these new conditions wrought by climate change emerges what I call a "carbonized nature," which produces distinctly gendered forms of knowledge in global climate policy. Indeed, when it comes to indigenous peoples, there is an unequivocal interrelation among science, gender, and politics (Ulloa 2012). Though rooted in scientific evidence, global environmental and climate change policies have come to "naturalize" gender relations and localized forms of knowledge and identity, generating geopolitical perspectives on the environment, territorialization, and

The South Atlantic Quarterly 116:1, January 2017
DOI 10.1215/00382876-3749359 © 2017 Duke University Press

climate change itself that exacerbate inequalities and exclusions. The result, in short, is a kind of blockage of alternative ways of producing knowledge about climate change.

This view, of course, is based on the notion that the global phenomenon of climate change has taken on its own distinct discourse, a set of geopolitical articulations that mediates the relation between nature, knowledge, and power. It takes on, in the Foucauldian sense, a discursive formation, a language through which climate change knowledge is produced and represented. These processes establish what I have called an "ecogovernmentality of climate change" (Ulloa 2005, 2008, 2010, 2011a, 2011b), which involves a particular form of rationality about climate change mitigation (carbon sinks, reductions of greenhouse gases, reducing emissions from deforestation and forest degradation) and a particular economic logic based on the certified reduction of greenhouse gas emissions. Operating both locally and globally, this ecogovernmentality institutes a kind of green colonialism that seeks to reverse long-standing environmental practices in local communities, consolidating diverse ways of thinking about the environment into a single knowledge system. The particular ways women and indigenous peoples live and conceive of their own environments have been systematically excluded in this new modality of colonialism in Latin America.

My focus in this essay is on the geopolitics of climate change knowledge and policy and what gets lost when local and global approaches converge. The consolidation of global climate change knowledge and policy takes place at universities and institutions in developed countries, where experts and officials determine the practices to be implemented throughout the world. Climate change, in other words, is an instantiation of what Walter Mignolo (2000: 4) refers to as "the equation between geographical location and theory (as well as the technological production of knowledge) [that] is related to the modern equation between time and theory (and technological production of knowledge)." It is this imposition by developed nations—locations deemed more knowledgeable, more technologically and theoretically advanced on issues of climate change—that gives shape to this monolithic view on climate and weather.

Another critical axis of this new geopolitical landscape of knowledge is derived from feminist critiques of environmental discourses, specifically those concerning climate change science and policy. A gendered analytical lens on climate change can indeed be crucial to exposing the absences and elisions in global warming policy, as well as inherent biases in representations of nature itself. A feminist perspective allows us to see how climate change policies reproduce a system of knowledge and power that has an impact on gendered positions and identities, reinforcing the ways science, knowledge, and power have historically used dualist associations, such as woman and nature, to generate inequalities.

In what follows, I present in more detail the associations among climate, gender, and indigeneity, focusing on how knowledge on climate change is produced and circulated based on the ideas of carbonized nature and the zero carbon citizen. I then present some conclusions, highlighting some possible alternatives and counterrepresentations from a localized perspective.

Geopolitics of Carbonized Nature and Its Effects

In recent years a body of work produced by universities and nongovernmental organizations (NGOs) on gender and climate change has emerged, focusing on the mitigation of inequalities at the policy and policy-making levels.[1] From my own review of many of these reports, I have noticed several persistent lines of thought. First, that questions related to the effects of climate change disproportionally affect women's access to resources. Second, that there is a pervasive masculinization of the political spaces of climate change, with markedly low participation of women in institutions and decision-making processes. And third, that many of these documents implement a form of ecofeminist critique that seeks to undercut the historical identification of women with nature, resulting in proposals to better account for the differentiated roles of both men and women in the management of climate change.

As one might expect, gender differences in relation to climate change were initially studied because of the noticeable dearth of women in policy programs and institutions (see Aguilar et al. 2009; FMICA 2010; Jungehülsing 2012; Ulloa 2008). These studies have called for increased attention to the role of gender stereotypes in the policy-making process and have criticized instrumentalist inclusions of women to compensate for gender inequities. Commenting on the work of Sybille Bauriedl, German researcher Sandra Bäthge (2013: 19) underscores these critiques, suggesting that "she [Bauriedl] criticizes the tendency within gender-related climate research to rely on oversimplified and homogenizing gender stereotypes, which fail to account for the complex interaction of multiple social dimensions of which gender is but one." Indeed, climate change gender analysis must transcend environmental policy and raise the question of how knowledge itself is produced. To date, most climate change discourses reproduce Western dualist forms of knowledge, creating a decidedly androcentric focus that excludes women from that knowledge-making process.

The stereotypes are well known. The natural world is often conceived of as pristine, wild, or chaotic. The notion of the "natural" is indeed a fluid, heterogeneous formation. But, specifically, it is the idea of a pristine nature that buttresses global environmental discourses, and its central figure is Mother Nature. She is the image of life upon which we all depend, from whom we feed. She, our caring and generous, lush and fertile mother, guarantees our survival.

These images for years have been compressed and expanded and associated with economic, political, and cultural processes. But with the growing cultural awareness of global climate change, a new image of nature has begun to appear. On the one hand, this new discursive formation is an external nature, wild and out of control—think hurricanes, earthquakes, floods—requiring expert knowledge and technical management. It demands new ways of controlling, organizing, and governing, and its inhabitants require the same forms of control, reminiscent of colonial practices. Unsurprisingly, indigenous conceptions of territory and nature remain outside this new geopolitics of knowledge. On the other hand, this new formation is also a biodiverse nature, one that requires protection and control to maximize the use value of the world's ecosystems. It is within this nexus of biodiversity and disaster management that the notion of "carbonized nature" appears, generating specific forms of knowledge in global policy, fragmenting long-held notions of nature. This emergent nature takes on a new valuation in terms of carbon markets, one that extends globally and has the potential to transform subjectivities, identities, and social practices.

This "carbonized nature" can be wild or in need of protection. It responds to the two visions upheld by the colonial power: nature as conquered, nature as safeguarded. And the expert scientific knowledge generated within this new carbonized nature paradigm is what implicitly naturalizes gender relations, dictating roles for men and women, subsuming localized identities and knowledge systems. A carbonized nature favors a culturally whitewashed global population in which the differences of gender, class, or ethnicity are negligible. The discourse of climate change returns us to the long-standing opposition between nature and culture: an unwieldy, untamed nature, on the one hand, and culture, on the other, as a possible way to mitigate and adapt to that unwieldiness. Within this opposition women are associated with nature, becoming "naturalized," as it were, denied entry into the "cultural" scene of technical action and decision making. And if policy approaches to climate change implicitly exclude women, indigenous women are far and away the most excluded from the cultural sphere, relegated even further as fixtures of an environment to be tamed. The notion of the "zero carbon citizen" so prevalent in global public discourse on climate change exposes all of that: it is a citizen deterritorialized, neutral, and culturally homogeneous, without ethnic, class, or gender difference.

The reasons for this elision of difference in climate policy are evident. There is a perceived lack of relevance of the different ways men and women relate to nature and little attention given to those differences. Important, too, is the production and circulation of dominant images and representations that highlight particular relationships with nature. And, perhaps, above all, there is the idea that the problem of climate change is global, that it uniformly affects the entire planet (Röhr 2007). Indeed, to discount difference hides the critical need to understand the specific impacts of climate change according to gender and ethnicity, how climate change is differentially perceived, experienced, and understood. While several studies demonstrate the need for a gendered perspective on climate change (Röhr 2007; Skinner and Brody 2011), it is important to recognize that beyond the simple question of erasure, we need to consider how such absences correspond to a more nuanced conception of cultural difference, how discourses and representations produce certain cultural ideals of, and historical associations with, nature.

Moreover, the implications of this new carbonized nature must also be understood geopolitically, in the sense that the knowledge it produces has a direct bearing on global discursive and socioeconomic imbalances. Crucial, here, as Mignolo (2003: 159) puts it, is "the relationship between geohistorical locations and the production of knowledge." Within the discursive geopolitical landscape that produces the Mother Nature and carbonized nature paradigms, "developed countries" emerge as the primary generators of climate knowledge and discourse. The result is a hierarchical order in the production of knowledge on nature, particularly as it pertains to economic dimensions (such as the commodification of biodiversity and ecosystem services), new eco-efficient technologies (such as wind and solar energy), and the capacity to detect threats and vulnerabilities and generate strategies to confront biodiversity loss or climate change at the global level.

In the production of knowledge about climate change, it is essential to establish the source of that knowledge, how that knowledge is conceived and developed, how it is disseminated, and how all of these facets relate to existing global imbalances in knowledge production. Academic institutions and NGOs, including the Intergovernmental Panel on Climate Change (IPCC)—the "official" generator of climate change knowledge worldwide—all have these elements in common: source location, scientific practice, knowledge representation and mobilization, and positioning in global discursive networks.

Consequently, the geopolitics of carbonized nature becomes spatially distributed, inaugurating new modes of territorial control. In the cartographic representations of climate change—understanding maps as "cultural products, geopolitically situated, and as epistemological statements of power" (Montoya 2007: 165–66)—the new territorial configurations are displayed to project the future effects of global warming. These future projections will become the basis for the appropriation and use of territories by subsequent generations as local landscapes and ecosystems continue to change. No doubt in this new ecogovernmentality of climate change, surveillance technologies of environmental transformations will become increasingly prevalent.

To be sure, this ecogovernmental conception of territory is not far removed from the idea of nature operative in the colonial imaginary, in which the environment was largely seen as an exploitable resource. The valuation several hundred years ago of gold or platinum finds a kind of contemporary correlate in the value of, say, biodiversity today. And this connection to colonialism becomes all the more evident when we consider the effects of global warming on indigenous territories. Though these spaces are often associated with significant losses of biodiversity, rarely is local knowledge and experience incorporated into strategies to combat environmental devastation (Blanco and Fuenzalida 2013). This is often evident in climate adaptation programs, such as those developed under IPCC regulations, which implicitly operate under capitalist notions of nature contrary to indigenous logics (see Dietz 2013). Many indigenous are thus excluded from the process of managing and curtailing the effects of climate change despite ancestral claims to land and forests. Governments redraw territorial boundaries and implement projects so as to maintain control of the land. Compounding these impositions by the state are the armed conflicts that have ravaged many of these indigenous spaces. All these processes are reconfiguring territorial jurisdictions, confronting indigenous social practices, and denying previously recognized indigenous rights in the name of progress, development, and economic opportunity.

The result is that cultural particularity threatens to become erased in the process of addressing national and global interests. Latin American indigenous populations are in the precarious position of facing the doubled threat of climate change and the imposition of state and nongovernmental policies that often run against their own beliefs, practices, and interests. At risk is the lived reality of indigenous peoples—their territorial autonomy, their food sovereignty, and their cultural and material continuity.

Conclusion: Decarbonizing Climate?

I want to underscore the necessity of a radical gesture of inclusion in climate change discourses and mitigation practices. That certainly means incorporating indigenous history and experience, but also specific forms of indigenous knowledge, such as perspectives on nonhuman forms of life. Such an inclusion would reveal different logics of relationality to nature, generating variegated uses and appropriations of resources that stand against the exclusions of contemporary climate change knowledge (Ulloa 2010). It would entail the expansion of the modern idea of nature to encompass other relational ontologies and geopolitical formations to build alternative ways of relating to the nonhuman (Ulloa 2015), thereby establishing an alter geopolitics imbued with localized ways of reading historical environmental transformations.

What seems evident is that our carbonized world necessitates critically rethinking policies regarding the problems caused by climate change at the local, national, and global scales. With this rethinking must come a willingness to reimagine contemporary climate change discourse, to allow for the emergence of other knowledges—what Mignolo (2003) calls *pensamiento fronterizo* (border thinking)—based on alternative ecological conceptions and logics. A new, inclusive constellation of knowledges, temporalities, and recognitions is needed to confront and present alternatives to facing climate change, following Boaventura de Sousa Santos (2006), in which indigenous knowledge is recognized and other nonhuman ontologies are included. Indigenous peoples are demanding the restitution and reappropriation of their territories and resources. They seek to reverse those policy decisions on climate change plagued by unequal gender and ethnic implications in their local contexts. Any rethinking of national and transnational policies on climate change must take their lived political and cultural realities into account.

As I have tried to show, two interrelated processes must be pursued in the realm of climate change knowledge and policy: on the one hand, the exclusions inherent in dominant climate change political discourse and, on the other, the cultural strategies for making that discourse more inclusive and heterogeneous. The first is necessary to demonstrate how women and indigenous peoples have been historically excluded from decision-making processes on environmental issues. Indigenous women in particular have been critical actors on the front lines of climate change, defending everyday livelihoods by focusing on food sovereignty and the construction of new femininities and masculinities. The second is pivotal to opening up those sedimented, hegemonic discourses on climate, clearing room for new ways of imagining landscapes, histories, cultures, and knowledges. The articulation and pursuance of these two processes would allow for new modes of comprehending not just the causes and effects of climate change but how culture and gender permeate the everyday experience of climate change, moving us closer to a decarbonization of our natural world.

Notes

All translations are mine, unless otherwise specified.

1　Ulloa et al. 2013 analyzes one hundred national and international documents related to gender and climate change.

References

Aguilar, Lorena, et al. 2009. *Manual de capacitación en género y cambio climático (Training Manual on Gender and Climate Change)*. San José, Costa Rica: International Union for Conservation of Nature (IUCN) and United Nations Development Program (UNDP) in collaboration with Gender and Water (GWA); International Network on Gender and Sustainable Energy (ENERGIA); United Nations Educational, Scientific, and Cultural Organization (UNESCO); Food and Agricultural Organization of the United Nations (FAO); and Women's Environment and Development Organization (WEDO), as part of the Global Gender and Climate Alliance (GGCA).

Blanco, Gustavo, and María Ignacia Fuenzalida. 2013. "La construcción de agendas científicas sobre cambio climático y su influencia en la territorialización de políticas públicas: Reflexiones a partir del caso chileno" ("The Construction of Scientific Agendas on Climate Change and Its Influence on Territorialization of Public Policy: Reflections from the Chilean Case"). In *Cambio climático, movimientos sociales y políticas públicas: Una vinculación necesaria (Climate Change, Social Movements and Public Policy: A Necessary Link)*, edited by Julio Postigo, 75–102. Santiago, Chile: Instituto de Ciencias Alejandro Lipshutz.

Bäthge, Sandra. 2013. "Global Climate Change Politics and Discourse from a Gender Perspective: Seeing Redd through Feminist Lenses." Master's thesis. Joint program between Freie University, Berlin; Humboldt University, Berlin; and Potsdam University.

Dietz, Kristine. 2013. "Hacia una teoría crítica de vulnerabilidad y adaptación: Aportes para una reconceptualización desde la ecología política" ("Toward a Critical Theory of Vulnerability and Adaptation: Contributions for a Reconceptualization from Political Ecology"). In *Culturas, conocimientos, políticas y ciudadanías en torno al cambio climático (Cultures, Knoweldge, Policies, and Citizenships on Climate Change)*, edited by Astrid Ulloa and Andrea Prieto-Rozo, 19–46. Bogotá: Universidad Nacional de Colombia, Colciencias.

FMICA (Foro de Mujeres para la Integración Centroamericana). 2010. *Género y cambio climático: Aportes desde las mujeres de Centroamérica a las políticas regionales sobre cambio climático (Gender and Climate Change: Contributions from Women in Central America to Regional Policies on Climate Change)*. San José, Costa Rica: FMICA.

Jungehülsing, Jenny. 2012. *Gender Relations and Women's Vulnerability to Climate Change: Contribution from an Adaptation Policy in the State of Tabasco toward Greater Gender Equality; the Reconstruction and Reactivation Program to Transform Tabasco.* Mexico City: Heinrich Böll Stiftung.

Mignolo, Walter. 2000. "Espacios geográficos y localizaciones epistemológicas: La ratio entre localización geográfica y la subalternización de conocimientos" ("Geographical Spaces and Epistemological Locations: The Ratio between Geographical Location and Subalternization of Knowledge"). *Instituto Pensar, Pontificia Universidad Javeriana.* www.javeriana.edu.co/pensar/Rev34.html.

Mignolo, Walter. 2003. *Historias locales / diseños globales: Colonialidad, conocimientos subalternos y pensamiento fronterizo (Local Histories / Global Designs: Coloniality, Subaltern Knowledges, and Border Thinking).* Madrid: Ediciones Akal.

Montoya, Vladimir. 2007. "El mapa de lo invisible: Silencios y gramática del poder de la cartografía" ("The Map of the Invisible: Silences and the Grammar of Power in Cartography"). *Universitas Humanística,* no. 63: 155–79.

Röhr, Ulrike. 2007. "Gender, Climate Change, and Adaptation: Introduction to the Gender Dimensions." Background paper prepared for Both Ends briefing paper "Adapting to Climate Change: How Local Experiences Can Shape the Debate." Berlin: Genanet—Focal Point Gender, Environment, Sustainability.

Santos, Boaventura de Sousa. 2006. "La sociología de las ausencias y la sociología de las emergencias: Para una ecología de saberes" ("The Sociology of Absences and the Sociology of Emergences: For an Ecology of Knowledge"). In *Renovar la teoría crítica y reinventar la emancipación social (Encuentros en Buenos Aires) [Renew Critical Theory and Reinvent Social Emancipation (Meetings in Buenos Aires)],* 13–41. Buenos Aires, Argentina: CLASCO. bibliotecavirtual.clacso.org.ar/ar/libros/edicion/santos/Capitulo%20I.pdf.

Skinner, Emmeline, and Alyson Brody. 2011. "Género y cambio climático" ("Gender and Climate Change"). *Género y Desarrollo en breve, Boletín BRIDGE,* November 22. http://docs.bridge.ids.ac.uk/vfile/upload/4/document/1112/EnBreve22-Web.pdf.

Ulloa, Astrid. 2005. *The Ecological Native: Indigenous Movements and Eco-governmentality in Columbia.* New York: Routledge.

Ulloa, Astrid. 2008. "Implicaciones ambientales y culturales del cambio climático para los pueblos indígenas" ("Environmental and Cultural Implications of Climate Change for Indigenous Peoples"). In *Mujeres indígenas y cambio climático: Perspectivas Latinoamericanas (Indigenous Women and Climate Change: Latin American Perspectives),* edited by Astrid Ulloa et al., 17–34. Bogotá: Universidad Nacional de Colombia and Fundación Natura. unodc.org/documents/colombia/2013/Agosto/DA2013/MUJERES-INDIGENAS-CAMBIO-CLIMATICO.2008.pdf.

Ulloa, Astrid. 2010. "Geopolíticas del cambio climático" ("Geopolitics of Climate Change"). *Anthropos,* no. 227: 133–46.

Ulloa, Astrid. 2011a. "Construcciones culturales sobre el clima" ("Cultural Constructions of Climate"). In *Perspectivas culturales del clima (Cultural Perspectives on Climate),* edited by Astrid Ulloa, 33–53. Bogotá: Universidad Nacional de Colombia and Instituto Latinoamericano para Sociedad y un Derecho Alternativos.

Ulloa, Astrid. 2011b. "Políticas globales del cambio climático: Nuevas geopolíticas del conocimiento y sus efectos en territorios indígenas" ("Global Climate Change Policies: New Geopolitics of Knowledge and Its Effects on Indigenous Territories"). In Ulloa, *Perspectivas culturales del clima,* 447–93.

Ulloa, Astrid. 2012. "Producción de conocimientos en torno al clima: Procesos históricos de exclusión/apropiación de saberes y territorios de mujeres y pueblos indígenas" ("Production of Knowledge about the Climate: Historical Processes of Exclusion/Appropriation of Knowledge and Territories of Women and Indigenous Peoples"). Working paper. desiguALdades.net.

Ulloa, Astrid. 2015. "Environment and Development: Reflections from Latin America." In *The Routledge Handbook of Political Ecology*, edited by Tom Perreault, Gavin Bridge, and James McCarthy, 320–31. London: Routledge.

Ulloa, Astrid, et al. 2013. *Informe final proyecto Perspectivas Culturales y Locales sobre el Clima en Colombia (Final Report of Project: Cultural and Local Perspectives on Climate in Columbia)*. Bogotá: Universidad Nacional de Colombia, Colciencias. Manuscript.

Michael Segal

The Missing Climate Change Narrative

Here are two sets of statements from far-distant opposites in the climate change debate.

The first is from Naomi Klein (2014: 60), who in her book *This Changes Everything* paints a bleak picture of a global socioeconomic system gone wrong: "There is a direct and compelling relationship between the dominance of the values that are intimately tied to triumphant capitalism and the presence of anti-environment views and behaviors."

The second is from Larry Bell, professor of architecture and climate skeptic, whom Klein quotes in her book. He argues that climate change "has little to do with the state of the environment and much to do with shackling capitalism and transforming the American way of life . . . " (Bell quoted in Klein 2014: 33).

Let us put aside whether we agree or disagree with these statements or are offended by them. What concerns us is their scope: Both attach a breadth of narrative to climate change that far exceeds what is, at base, a relatively well-understood set of climate mechanics (human-produced carbon emissions are changing the composition of our atmosphere and warming the planet) and a well-developed set of solutions (renewable and

The South Atlantic Quarterly 116:1, January 2017
DOI 10.1215/00382876-3749370   © 2017 Michael Segal

possibly nuclear energy, efficiency improvements, consumer education, and the appropriate pricing of carbon).

Each side of the climate debate accuses the other of exaggeration and suffers from its own. Skeptics ignore basic climate facts and perils, while those who point their finger at capitalism itself, like Klein, discard one of the best tools at their disposal. It is in part market forces, after all, that have produced a thousandfold reduction in the cost of solar power over the past three decades (guided by policy).

There is a swirl of other, orthogonal narratives, too. American conservatives worry about global agencies interfering in domestic affairs. Some Europeans mistakenly dismiss climate change denial as uniquely American—in December of 2015, Richard Branson told CNN that skepticism is not something he has to deal with in Europe, despite the fact that the percentage of people who believe climate change is caused by human emissions is *higher* in the United States than in the United Kingdom.

The climate conversation can sometimes feel like a shouting match in a roomful of children wearing earplugs. Each narrative doesn't just oppose the next but is deeply incompatible with it. Partly this is a natural result of what is at stake. But it is also because something is missing. We have allowed our political, national, economic, and cultural narratives free play in the modern climate change debate. But where, in this shouting match, are the narratives from science itself? Where is the science teacher?

Peter Sheridan Dodds has a nickname for us humans: *Homo narrativus.* Dodds, a professor at the University of Vermont, uses mathematics to study social networks. He has argued that people see the stories of heroes and villains, where there are really just networks and graphs. It's our desire for narrative, he says, that makes us believe that something like fame is the result of merit or destiny and not a network model quirk (see Dodds 2013).

That we love heroes is something we can all intuitively understand. Less obvious is that climate, too, has a considerable narrative weight and that it is something we understand through storytelling. "Climate cannot be experienced directly through our senses," writes Mike Hulme in his book *Why We Disagree about Climate Change.* "Unlike the wind which we feel on our face or a raindrop that wets our hair, climate is a constructed idea that takes these sensory encounters and builds them into something more abstract" (Hulme 2009: 4). That abstraction has a moral and a historical quality: from the portrayal of flood myths as part of our relationship with the divine, to the birth of fictional monsters like Frankenstein in the wake of climate events, to our association of storms and earthquakes with emotional states—climate has always been more than a mathematical average of weather. In fact, Hulme says, it is only recently, and primarily in the West, that the cultural and physical meanings of climate have become so separated.

That separation has contributed to a narrative vacuum—and, like nature itself, people abhor a vacuum. We fill it with the narratives we have at hand, even if they are powerfully at odds with each other. This goes some way to understanding the vitriol of the climate debate. "The ideological freightage we load onto interpretations of climate and our interactions with it," writes Hulme (2009: 28), "are an essential part of making sense of what is happening around us today in our climate change discourses." Stories about the virtues and evils of capitalism, the role of divine control (C-SPAN 2013), nationalist values, and so on, are not so much maliciously inserted into what could be a sober conversation but are an inevitable response to a story that is incomplete without them.

That is not to say, though, that the climate conversation is irreparably broken. It's true we can't take away those unhelpful narratives that have already been attached to it. But we can add new ones, and some narratives are more powerful than others. Scientific narratives are some of the most powerful of all. They teach us more than facts, mechanisms, and procedures. They convey a worldview of skeptical empiricism and indefinite revision, show us how to negotiate the boundary between our rational and emotional selves, teach us to suspend judgment and consider all the possibilities, and remind us that a belief in objective truth is a deep kind of optimism with massive dividends. Perhaps most important of all, they situate us in the world.

The successful assimilation of broad narratives from astronomy and genetics reminds us how powerful science narrative can be. We think of ourselves today as genetic machines, carrying around an adaptive program, which we inherit and pass on, doing so on this one habitable planet among countless others in a universe with a finite age. These facts have become intuitions, and it has become hard for us to imagine how we might have constructed our identity before they were discovered. The goal of climate change coverage should be no less of a creation of intuition from fact.

Are we getting that done? The mass media has communicated the basic facts behind climate change well enough: the famous line graph of rising carbon dioxide levels, the 300 parts per million line in the sand, the northward migration of adapting species, and the endangerment of those left behind. But the narrative around these facts is more obscure. What does it mean for there to be a scientific consensus? How is the scientific method properly applied to a system that resists experimentation? What does a complex system look like? What is the nature of risk and probability?

Each of these questions has a direct bearing on the climate change conversation without necessarily being about climate change. They, and others like them, constitute a suprascientific narrative that is necessary for science to become culture. In a way, every good science story is a story about all of science and helps us understand every other science story. And we are probably not telling this supranarrative well enough.

Kirk Johnson (2016), director of the Smithsonian National Museum of Natural History, puts it this way: "If you look at how the media treats scientific discoveries, they'll go to the wonder. . . . [They'll say] 'here's this thing that's been discovered,' not the process of how we figured it out. And I think that understanding of how we know what we know is so critical . . . If you don't help people understand what those processes are, [if] you just say 'here's the answer,' now they can go onto the web and dial up an alternate answer. I think we're seeing an erosion of credibility of science to the public because of this huge flood of technology and information."

This erosion is essential to understanding the modern climate debate. In the words of the philosopher Richard Rorty (1981: 170), "We understand knowledge when we understand the social justification of belief, and thus have no need to view it as accuracy of representation." In the absence of social justification, the public ends up being called on to be the judge of accuracy of representation—in other words, of scientific content. Sure enough, quasi-scientific arguments based on misinterpreted data fragments abound in the skeptic community (see Meredith 2012). Why did temperatures stay flat during World War II, despite an emissions increase? Why was there an eighteen-year pause in temperature rise? The only reasonable answers to these questions lie with the scientific community, but they will be ignored if that community hasn't earned an authoritative public voice. That is especially true when the answer is, "We're not sure yet."

The question of authority is complicated further by the multidisciplinary nature of climate change. Authority within the sciences revolves tightly around narrow silos of expertise. As the academics Simon Shackley and Brian Wynne (1996: 278) put it, "A common response by scientists to challenges to their authority is to demarcate the realm within which their expertise is autonomous." In other words, there is a retreat to the silo. But at the policy level, climate change involves atmospheric chemistry, plant and ocean biology, solar physics, geochemistry, soil science, and glaciology, among other disciplines. Building authority in climate science is therefore not well served by the tendency of the scientist to retreat to home turf. Here, too, narratives can help.

But most of the communication effort from the traditional core of science media (magazines, newspaper science sections, radio, and TV) steps around the narrative fray and focuses on reiterating the naked facts of climate change: rising average temperatures, more frequent extreme weather events, and so on. In the words of social scientists Susanne Moser and Lisa Dilling (2011: 163), science communicators "often assume that a lack of information and understanding explains the lack of public concern and engagement, and that therefore more information and explanation is needed to move people to action." But many of these facts are, by now, either uncontested or unsurprising. It is the narratives around them that are missing.

The avoidance of narrative here stems partly from the constraints of modern media—online readers are more easily distracted than print readers, and television and radio segments are short. It also flows from the fact that a focus on narrative context, despite all the lip service paid to it these days, still enjoys a mixed reputation among the traditional science media. I've heard some defend the idea that if the reader's not interested, it's his or her problem. But even scientists need to lure each other with narratives.

The philosopher Rom Harré offers up that pillar of modern professional science, the scientific paper, as exhibit A. He argues that the three-part structure of the typical paper (hypothesis, results, and inductive support) is a post facto interpretation: "Anyone who has ever done any actual scientific research knows that this is a tale, a piece of fiction. The real-life unfolding of a piece of scientific research bears little resemblance to this bit of theatre" (Harré 1990: 89). Speaking as both a former scientist and a former academic editor, I can attest to the truth of this statement. From the lab to the publisher's desk, narrative is constantly helping to organize, sell, and drive science. As Harré puts it, "Science must present a smiling face both to itself and to the world" (89).

If narrative is necessary for one scientist to convince another of his or her result, can we let ourselves believe that it is unnecessary to engage and convince the public? If we consider science to be society's eyes and ears, gathering information about the world, then we can even take a lesson from physiology. Before the mid-1900s, scientists believed that the mammalian eye was a passive recorder of information, like a photographic plate, passing on raw data to the brain. That was until a set of experiments at the Massachusetts Institute of Technology in 1959 showed that the eye is actually analyzing information before passing it on—the brain never receives the naked data and presumably wouldn't know what to do with it if it did (Gefter 2015). Will naked, uninterpreted scientific data work any better for us?

Without new narratives informed by science, we revert to old ones. That is especially clear when it comes to two of the oldest: utopia and dystopia. The skeptic story line of the rise of a dictatorial world government usurping American values must be considered not as a unique reply to climate change but as the latest instance of a well-established dystopic trope, stoked by the climate narrative vacuum. Something similar can be said for attacks on the capitalist enterprise from the left. The public, for its part, is served visions of an apocalyptic future, whether it's from politicians or from Hollywood—and, simultaneously, the utopianism of far-distant science fiction, which as a category is consumed in greater quantity than science journalism and which reflects and encourages what sociologists call "optimism bias" or "technosalvation." These utopian instincts are strengthened by a historical data point obvious to all: our species has survived every obstacle we've encountered, and we are still here.

Utopia and dystopia pervade even the narratives of high-level authorities. The Intergovernmental Panel on Climate Change (IPCC), a United Nations body tasked with stabilizing greenhouse emissions, exhibits them both. Mattias Hjerpe and Björn-Ola Linnér, from the Centre for Climate Science and the Department of Water and Environmental Studies at Linköping University, in Sweden, point out that utopian elements can regularly be found in IPCC planning documents. The IPCC's special reports on emissions scenarios, for example, "all envision a radical narrowing of global income gaps between rich and poor countries. This vision is outright utopian thought" (Hjerpe and Linnér 2009: 240). Not only has the per capita income gap between rich and poor countries grown over most of the past three decades, but the economic development required for a significant narrowing of the gap seems at odds with the IPCC's own sustainability goals. That, say Hjerpe and Linnér, "is utopian in the sense that it is not a projection based on current trends, but rather an extrapolation of current policy goals" (240).

Both dystopian and utopian narratives have their own rationales and evidentiary support, and there's no doubt that climate change presents a real and severe danger. But in the public realm, these types of narratives also have a tendency to be useless. They leave the public spectating a stalled debate between extremes and generate ample motivation to check out.

Things are getting better. There is a common understanding inside science media that a resurgence in long-form science writing is under way. Magazines like *Quanta, Matter, Aeon, Undark,* and *Nautilus* (which I cofounded and edit) are joining established outlets for long-form narrative science writing. At *Nautilus,* themed issues address a single, broad narrative (such as "time" or "chance") through a variety of dissimilar scientific perspectives. This structure, together with a strong contextual focus in the selection and editing of stories, encourages the creation of bridges among the sciences and between science and culture.

The positive critical and reader responses to this experiment and others like it are showing us that readers are hungry for context and narrative in scientific storytelling and appreciate being given the credit of expecting that they will understand the hard stuff. Not only are we able to invite science into the same messy conversations that are usually ruled by culture, or art, or politics—we need to.

References

CNN. 2015. "Sir Richard Branson on Climate Change." December 13. Video.www.cnn.com /videos/world/2015/12/13/climate-change-branson-harlow-nrcnn-intv.cnn.

C-SPAN. 2013. "'God Won't Allow Climate Change': Clip of Senate Session, Part 2, May 8." Video. www.c-span.org/video/?c4450639/god-wont-allow-climate-change.

Dodds, Peter Sheridan. 2013. "Homo Narrativus and the Trouble with Fame." *Nautilus,* no. 5. nautil.us/issue/5/fame/homo-narrativus-and-the-trouble-with-fame.

Gefter, Amanda. 2015. "The Man Who Tried to Redeem the World with Logic." *Nautilus,* no. 21. nautil.us/issue/21/information/the-man-who-tried-to-redeem-the-world-with-logic.

Harré, Rom. 1990. "Some Narrative Conventions of Scientific Discourse." In *Narrative in Culture: The Uses of Storytelling in the Sciences, Philosophy, and Literature,* edited by Cristopher Nash, 81–101. New York: Routledge.

Hjerpe, Mattias, and Björn-Ola Linnér. 2009. "Utopian and Dystopian Thought in Climate Change Science and Policy." *Futures* 41, no. 4: 234–45.

Hulme, Mike. 2009. *Why We Disagree about Climate Change: Understanding Controversy, Inaction, and Opportunity.* New York: Cambridge University Press.

Johnson, Kirk. 2016. "Ingenious: Kirk Johnson." Interview by Kirk Steel. *Nautilus,* no. 33. nautil .us/issue/33/attraction/ingenious-kirk-johnson.

Klein, Naomi. 2014. *This Changes Everything: Capitalism vs. the Climate.* New York: Simon and Schuster.

Meredith, Charlotte. 2012. "One Hundred Reasons Why Climate Change Is Natural." *Daily Express,* November 20. www.express.co.uk/news/uk/146138/100-reasons-why-climate -change-is-natural.

Moser, Susanne, and Lisa Dilling. 2011. "Communicating Climate Change: Closing the Science-Action Gap." In *The Oxford Handbook of Climate Change and Society*, edited by John Dryzek, Richard Norgaard, and David Schlosberg, 161–74. Oxford: Oxford University Press.

Rorty, Richard. 1981. *Philosophy and the Mirror of Nature*. Princeton, NJ: Princeton University Press.

Shackley, Simon, and Brian Wynne. 1996. "Representing Uncertainty in Global Climate Change Science and Policy: Boundary-Ordering Devices and Authority." *Science Technology and Human Values* 21, no. 3: 275–302.

Tom Cohen and Claire Colebrook

Vortices: On "Critical Climate Change" as a Project

When William Blake (in 1805) wrote about the earth as a vortex that had not yet been passed through, he seemed to express the infinite human yearning or Romantic pioneer spirit for "something evermore about to be" that would see this actual earth in all its finitude as a material limit that ought to be surpassed by spirit (Wordsworth 1970: 100). One might argue that it is just this self-surpassing spirit of the sublime that played a constitutive role in the crisis that has come to be known as the Anthropocene. And yet Blake writes about vortices; every thing opens to its own infinite, suggesting that there are as many generations of the infinite as there are points of view (human and inhuman):

> THE NATURE of Infinity is this: That every
>   thing has its
> Own Vortex; and when once a traveller thro'
>   Eternity
> Has pass'd that Vortex, he perceives it roll
>   backward behind
> His path, into a Globe itself enfolding,
>   like a sun,
> Or like a moon, or like a universe of starry
>   majesty,

The South Atlantic Quarterly 116:1, January 2017
DOI 10.1215/00382876-3749381   © 2017 Duke University Press

While he keeps onwards in his wondrous journey on the Earth,
Or like a human form, a friend with whom he liv'd benevolent.
As the eye of man views both the East and West, encompassing
Its vortex, and the North and South with all their starry host,
Also the rising sun and setting moon he views, surrounding
His corn-fields and his valleys of five hundred acres square.
Thus is the Earth one infinite plane, and not as apparent
To the weak traveller confin'd beneath the moony shade.
Thus is the Heaven a Vortex pass'd already, and the Earth
A Vortex not yet pass'd by the traveller thro' Eternity. (Blake 1982: 109)[1]

This might raise the question, when we talk about "earth system science," "the Anthropocene," and even climate change (in the singular) are we drawing upon a presupposed "we" that the very events of the past century place under pressure? Does climate change with all its volatility, unpredictability, and exposure to nonhuman forces and losses once and for all bring to an end a single scale and even the notion of "the climate" or "the earth," *or* does the predicament of earth system change impose a new unity and new "we" upon "us" all? It is in the spirit of this second question that Dipesh Chakrabarty (2009: 222) refers to a "negative universal history": there is no human essence that unfurls and realizes itself through time, but there is a contingent historical event—human imperialism and industrialism, with its infinite quest that knows no limits—that ultimately generates a global and inescapable "human condition" from which there is (now) no escape. For all the talk of posthumanism and multiple worlds, material conditions demand a new conception of human unity, tied as "we" all are to this planet, its limited future, and nature's incapacity (despite Romantic striving) to be infinitely generative of unlimited futures.

The concept of *critical* climate change accepts and refuses Chakrabarty's premise: to imagine that one might simply exit, refuse, or abandon "the human" is to ignore the extent to which history has generated a human unity constituted not by what humanity has done but by the damage inflicted by some humans that subsequently implicates and threatens every human. Humanity is an effect of being unified by a critical condition. And yet, while we accept this humanity that is a "kluge" (not driven by any intentionality, but cobbled together after encountering one obstacle after another to the point that it retains a series of less-than-optimal design features [Marcus 2008]), we invoke the practice of critique to think about climate change in ways that extend beyond climate defined as environment, earth, Gaia, living system, or earth. That is, we are at once critical of this universal striving of infinite "man" that generates a "we" ex post facto, while also being critical of considering the earth, the planet, environment, and life as prima facie goods that "we" ought to preserve, even if for a good beyond our all-too-human selves.

To return to Blake and the vortex: the theoretical vogue for thinking beyond the human toward a geological, Real, materialist, universal register is at one and the same time an extension of the cognitive imperialism that destroyed the planet *and* a necessary gesture to combat all the uncritical parochialisms that would regard climate change as nothing more than a wake-up call or an opportunity for a human justice and felicity. There are, as already indicated, two ways to read Blake's vortex and (in turn) two tendencies of critique that "critical climate change" seeks to maintain. The vortex is *both* an infinite force that destroys the myopia and stability of the present *and* an infinite drive that has always imagined itself as self-surpassing. To imagine that every grain of sand harbors an infinity is at once to decenter thinking away from the human subject, while also allowing that same subject to achieve a perception of a world beyond its own. The first way to read Blake's vortex is to see it as a symptom of an expansionist drive that can only regard the bounded planet as a limit to be surpassed; spirit would have an infinite trajectory that must rise to its own potentiality and exceed material limits. This Romantic hyperhuman and proto-posthuman spirit might find its contemporary resonance in the aftermath of the work of Gilles Deleuze and Felix Guattari, where a perception of the world of fixed forms ought to give way to a sense of moving at infinite speed, surpassing itself to be nothing more than its pure becoming. It is not only accelerationism in its intense and hypertheoretical forms that wants to regard the seeming death sentence of climate change as the opportunity for a new world. When, today, notions of closed windows and tipping points are met with an insistence that there is always a future to come and that there is always a humanity that cannot be contained by the pessimism of the Anthropocene, it is this same sense of passing through the vortex that generates an uncritical future. It is by way of perceiving his limits and imminent destruction that "man" can posit the planet earth as a *seeming* limit that will elicit everything from a "good Anthropocene" of geoengineering (Asafu-Adjaye et al. 2015) to a final liberation from capitalism and justice for all (Klein 2014). Rather than see the drive for futurity, self-overcoming, and an abundant future as extensions of the acquisitiveness and greed that powered the present, one finds a heaven in the collapse of capitalism. It will be capitalism's own violent energy that annihilates any closed, limited, and distributed economy (of the 1 percent), generating a justice for all. And one might say that from Blake, through modernist vorticism, to accelerationism and Naomi Klein, one way of avoiding the violence of the fetish for the unlimited future has been to regard one's striving for life beyond limits as the only drive that will save "us" from the limited. In this respect a certain notion of critique, where one surpasses the limits of the present to find a pristine future or "outside" is symptomatic rather than destructive of all that has come to be known as capitalist industrialism. But while this may be so, any simple return to the immanent, to a refusal of critique, or to a mere embrace of life as we know it in all its glorious vibrancy is perhaps, to quote Jacques Derrida (2001: 400), the "worse violence."

Another way to read Blake's vortex is to imagine the surpassing of the earth *not* in the sense of an overcoming of the planet's seeming limits for the sake of human survival and justice but rather as a critical experiment of contemplating a life beyond the earth, or a life beyond life. "Man's" attachment to this human earth, "the rising sun and setting moon he views, surrounding / His corn-fields and his valleys of five hundred acres square," is a contingent and unjustifiable parochialism that one can observe, and *possibly* do without. The idea of passing through a vortex and thinking beyond the level of this planet, of "climate justice," is perhaps unthinkable and yet critical.

Of these two modes of reading—seeing self-surpassing as the very annihilative drive that got us into this mess *or* struggling to discover what it might really mean to say farewell to parochial conceptions of humanity— critical climate change aims to think both at once. Climate change is *critical* not because it prompts "us" to do something now, once and for all, given our critical condition. Critical climate change is at one and the same time critical of the notion of climate change, or that there is *a climate that we occupy that is going through change*, while also being wary of the rhetorical tactics of "game over" that legitimate new states of emergency that preclude any thought of genuine climate change (a change in cognitive, critical, perceptual, and affective climates). At one and the same time, we aim to contemplate what genuine climate change might be: What would eventuate if one were to lose the sense of this earth as being bounded by the starry heavens and parceled out into properties of *our earth, our climate?* And yet, at the same time, we also question all the popular and high-culture exits that imagine a thought, life, or futurity that would redeem "us" from the present.

When we embarked upon a series of projects under the rubric of "critical climate change" (including a series of books published as open access texts through Open Humanities Press), we did not envision a turn toward climate change as either a new topic of concern or an expansion of context to include a nature that would now be inextricably bound up with humanity. Even though the notion of "environmental humanities" did not have the purchase it has today, we were already seeking to open a project distinct from ecocriticism, environmental humanities, and various other projects that take up an awareness of ecology as part of an interpretive project. Although "critical climate change" distanced itself from the premises of ecocriticism and environmental humanities, its first impulse was positive. By understanding climate change as "critical," we wanted to suggest that climate change in its meteorological sense was a symptom or an expression of a broader critical climate. Rather than say that the destruction of the environment or the recognition of the Anthropocene is a "wake-up call" that will draw "us" back to a sense of ecological attunement, mindfulness, or social justice, we propose that conceptions of redemption, retrieval, sustainability, and ecology (or benevolent interconnectedness) are the macroaggressions that have generated a lure of humanity that has the destruction of the planet as one of its many expressions. To think about *critical* climate change, we propose, is to deconstruct the relation between humanity and ecology: there is no ecology that humanity unfortunately comes along to destroy; there is a relatively stable ongoing habit of voracious and rapacious consumption *from which* the twinned notions of "the human" and "the environment" emerge. To talk about "ecology," "environment," "the human," "sustainability," or "the" Anthropocene is to be seduced by notions of various levels and registers of unity. Critical climate change seeks to change this discursive, habitual, and cognitive climate. It follows, then, that rather than "ecocriticism" where the concerns of ecology expand the range of what counts as a critical context, we are critical of the "eco" and "oikos." Rather than expanding scale or context, rather than scaling up to include the earth, we entertain the thought of collapsing scale: any supposed ecology, environment, or climate is the effect of a stabilizing and self-sustaining practice of inscription. As such, there can be no proper scale that could judge or incorporate the contingency of inscription. If there is no ecology—no relatively unified milieu of interconnectedness—then what remains is climate change, a series of shifting, unstable, and continuously receding *climates* that open a series of multiple and unsettled registers for inquiry. We do not want to expand or enrich the humanities: on the contrary, the very notion of "the human" (however varied, diverse, or multicultural) is the false commonality from which other violent captures have emerged, including the notion of "the planet" that "we" must save. A change in critical climates would require situating the human as one of the effects of a broader milieu of multiple, conflicting, and diverging forces, where "the human" both occupies a position of seeming universality *and* appears as an odd parochial exception.

It is for this reason that the texts that have appeared in our Critical Climate Change series for Open Humanities Press range from works that aim to think in visual and multimedia terms to more traditionally "critical" texts such as Joanna Zylinska's *Minimal Ethics for the Anthropocene* (2014), which adopts the theoretical terminology of ethics while questioning its very figurations of "ethos" and (more importantly) "anthropos." In the recent multiauthored *Twilight of the Anthropocene Idols* (Cohen, Colebrook, and Miller 2015), we sought to take advantage of, and destroy, the concept of the Anthropocene, at once refusing the referential force of "Anthropos" while nevertheless insisting upon its force as a lure. In the wake of a widespread questioning of the elevated and condescending comportment of critique, we at once wanted to join forces with those (such as Rita Felski [2015] and Bruno Latour [2004]) who had become tired of the unruffled cool of distant mastery, and yet we wanted to sustain "critical" force *not* as something "we thinkers" impose upon a climate but as a climactic field that happens *to thinking*. When we wrote of the "twilight of Anthropocene idols," we saw ourselves less as valiant dragon slayers and more as caught up in the great climate change "hoax" (Delingpole 2015). That master delusion is *not* the Fox News hoax that there are left-wing scientists trying to bring down capitalism by cooking the books on climate change. No, it is the ongoing fraud that calls itself "Anthropos": bringing itself into being by admitting to destruction on a geological scale and then concluding that *by way of this destructive unity* "we" ought to survive. The cogito of the twenty-first century is, "We are united by the threat of extinction; therefore we are." The very concepts that shore up this newfound human unity—climate, ecology, environment—are those that may also operate destructively. In short, we are seeking something like "destructive writing" (a counterpoint to the "creative writing" through which we have come into being). How, we hope to continue asking, does what appear as climate, environment, the Anthropocene, and ecology destroy all the interconnectedness that such notions seem at first to promise?

The phrase *critical climate change* appears simple enough. Even though we open with a reversal—arguing that what have become known as ecocriticism and environmental humanities may be seen as the symptoms that mistake themselves for the cure—we nevertheless hope to generate a notion of "critical climate" that opens and expands the force of all the concepts, figures, techniques, and tendencies that have been generated in the past half century of "theory." Put more concretely, whereas some claims have been made that the Anthropocene would oblige us to throw out posthumanism and any form of the social construction of humanity and attend to the inescapable reality of the species (Chakrabarty 2009; Hamilton 2013), we claim quite the opposite: what has come to be known as "theory" was anything but a suspension of inhuman materiality and is now more pertinent than ever in the wake of a reaction formation that strives to reassert the human, life, futurity, and matter. It is in this respect that the materiality to which we refer is not an unproblematic referent but a referential lure, a series of inscriptive traces that generates a ground or earth that offers itself as ours.

Materiality is not some unified, real, present, and empirical field that will enable "us" to grasp things as they really are now that we have overcome our anthropocentric myopia; the complexities of materiality preclude any such simple return to the things that matter. Every constituted thing is haunted, disturbed, and rendered multiple by the forces of materiality that enable it to come into being. Rather than say that the humanities can save themselves by becoming environmental or that ecocriticism must be the future of a world whose priority ought to be survival, we think of matter as too plural, volatile, and inhuman to provide any such escape. Matter is textual and certainly not something that can justify a posttheoretical literalism, anticritique, or surface reading; the events of climate change and the Anthropocene *intensify* the textual recalcitrance of materiality, precluding any notion of a return to what would supposedly precede and cause the text.

By critical climate change we therefore see climate *change* as precluding any reprieve from critique, while also warding off any critique that would allow disturbance, volatility, and multiplicity to generate "a" privileged outside or beyond. To take just one example: while there is certainly a redemptive (and industry standard) deconstruction that insists upon a necessary future and justice to come, there is also (and unavoidably) another deconstruction where what appears as nature, earth, the future, humanity, and ecology are effects of multiple forces that are critical or that generate an ongoing disruption of any event that one might hope would count as salvation. Irreducible to any one thematic, critical climate change opens a destructive field that draws in a range of critical concepts, referentials, and political imaginaries. Situated in the field of critical climate change these terms are reconfigured, with their moral precepts and premises discarded as having fueled the ecocidal vortex.[2] To that extent, critical climate change is not only a platform but a sort of incubation trap.

But if there is the Blakean vortex to consider, one might supplement it with Edgar Allan Poe's maelstrom funnel or Alfred Hitchcock's vertigo swirl— figures less cosmic than semio-mnemonic, en route to an accelerating back loop that is also an irreversible descent. One might say that if *critical climate change* has morphed, what is its value, in 2016, after an array of leading critical voices have entered this horizon? The voices turning to address these transformations advanced through a series of stages: from the ecological thought to absorbing the irreversibly ecocidal structure and entropy of the "anthropocene" as a negotiation with mass extinctions. And rather predictably, not only have geopolitical maps and legacy accords ("international law," financialization, "human rights") begun to roll over along with the petrodollar and state institutions, but climate proxy wars—the much-commented-on desertification of the region, Egypt's bread inflation, Syria's agrarian collapse, Iran's desiccation, Saudi Arabia's glimpses of unlivable heat waves, Tunisia's self-immolated climate refugees (Africans will come later) have already bucked the European's last Enlightenment protocols or pretexts. In Southeast Asia, the Rohinga give a glimpse of what open denial of place by all looks like, for which the sea becomes an impersonal disposal site. The domino effect of right-wing and retro-nationalist turns globally, focused on exclusion and securing resources, cannot be read today outside of the masked climate panic.

To the flaneur of critical climate change, another implication of the vortex enters, officially, once *tipping points* are passed (wherever they are artificially placed): the irreversible accelerations of physics, chemical shifts, melt-offs, a viral renaissance, mass extinctions, geoengineering reactions. Roy Scranton (2015b) posited this with literary acumen by asking, as if some curtain dropped, in a *New York Times* blog: So we're doomed—now what? But the public marker of the 2015 United Nations Climate Change Conference in Paris, or the phantom and "aspirational" accords referenced to that, obscures the public game board as very different rhetorical and power agendas emerge—in ways parallel to those of critical or cognitive resets. The literary vortex, so to speak, enters the real accompanied by the catalyst of mediacratic streaming and cultures of distraction, advancing a couple of spins down in the maelstrom.

If Derrida (1984: 21–22) analyzed the Cold War structural threat of nuclear apocalypse as a "fable" (since it had yet to occur) and located in that, nonetheless, the organizing fiction of sociopolitical realities, climate change would be an antifable—an ongoing mutation in the material premises of the biosphere, a one-way street without arrival. When Scranton bids to dissociate from the present and anticipate what those after the catastrophe may require, he ventures that that is the archive, "the Humanities" as such. It is not clear that a reading model that participated in the ecocidal acceleration is being conveyed to seed the fantasy of, again, a "new" world and "new enlightenment" (however diminished). The question emerges in 2016—in contrast to ecological or ecocidal thought—as what gets loaded onto the ark?

The responses are necessarily compromised by the same reflex that makes *Anthropos* assert, in the era of extinction, that above all else "he," or the archival trajectory of technoscience, must survive his own evisceration of living systems. Anthropos remains the proper name for a Western regime and *Logos*, devolved to calculation and utilitarian algorithms, that projects its "universality" despite being increasingly and publicly disowned by planetary stakeholders (hypocritical "Western values")—which raises the question of whether this critical struggle is not still Anthropos talking (or not) to himself, like Hamlet, and whether the better efforts of critical invention, today, are not in part therapeutic. Isabelle Stengers (2015) approaches the reset otherwise (for at issue, grammatically compromised, is as Scranton asks: What's next?), as her title *In Catastrophic Times: Resisting the Coming Barbarism* announces. Finding the present "suspended" between two historical "epochs," caught in mediatric "enclosures" as if shaped by, troping Plato, the "Guardians" (the invisible hand of a 0.001 percent and corporate levers), she fast forwards over any nod to ecological politics as too late or systemically doomed and focuses on the struggle to keep the "struggle" itself of a progressivist future by resisting "the coming barbarisms." Different from Scranton, Stengers finds the affirmation of struggle in a double negative, a resistance not to extinction economies, corporatocracies, and so on but to a "barbarism" marked less by Asian (or African) hordes inundating shores or Islamizing populations than the recoil to national savageries that follow the script (raised, recently, in a *New York Times* column titled "The Next Genocide" [Snyder 2015], rereading Adolf Hitler's motives as ecologically driven).

But does an insistent return to the familiar archival perks of "the Humanities," or of the technoscientific or proto-Enlightenment toolbox and ideals, not echo Nick Bostrom's (Anderson 2012) insistence on the survival of the adventure of technoscientific knowledge and transformation of the material universe, barely begun? What has not yet caught public attention is that, after tipping points pass, *per definition* there emerges implicitly and everywhere a "politics" of managed (or delayed) extinctions. The current gamble is on accelerating hyper-technologies such as gene editing, designer babies, AI integration, biohacking, and selectively gifted hyperlongevities for Anthropos's most refined heirs (Anthropos Inc.?)—if not an immortalizing "singularity" imaginary. Something had altered entering 2016, which, far down the food chain, implies a technoevolution in the critical climate change space.

What "Paris" indicates is that tipping points are (discretely) acknowledged as passed, conceded, but that the ecocide will be managed, delayed, stretched out—and kept within an indefinite "suspense" narrative (will we stay at five degrees or break seven?) as a herding device. What's the point, one might ask, of putting off extinction accelerations by a few score years and for whom? It doesn't take Sherlock Holmes to figure out textual patterns, particularly in the post-2008 superheist that Latour (2016) notes as the creeping of the 1 percent ever further in digital refinement (become 0.01 percent, become 0.001 percent?). Judging from the debacle of the 2009 UN Climate Conference at Copenhagen, an event/nonevent that would also be a crime scene of sorts—since "no decision" was a (passive) decision—we pass to the dissimulations of "Paris" (what I leave in quotation marks as naming an open rhetorical process). It is not the behind the scenes negotiating for winners and losers in the geoengineering boondoggles to come that tempts us to update Marx's formula to "first time as farce, second, kitsch." The same folks that streamed corporate media climate denialism knew very well the opposite and, looking ahead decades, did the only sensible thing—for them—which is to scoop up the majority of planetary wealth and resources, create a "breakaway civilization" unmoored from public megadebt and locale, privatize technoscience, and plan ahead like good anthropoi as the designated survivor caste, a technoeugenist caste per definition, eyeballing Arctic condos by late century and taking heart in Matt Damon's garden patch on Mars in the *The Martian* (2015), a film taken as a propaganda win for ex-terra colonization plans. Behind the fog of mass denialism and financial stress, a massive (digital) wealth transference occurs just as hypertechnologies accelerate exponentially, executing a literal *species split* in which synthetically enhanced groups would be gifted longevity and purged of bad or diseased DNA (entirely natural). The only thing missing from this technonarcissist trajectory is any remaining pretense of the old environmental concerns, sustainability, "keep the earth habitable for all" sort of stuff, the rhetorical expectation of "rational self-interest" writ large by the liberal legatees of Enlightenment memes, the ones who had imagined that bringing to light an existential threat would move some collective, naturally enough, to emergency countermeasures—as one would expect for an asteroid threat. Vortex.

But the project of a "sustainability" strategy—the pretext of Paris-related plans, number juggling, and media—was never on the table, despite a split-screen public narrative broadcast for the telemasses: a suspense tale begging the question "Will 'we' avoid 'the worst' by century's end?" after which the screens go black. Behind the facade of squabbling and walking away in Copenhagen, or agreeing and walking away at "Paris," it was understood that it was too late and to go to plan B. Caricatured, a bit, that would be something like: separate from the doomed herd, reengineer, and plan to get out of Dodge altogether when the time comes. In short, amazingly enough, double down. The banality of this script does nothing to tarnish amazement at how seamlessly it was inaugurated and rendered itself irreversible (short of general carnage). But was the imaginary of *Homo sapiens* or its desultory star, the Western Anthropos, ever attached to earth as such, any more than, today, technomedia is particularly terrestrial—and if not, the migratory feed, pillage, and move-on logic of what Elizabeth Kolbert in *The Sixth Extinction: An Unnatural History* (2014) calls the aesthetic or "madness gene" (or what amounts to permanent metonymic displacement) renders something in this otherwise embarrassing narrative recognizable. It was *never* about preservation, then?

Postmodernism patted itself on the back for giving up "grand narratives" voluntarily when they had been taken away, and climate change has swept up the micros—leaving the different terms of the proactive splintering and irreversible vortices to figure out how to neutralize or disfigure. We can now update a mutation in the *vortex*, which is not primarily concerned with mass extinction events—which hominids litter in their wake—and not only about accelerating feedback loops but rather about the lateral, tempophagic, and chemical networks that now advance according to *their own rules* yet which, in the era of digital totalization, perpetually update Anthropos's recollection of what is normative, in turn fueling the spin. It is small satisfaction to see Hubble shots of entire galaxies weaving similar pictorial symmetries.

This particular fable of the antifable, no less real for being B Hollywood stuff, or the more so for it, gives an example of the way the rhetorical management, dodges, and reactivisms of this transepochal period saturate and blur attention. George Marshall titles his study of public occlusion due to neural and social forces *Don't Even Think about It: Why Our Brains Are Wired to Ignore Climate Change* (2014). One may take "overpopulation" as a parallel example of how these *bans* circulate. When we need to be reminded that black lives matter; when Flint, Michigan, is triaged budgetarily for water, its young written off; when critically new antibiotics somehow don't become available to the public or an Ebola response is held off just a bit too long—well, paranoid minds might suspect that systemic reallocations were testing the triage tool kit. Yet *both* "overpopulation" as a sabotaging calculus tossed into Anthropos's hive (by a no doubt grinning Thomas Malthus [(1898) 1992]) *and* the suppression or ban on "population talk" were inventions of the West's own ratiocination regime. Moreover, one can only address them in trying to lift the ban, since no one else is listening to Anthropos (not) talking to himself anymore or cares—the majority sectors of ex-colonial enclaves and actively non-Western, "illiberal," or Asiatic actors (China, the Islamic world, Africa, Russia, and so on) retain entirely different value apparatuses for life and mass death and acceptable sacrifice of populations. To try to inspect "overpopulation" or reanimate it, even for the rational ends of a sustainability goal to come, has been prohibited for so many reasons, not least for its Hitlerian echoes, that every past variant of control (or eugenics) had been racist and tribalist in the extreme, and so on: one is damned to even address it, contaminated, fascist by necessity. "We" can never go there, and the liberal orders of political thought, the last Enlightenment thumbtack, condemn any possible . . . and so on. Here we get that rare delight, listening to Anthropos talking to himself about what he will not talk about, or not talking to himself in order to claim control of an occlusion he devised. The pattern writes large the recoil of postcolonial studies before the Anthropocene disruption (in which its priorities are suspended and its narrative programmatically regressive) by attempting to claim climate change as itself another extension of the colonialist trajectory—confirmed, certainly, by no less than James Cameron's *Avatar*. Yet the needle swings back, hard, if one marks that this refusal and keeping one's hands clean perhaps enables the very outcome most abhorred, permits an unheralded species split to occur unremarked before its (unseeing) eyes, preoccupied by (not) talking to itself. That is to say, the liberal progressive orders passively enable the future population culls of the peripheries to take place as if on their own (from which the wired and caffeinated urban intellectual cannot imagine being removed and, prospectively, benefits from in being kept within the survival zones). Vortex.

As Derrida remarked of the nuclear holocaust imaginary, who can say there is not a will to see and test this event, a desire to experience the postapocalypse one had been entertained by relentlessly to the point of wishing, like the teen gamers that ISIS recruits, to literalize the video-game carnage whose immersive realities had fully replaced mere existence? For, if so, they are just lower on the scale (or in the maelstrom) than the hyperelites *in medias* species split. "Overpopulation" presents an ethical impasse to address or resolve only as long as one is within the same species supposedly. Looking ahead decades, *passively engineered population culling* need have no overt fingerprints and presents no ethical agony for an advanced, if related, "species"—or, more accurately, a turbocharged version of what, all along, has been the *species that is not one*, since everything it had identified with and proprietized as archival arts, mnemotechnologies, semio-aesthetic sensoria, and digital totalizations were, already, *materialistic* signifying chains neither human, explicitly, nor living as such.

The above narrative can be seen confirmed everywhere today and be nonexistent at the same time—one of the anomalies of a climate change *unconscious* that, contrary to definition, is constituted by what, unsaid, *everybody knows*. It caricatures one of the plausible next mutations of the critical climate template, the value of a return to aesthetic and rhetorical forces of the era of extinction. This, particularly if it is the archival technoapparatus that has designated *itself* as what is to "survive" the extinction, say, of Humanity 1.0 and hominid swarming as oceans acidify, food chains collapse, waste toxifies bodies and chronotopes, droughts claim agricultural planning, as bots and drones police safe zones and cities. Rather than a calculus of negotiated preservation, the covert logic is one of acceleration to achieve a kind of *escape velocity*—from the miasma of diseased human DNA, from the uninhabitable parts of the planet going forward, and, finally, as Stephen Hawking advises (he gives "us" two centuries tops), from an incinerated earth (think a mix of the animation film *Wall-E* and *Interstellar*). Specifically, to colonize hostile space rocks, mine asteroids, garden on Mars. Earth will have been something of a "birth" or incubation planet, merely, servicing the technoevolution of this *species that is not one*. The fond evocation of a Mother Earth, or Gaia, to respect as life-giving fertility is so "hominid," as is any switch to a Medea logic. One might recast the model to arachnids, of maternal insects providing the first meal for their offspring, or octopus mothers whose lives exhaust in producing the technomarvels they issue.

One cannot be sure when an initiative like critical climate change deflates, recedes from these intersections that appear so entirely remarkable in 2016 that one can lose oneself in endless speculation and prize witnessing the sociology of occlusion at the moment of peak humans: the brief decade or so in which the diversity of biota hundreds of millions of years hence has been catastrophically diminished. But it presents ever-bolder options for exploring and attending to, cataloging and entering, the menagerie of vortices that stand to revive near term attentions—among else as new referential seed and groups and perceptual regimes, so to speak, contest and as the last great era of megaextractivism unfolds. For the flaneur of critical climate change, there is no one "barbarism" and it was never *to come*.

Notes

1   Spelling and punctuation adjusted according to William Blake Archive: http://www
.blakearchive.org.

2   Thus, for instance, the initial compilations of the Critical Climate Change initiative—
two volumes subtitled *Theory in the Era of Climate Change*—invited diverse contributors to choose a key term or concept to feed into this horizon, concepts including time,
ecotechnics, care, war, sex, and so on, to traverse samplings of how each term mutated
or redefined itself before this shared conundrum, intersecting only on occasion.

References

Anderson, Rick. 2012. "We're Underestimating the Risk of Human Extinction." Interview
with Nick Bostrom. *Atlantic*, March 6. www.theatlantic.com/technology/archive/2012
/03/were-underestimating-the-risk-of-human-extinction/253821/.

Asafu-Adjaye, John, et al. 2015. "An Ecomodernist Manifesto." www.ecomodernism.org/manifesto.

Blake, William, 1982. *The Complete Poetry and Prose of William Blake*. Edited by David V. Erd-
man. Berkeley: University of California Press.

Chakrabarty, Dipesh. 2009. "The Climate of History: Four Theses." *Critical Inquiry* 35, no. 2:
197–222.

Cohen, Tom, Claire Colebrook, and J. Hillis Miller. 2015. *Twilight of the Anthropocene Idols*.
Michigan: Open Humanities Press. openhumanitiespress.org/books/titles/twilight-of
-the-anthropocene-idols/.

Delingpole, James. 2015. "Climate Change: The Hoax That Costs Us $4 Billion a Day." Fox
Nation, August 10. nation.foxnews.com/2015/08/10/climate-change-hoax-costs-us
-4-billion-day.

Derrida, Jacques. 1984. "No Apocalypse, Not Now (Full Speed Ahead, Seven Missiles, Seven
Missives)." Translated by Catherine Porter and Philip Lewis. *Diacritics* 14, no. 2: 20–31.

Derrida, Jacques. 2001. *Writing and Difference*. Translated by Alan Bass. London: Routledge.

Felski, Rita. 2015. *The Limits of Critique*. Chicago: University of Chicago Press.

Hamilton, Clive. 2013. "Climate Change Signals the End of the Social Sciences." The Conversation, January 24. theconversation.com/climate-change-signals-the-end-of-the-social
-sciences-11722.

Klein, Naomi. 2014. *This Changes Everything: Capitalism vs. the Climate*. New York: Simon and
Schuster.

Kolbert, Elizabeth. 2014. *The Sixth Extinction: An Unnatural History*. New York: Holt.

Latour, Bruno. 2004. "Why Has Critique Run out of Steam? From Matters of Fact to Matters
of Concern." *Critical Inquiry* 30, no. 2: 225–48.

Latour, Bruno. 2016. "A New Political Circle"/ "Terror, Globe, Earth—a New Political Trian-
gle." www.academia.edu/20202424/Bruno_Latour_A_New_Political_Circle.

Malthus, Thomas. (1898) 1992. *An Essay on the Principle of Population*. Cambridge: Cambridge
University Press.

Marcus, Gary. 2008. *Kluge: The Haphazard Construction of the Human Mind*. Boston: Hough-
ton Mifflin.

Marshall, George. 2014. *Don't Even Think about It: Why Our Brains Are Wired to Ignore Climate
Change*. London: Bloomsbury.

Scranton, Roy. 2015a. *Learning How to Die in the Anthropocene: Reflections on the End of a Civilization*. San Francisco: City Lights Books.

Scranton, Roy. 2015b. "We're Doomed. Now What?" *Opinionator* (blog), *New York Times*, December 21. opinionator.blogs.nytimes.com/2015/12/21/were-doomed-now-what.

Snyder, Timothy. 2015. "The Next Genocide." *New York Times*, September 12. www.nytimes.com/2015/09/13/opinion/sunday/the-next-genocide.html.

Stengers, Isabelle. 2015. *In Catastrophic Times: Resisting the Coming Barbarism*. Translated by Andrew Goffey. Ann Arbor, MI: Open Humanities Press.

Wordsworth, William. 1970. *The Prelude: Or, Growth of a Poet's Mind (text of 1805)*, edited by Ernest De Selincourt. London: Oxford University Press.

Zylinska, Joanna. 2014. *Minimal Ethics for the Anthropocene*. Ann Arbor, MI: Open Humanities Press.

Matthew Burtner

Climate Change Music:
From Environmental Aesthetics to Ecoacoustics

Several meters back from the riverbank, the
microphone points out and slightly upward, as if
trying to hear the treetops on the far bank, or the
distant mountains. The river and wind roar, amplified
through the headphones, louder than my normal
hearing. The sound is also spatially altered by the
microphone characteristics. Small spectral shapes
dance in the noise; am I imagining them? Perhaps
they are a by-product of the electroacoustics of the
recording system, or of my hearing. Perhaps they
result from some interaction between the acoustics
of the wind and the river. In the headphones, I hear
the wind and the river pressed into a single complex
mass of noise. My creative mind follows the listening,
and I wonder: Are the wind and river really separate?
—EcoSono Field Journal: Hearing Mountains Sing in
the Sound of Wind and River

Introduction to Climate Change Music

Climate change music applies real-world environmental dynamics as musical methods. The
composer employs changing environmental conditions as music theory, and musicians perform
the music using natural materials in addition to
human-designed instruments. In a time of rapid
and impactful climate change, music made with

The South Atlantic Quarterly 116:1, January 2017
DOI 10.1215/00382876-3749392 © 2017 Duke University Press

environmental systems may resound with listeners in new ways, bridging transformations in the physical world around us with conceptual and emotional dimensions of our lives.

My field journal excerpts, such as the text above, are interspersed throughout this writing to offer a parallel, more evocative analysis of hearing "climate" and "change" in the natural world. I hope that this active listening report offers another kind of insight into the compositional approach described in the main body of the article. This music is built on techniques of environmental temporality and interrelated energy fluctuations, inspired by an uncommon way of listening to the natural world. The field journal offers a real-world account of this way of listening.[1]

Music is a time-based art form, and, like ecology, it operates on several temporal scales simultaneously. Composers work with sonic energy across time, and climate change music attempts to capture the multiply directed characteristics of environmental time into a human experiential frame. The listener can experience the complexity of climate change through sound—hours, days, or decades of change set in counterpoint with real-time events. To help facilitate this experience, my music uses techniques well familiar from Western classical music, techniques found in the music of Ludwig van Beethoven, for example, where small motifs, larger phrases, sections, and macro form work together to move the music on multiple scales simultaneously (Kramer 1988). I learned these techniques as a music student, and I apply them now to ecoacoustics.

In my music, time relates to some environmental parameter of change outside the music, giving it an extramusical grounding in the natural world. Such experiential sources may be widely shared among people who have spent time outdoors with environmental conditions such as wind, waves, snowfall, and so on. The music draws on these experiences.

Climate is the integration of the various weather systems in the environment, and in this music the multithreaded aspects of weather are represented through counterpoint. I treat climate as an ensemble, scoring the multiple systems as musical harmony. Climate structures occur across a spectrum of environmental conditions including cryospheric, atmospheric, hydrospheric, and biospheric. As the interleaved patterns of weather form climate across time, so do the contrapuntal layers of my music evolve into musical forms.

In a work such as *Auksalaq* (Burtner 2012), the environmental systems of hydrologics and atmosphere interact as contrapuntal layers of the music. Real-time sounds are set to sonifications of data and performed by musicians using natural materials (Burtner 2011b, 2016a).[2] The works analyzed here—*Syntax of Snow*, for amplified snow, bells, and electroacoustics (Burtner 2010), and *Six Ecoacoustic Quintets No. 1: Water (Ice)*, for amplified melting ice, water percussion, and electroacoustics (Burtner 2009)—pursue a similar approach. I discuss this music within a philosophical framework articulated by Emily Brady (2003), who builds on Immanuel Kant's theory of aesthetics and imagination, refitted for environmental aesthetics.

A look at the broader field of environmental sound art will help contextualize the analysis of specific works.

> The river and the wind originate in the mountains, many miles away. Geographers describe these mountains as "young" and "dynamic." I imagine them that way, collapsing time in my mind to feel how tectonic forces push plates together and the earth's crust buckles and juts into an impressive ridge, rippling like the river in front of me, but on a geological timescale. Then in my mind I try to reconcile the scales of time. How does that tectonic dynamism shape the experience of this wall of wind/river noise in my ears?
>
> —EcoSono Field Journal: Hearing Mountains
> Sing in the Sound of Wind and River

Environmental Sound Art

Composers have long sought musical inspiration in nature, depicting places and forces of the environment through instruments and dynamic musical forms. Ancient Alaskan composers of the Arctic imitated seals and geese to celebrate the animals in times of hunting through a form of vocalization called *katajjak* (throat singing).[3] Ancient Greek composers harnessed the wind and water to create musical instruments such as the aeolian harp and the hydraulis.[4] Millennia later, European composers depicted complex scenes and stories through orchestrated "tone poems." For example, Czech composer Bedřich Smetana's orchestral work *The Moldau* (1874) depicts streams that combine into the Vltava River as it makes its way to the North Sea. Smetana composes the intertwining rivulets of water, as they move toward the river.

La mer (*The Sea*) by French composer Claude Debussy (1905) explores the light on the turbulent surface of the ocean as a musical system. Debussy blends dynamics, timbre, and texture into a tonal painting of the sea. Such impressionist works reveal a fascination with the technology of transcription of the natural world into music. French composer Olivier Messiaen (1964)

Figure 1. Flute and clarinet part, Smetana, *The Moldau*, mm. 17–19

pushed the boundaries of musical transcription, using his outstanding ears and musical knowledge to transcribe the songs of birds in *Catalogue d'oiseaux* (*Catalog of Birds*), which he completed in 1958. Messiaen's bird transcriptions coincide with the emergence of the tape recorder as a musical technology in Paris (repurposed from its role as a strategic weapon used by the Nazis during the invasion of France). Tape music, or *musique concrète*, as described by its inventor, composer Pierre Schaeffer ([1952] 2012), gave musicians another technique for composing human-nature music through the ability to capture sounds of the natural world and manipulate them as audio in a laboratory.

The new audio technology and theoretical approaches of the 1950s and 1960s enabled a deeper relationship between the composer and the environment. Composers found new ways to describe nature as music and to recognize the changeability of the environment as part of the musical form. For example, in the 1960s and 1970s, Canadian composer R. Murray Schafer (1977) created music designed for outdoor performances in which the musicians and the audience were spatially situated in specific places and the sounds of nature were considered part of the musical composition. Schafer and his students, Barry Truax (1996) and Hildegard Westerkamp (2002), created a new form of music called *soundscape* composition. In soundscape music such as Westerkamp's 1996 composition *Beneath the Forest Floor*, the sounds of the environment become musical instruments alongside electronically generated sounds. Such works use advances in theory and technology to bring nature and music closer together. These soundscape composers were also part of an environmentalism movement, and they connected artistic practice and political activism, lobbying against the advance of human industrial noise and the preservation of the natural world.

I imagine how the steep mountain slope causes a temperature difference corresponding to the rapid change in altitude. The warm air rises and surrounding air is drawn in to fill the low pressure zone left by its passing. The result is a movement of air we experience as wind, and it carries with it the form of the mountains. I imagine how that contour is contained in the noise of the wind in my headphones. In this way, I can *hear* the shape of the mountains in the noise of the wind. The mountains sing through the wind.

—EcoSono Field Journal: Hearing Mountains
Sing in the Sound of Wind and River

From Environmental Aesthetics to Ecoacoustics

Emily Brady, a philosopher, describes in her book *Aesthetics of the Natural Environment* (2003) an "integrated" aesthetic in which the experience of nature is more immersive than distant. She decenters cultural aesthetics, placing the work of art alongside an equally aestheticized nature. She does so through the philosophy of aesthetics, creating a framework that balances the subjective and objective approaches to aesthetic appreciation. Environmental artists who try to bridge distinctly nonhuman environmental energy and human aesthetics find her work particularly helpful. Her theory of the "integrated aesthetic" challenges culture to take a secondary role in the production of aesthetics, giving the philosophy an environmentalist tendency. The integrated aesthetic moves the frame of art toward the otherness of nature. The implications of this theory are massive because, unlike nature, art often presupposes the comfort, pleasure, and entertainment of humans. Aesthetic appreciation shifts when confronted with a powerful, non-human-centered theory of art.

Brady (2003: 121) writes: "The aesthetic situation reflects the complexity of environmental appreciation, where appreciation is more like a *happening*, and where that happening creates the conditions of the situation we are in." Indeed, the environmental music of the 1970s was indebted to the artistic genre of *happenings* in which multiple artworks unfold in parallel and in dialogue with one another. The musical proponents of happenings, such as John Cage and David Tudor, were also advocates for the use of everyday noise sounds as part of music. Brady's integrated aesthetics provides a philosophical framework for understanding an emerging ecological-acoustics approach to music. Happenings, electroacoustic technology, soundscape composition, and the environmental activism movement together form a foundation for ecoacoustic music.

In the 1990s I started composing musical works that brought together experiences of my youth in Alaska with my studies of music, technology, and philosophy. As a music technologist, I developed ecoacoustic approaches out of a love of my native environment. But as the effects of climate change began to dramatically reshape the Arctic, and as it became clear that the transformations we were experiencing in the north were only the first signs of a massive global shift of climate, my regionally focused music found a more global political purpose.

Works such as *Sikuigvik (The Time of Ice Melting)* (Burtner 1998; MiN Ensemble 2001) for piano and ensemble today feel more like fearsome elegies for the loss of ice than the celebrations of the harsh beauty of the Arctic environment I intended. In 2010 I revisited the harmonic system of *Sikuigvik* to compose *Iceprints*, a work for piano and electronics using recordings in the Chukchi Sea and sonifications of ice-extent data. In this piece, the ice deformations play the piano through a process of sonification, and the harmonic modulation is driven by climate change across forty years (Burtner 2010). In 2015 I composed *Threnody (Sikuigvik)*. The title of the work alone reveals how my own experience of climate change has shifted. The techniques I developed out of a search for beauty became tools for activism that I now deploy in collaboration with politicians and scientists.[5]

The places where I grew up were rapidly transformed as glaciers and the polar ice melted. Global warming brought new foliage and fauna into the region, and animals disappeared. Meanwhile, human development threatened a sustainable human lifestyle that had been dominant for thousands of years. Ecoacoustics became a multifaceted form of conservation that at once preserved and documented places in time and also proposed positive forms of human-nature interaction with the hope of finding a sustainable future through music.

> The air, moist with evaporated snowmelt, rises up the mountain slope and flies off above the peaks, cooling rapidly until the moisture in the air dews and forms clouds. The mountains collect cloud cover throughout the year, and the clouds shed precipitation in the form of snow. The snow builds up and compresses under its own weight into glacial masses. During the summer months, the glacier ice melts and flows down the mountain. The landscape shapes the movement of the water and collects it together into this river. The water carries with it the form of the mountains, and that contour is contained in the noise of the river in my headphones. I can hear the mountains singing in the sound of the river.
> —EcoSono Field Journal: Hearing Mountains
> Sing in the Sound of Wind and River

Figure 2. Ecoacoustic instruments in *Syntax of Snow*

Composers have often created new musical approaches sympathetic to the sciences or philosophies of their time. Like musical *serialism* (Perle 1977; Schoenberg 1925, 1975) or *spectralism* (Grisey 1974–85; Fineberg 2000; Harvey 2001), ecoacoustic music offers an aesthetically flexible method for composing. This makes it highly useful as a pedagogical tool for exploring climate change through music composition.[6]

> Compared to the wind and river I am slow, lingering on the riverbank while the water and air rush by. Meanwhile, the hours I spend here, in spite of being profound for my life, don't even register in the temporal scale of the mountains. Human time, perception, and life are caught between extreme scales of environmental time. My listening to the river and wind could not possibly alter their course. And it seems similarly impossible that my listening to the river and wind could change the mountains. And yet . . .
>
> —EcoSono Field Journal: Hearing Mountains
> Sing in the Sound of Wind and River

Using semiotics, sonification, and electroacoustics, I explore the orchestration of human-performed environmental systems (Burtner 2011a, 2011b). These techniques for scoring climate change as music are best described through a look at specific musical works.

The musical score for *Syntax of Snow* (Burtner 2010) for snow and bells offers the performer and listener a way to connect environmental change and music through the intricate performance of musical snow. Musical notes couple with invented graphic symbols describing specific gestures performed on the snow.

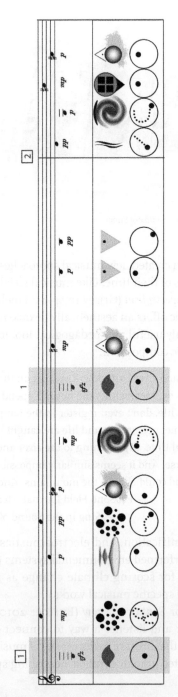

Figure 3. The opening measures of *Syntax of Snow*

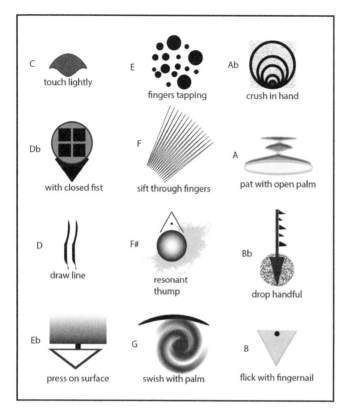

Figure 4. Symbolic snow notation instructions in *Syntax of Snow*

The upper staff shows the glockenspiel notes, and the lower staff shows the snow gesture and hand motion. The performer plays the bells with a mallet held in one hand and the snow with the other (gloved) hand. The snow is amplified by microphones so that the sounds balance with the glockenspiel in performance. The two hands are coupled such that each note on the glockenspiel corresponds to a movement in the snow. In this way, the notation extends the syntactical musical structure to the environmental material. For example, an E on the glockenspiel will always accompany a gesture of fingers lightly tapping on the snow. Each pitch class (A, B-flat, C-sharp, etc.) corresponds to a unique gesture in this manner.

The piece has been performed in concert halls or outdoors in the snow. In either case, the transformation of the snow through various states of melt and noise contrasts with the unchanging and pitched character of the glockenspiel.

The musical form models drifting, amassing harmonic material gradually. Each new section builds on top of what came before, and the performer may choose to echo fragments of previous music at any time. In the score, the past material is differentiated by color, and the current material is notated in black. Late in the piece, the performer interprets four distinct layers of colored note heads, representing the amassed harmonic energy.

Syntax of Snow allows the changing material quality of the snow as it melts to create musical form. Transformation is an inherent characteristic of the snow "instrument" when it is brought into the musical work, rather than a parameter manipulated by the musician. By the end of the piece, the snow will have become damp or slushy, noticeably affecting the sound of the music.

> We humans have more profoundly impacted the planet than any other animal before. Our presence, multiplied by billions, does change the shape of glaciers, the path of rivers, and the time of mountains. Humans alter the atmosphere in ways that drive new planetary conditions. These conditions not only melt the glaciers, but they alter every part of earth's surface.
>
> —EcoSono Field Journal: Hearing Mountains
> Sing in the Sound of Wind and River

In *Six Ecoacoustic Quintets No. 1: Water (Ice)* the musicians play tubs of water containing large chunks of ice. Microphones in the air, underwater, and frozen inside the ice amplify the vibrations generated by each performance gesture in air, water, and ice. The technology allows listeners to hear across the material threshold in a way they cannot with their normal hearing. Listeners may observe how the human energy ripples through various hydrologic states of gas, water, and ice.

A closer look at the score illuminates how this action is scripted. Four percussionists play the water with their hands, and the fifth player applies heat to the ice by pouring hot water onto it. The piece opens with the following four-measure sequence.

A unison quintuplet figure across a 5/4 measure leads to a free 5/4 measure of stirring and tapping the water, marked with a fermata. This is followed by a 3/4 measure of rest, also marked with a fermata, and the indication "wait for loud ice cracking sounds." The fifth player staff shows the intensity of the heat applied to the ice. In the first two measures the performer applies

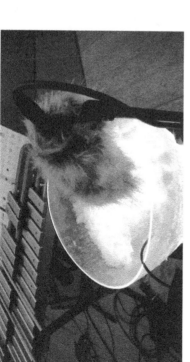

Figure 5. Indoor and outdoor performance of *Syntax of Snow*

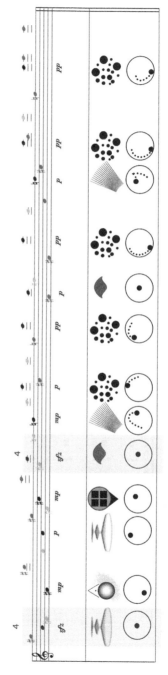

Figure 6. A musical excerpt from *Syntax of Snow*

Figure 7. Performance setup for *Six Ecoacoustic Quintets No. 1: Water (Ice)*. Left: Amplified tub of ice/water. Right: microphone frozen inside a block of ice

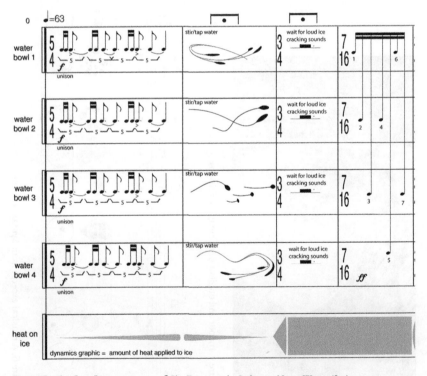

Figure 8. The first four measures of *Six Ecoacoustic Quintets, No. 1: Water (Ice)*

a very slight crescendo/decrescendo of heat that amplifies to full intensity leading into the third measure. The quick application of heat should cause internal cracking in the ice due to the rapid expansion of the molecules generated by the heat. When they hear the loud cracking the musicians move on to the 7/16 measure alternating on sixteenth notes. These first measures reveal several approaches to scored human/nature interaction. Precise rhythmic music notation (measure 1) alternates with evocative graphic notation (measure 2), and the performers listen to the material for cues (measure 3) and listen to one another as an ensemble (measure 4). Meanwhile, the fifth player applies some systemic force to the instrument, altering the conditions of the whole system.

Each measure reveals a distinct way of interacting with the environment. In the first measure the musician is asked to faithfully play the notated musical material, but the water splashes and ripples, creating aleatoric microrhythms and imprecision. The sounding result does not quite match the notes in the music because of the behavior of the water. The second measure gives a suggestive graphic notation, encouraging the musician to play *with* the water, not in spite of it. Here the relationship between the water and the performer is more consonant, but the invented graphical notation is less clear to the musician. To discover how to interpret the notation, the musician must actually play the water. The third measure instructs the musician to "wait," to wait for a sound. The score only provides a rest, a symbol of silence, but it says that the ice will create some sound as a result of the force of applied heat over time. The musician is asked to wait and listen to the world for a cue, to let environmental change trigger human movement. In the fourth measure the musicians respond in sequence. This measure is already difficult to play because the performers must alternate precisely at a sixteenth-note pulse. But the water is also distorting the precision of their articulation. To play this measure, members of the human group must be acutely in balance with one another and with the water. The measure suggests that human-nature collaboration requires a deep sense of both human and environmental agents.

These first four measures of the *Six Ecoacoustic Quintets* reveal an approach to human-environment interaction played out repeatedly in the 160 pages of the full score. Next, the percussionists lower metal tubular bells into the water and build a harmonic polyphony above and below the surface of the water. Like scientists taking core samples of ice, the musicians carefully measure the depth of the chimes, varying pitch and speed to create harmonies and polyrhythms. The polyrhythms eventually transform into

Six Ambient Extensions: No. 1, Water (Ice)
Matthew Burtner

Figure 9. Page from the score of *Six Ecoacoustic Quintets No. 1: Water (Ice)*

unison pulsing. The fifth player continues melting the ice according to the heat intensity staff as, one by one, the performers fill containers of water, parceling out the melted ice into receptacles of various shapes and sizes. They shake these measured resources like rattles, expanding the original rhythmic motif into a canon. The music is particularly impactful when experienced as a performer. For this reason, I composed an accompanying score that can be performed simultaneously by any number of musicians or even by untrained audience members. This accompanying score maintains the experiential and performative traits of the music without being highly technical. For example, here is one page from the *Six Ecoacoustic Quintets No. 1: Water (Ice)*.

> Just as I puzzled about how the dynamism of mountains is contained in the sound of the wind and river, I now wonder how my listening here on the edge of the river is a performative action that could alter the shape of the mountains. Human activity drives global climate change, so if billions of people could hear the music of the environment the way I hear it now, would it change the way we behave on the planet? Would it change the planet?
> —EcoSono Field Journal: Hearing Mountains
> Sing in the Sound of Wind and River

Conclusion: Toward a New Tonality of Climate Change Music

In the EcoSono Field Journal excerpt I ponder the relationship between one person's listening experience and climate change. Using an imaginative extrapolation of the experience, I wonder how the actions and thoughts of one person might be shared by others, perhaps even by billions of people. In a time of human-caused climate change, we understand abstractly that our collective behavior alters the world and that we can no longer underestimate the impact of human action on the planet. Every action, every tendency, every thought is likely shared by others. We humans are so numerous and the speed of our technology so fast and impactful that we can change the planet relatively quickly. Considering this understanding, how might listening be a starting point for activism? The EcoSono Institute set up the conditions for that listening experience, and those of us who heard the sound of the wind and river that day were changed by it. It was a planned action that could be repeated, and it leads to a repeatable creative practice.

Through Brady's framework of an integrated aesthetic and the ecoacoustic works described here, a new musical "tonality" emerges. Some tonal structures are widely understood by humans because of the physics of vibration, and the physiology of the human ear allows us to differentiate between degrees of harmonic and inharmonic vibration. Ecoacoustics also relies on human physiology and a widely shared understanding of nature to create an aesthetic experience. The listener's experience with nature provides a foundation upon which the composer can build the musical artwork.

For example, in daily life, people may not think about the wind even as it envelops them and fills their ears with noise. But a musical artwork using the wind as an instrument will trigger memories of the real wind in the listener. This hypothetical wind music will ask the listener to aestheticize the experience of the wind by connecting those memories to an artistic experience. In this way, the artwork relies on the listener's preformed experience of wind. The wind is the shared structure around which the listener and the artwork connect.

In this manner, ecoacoustic music frames an experience as a work of art and simultaneously relies on the inherent aesthetic attributes of the human experience. In the musical context, sonified energies from the natural world, such as the sounds of wind, a river, a sand dune, a glacier, and so on, become tonal centers within which the composer can build a musical syntax. The tonality provides the pervasive connective fabric of the music, the perceived logic of its operations.

Most people experience climate change through the gradual transformation of places they know well, perhaps the place where they grew up or one they have known for a long time. In a time of rapid climate change, we are confronted with the fragility of our habitats. Many will experience a sense of loss for the places they once knew—forests, coasts, wetlands, glaciers, lakes—transformed over a period of decades by climate change. Ecoacoustic music can draw on this shared sense of connection to place. Like a song that elicits emotion as we personalize the music, connecting the lyrics to our unique life situation, climate change music can connect an ecosystem with a personal experience of environment.

Notes

1   It would be helpful for a reader at this point to listen to a musical composition. Musical excerpts for this article are available at Burtner 2016b.
2   For more information and musical examples, see Burtner 2012.
3   The Nukariik *Inuit Throat Songs and Drumming* album (2008), performed by Karin and Kathy Kettler, offers an excellent modern recording of this tradition.
4   In 1992 the European Cultural Centre of Delphi recovered and reconstructed a first-century BCE hydraulis from the city of Dion. Hear it at Archaeology Channel 2016.
5   In 2015 I worked with the US State Department to create a soundtrack for President Barack Obama's visit to Alaska, where he addressed climate change issues in the Arctic. One of the pieces we used, *Fern*, was written in 1996, before the catastrophic effects of climate change were transforming Alaska's North Slope, but it has now become an elegy for the loss of Arctic permafrost and tundra ecosystems.
6   The EcoSono Institute (www.ecosono.org/) works closely with educational institutions such as the University of Virginia, University of Colorado, and University of Alaska. The University of Virginia has a course in ecoacoustics within its McIntire Department of Music.

References

Archaeology Channel. 2016. "The Ancient Hydraulis." Video, 9:5. archaeologychannel.org /video-guide/video-guide-menu/video-guide-summary/109-the-ancient-hydraulis (accessed January 4, 2016).

Brady, Emily. 2003. *Aesthetics of the Natural Environment*. Tuscaloosa: University of Alabama Press.

Burtner, Matthew. 1998. *Sikuigvik (The Time of Ice Melting)*. Score. matthewburtner.com/sikuigvik.

Burtner, Matthew. 2009. *Six Ecoacoustic Quintets*. Score. matthewburtner.com/six-ecoacoustic -quintets.

Burtner, Matthew. 2010. *Iceprints*. Musical score. matthewburtner.com/syntax-of-snow-2.

Burtner, Matthew. 2011a. "EcoSono: Adventures in Interactive Ecoacoustics in the World." *Organised Sound* 16, no. 3: 234–44.

Burtner, Matthew. 2011b. "Syntax of Snow: Musical Ecoacoustics of a Changing Arctic." In "Expressions of Climate Change in the Arts," chapter 8 of *North by 2020: Perspectives on Alaska's Changing Social-Ecological Systems*, edited by Amy Lauren Lovecraft and Hajo Eicken, 651–64. Fairbanks: University of Alaska Press.

Burtner, Matthew. 2012. *Auksalaq*. Score. matthewburtner.com/auksalaq.

Burtner, Matthew. 2016a. "Sounding Art Climate Change." In *Routledge Companion to Sounding Art*, edited by Marcel Cobussen, Vincent Meelberg, and Barry Truax, 287–304. New York: Routledge.

Burtner, Matthew. 2016b. "Climate Change Music." matthewburtner.com/climate-change -music.

Debussy, Claude. 1905. *La mer (The Sea)*. Score. Paris: Durand.

Fineberg, Joshua. 2000. "Spectral Music: History and Techniques." *Contemporary Music Review* 19, no. 2: 1–5.

Grisey, Gérard. 1974–85. *Les espaces acoustiques (The Acoustic Field)*. Score. Milan: BMG Ricordi Music Publishing.

Harvey, Jonathan. 2001. "Spectralism." *Contemporary Music Review* 19, no. 3: 11–14.

Kramer, Jonathan D. 1988. *The Time of Music: New Meanings, New Temporalities, New Listening Strategies*. New York: Schirmer Books.

Messian, Oliver. 1964. *Catalog d'oiseaux*. Musical score. Paris: Alphonse Leduc.

MiN Ensemble. 2001. *Arctic Contrasts*. Tromso, Norway: Euridice Turn Left AS. Compact disc.

Nukariik. 2008. *Inuit Throat Songs and Drumming*. Ontario: Nukariik. Compact disc.

Perle, George. 1977. *Serial Composition and Atonality: An Introduction to the Music of Schoenberg, Berg, and Webern*. 4th ed., rev. Berkeley: University of California Press.

Schaeffer, Pierre. (1952) 2012. *In Search of a Concrete Music*. Translated by John Dack and Christine North. Berkeley: University of California Press.

Schafer, R. Murray. 1977. *The Tuning of the World*. New York: Knopf.

Schoenberg, Arnold. 1925. *Suite für Klavier, Op. 25 (Suite for Piano, Op. 25)*. Score. UE 7627. Vienna: Universal Edition.

Schoenberg, Arnold. 1975. *Style and Idea: Selected Writings of Arnold Schoenberg*. Edited by Leonard Stein with translations by Leo Black. Berkeley: University of California Press.

Smetana, Bedřich. 1874. *The Moldau*. Score. EE 3642. London: Ernst Eulenberg.

Truax, Barry. 1996. "Soundscape, Acoustic Communication, and Environmental Sound Composition." *Contemporary Music Review* 15, nos. 1–2: 49–65.

Westerkamp, Hildegard. 2002. "Linking Soundscape Composition and Acoustic Ecology." *Organised Sound* 7, no. 1: 51–56.

Dipesh Chakrabarty

Afterword

"In *After Nature*," writes Willis Jenkins in this issue, "the legal scholar Jedediah Purdy . . . suggests that thinking through food allows environmental thought to reckon with key uncertainties of life in the Anthropocene." The contributors to this issue have accomplished something remarkably similar. Anchoring themselves in the everyday "bread and butter" concerns of the humanities— to speak the issue of food but on a metaphorical register—they have presented the reader with a veritable feast of ideas to reflect on what the Anthropocene could mean for the humanities and the humanities for the Anthropocene.

All of the contributors are in effective agreement that scholars in the humanities could not afford to remain indifferent to the Anthropocene (or to whatever the name signified). But, true to the tradition of the humanities, the agreement is merely an initial one. All signs of consensus disappear as we get into individual essays; they develop approaches that are not only varied but sometimes even opposed, if not hostile, to one other. Not quite the "shouting match" that climate conversations sometimes feel like to Michael Segal, but surely not a symphony either. I would probably place at one end of the intellectual spread Noel Castree's

The South Atlantic Quarterly 116:1, January 2017
DOI 10.1215/00382876-3749403 © 2017 Duke University Press

passionate plea for a "public sphere" humanities that proudly takes its place alongside science, economics, and policy prescriptions and brings its own concerns—including the critical skepticism that often marks social studies of science—to bear on public discussions of "climate change." Castree, incidentally, must be able to take some comfort from the mirror image of his argument in Segal's essay—especially from Segal's concern to ensure that big broad scientific narratives not only can sit at the same table as narratives from politics, identity, and culture but also are actually able to hold their own. At the other extreme from Castree and Segal is perhaps the essay by Claire Colebrook and Tom Cohen, who advance their ideas about what it might mean to practice "critical climate change" discourse. In the tradition of schools of thought that come preceded by the self-describing epithet "critical," they "propose that [very] conceptions of redemption, retrieval, sustainability, and ecology (or benevolent interconnectedness)" are symptomatic of "the macroaggressions that have generated a lure of humanity that has the destruction of the planet as one of its many expressions." They posit that "the twinned notions of 'the human' and 'the environment'" emerge from the same "relatively stable ongoing habit of voracious and rapacious consumption." They expressly do not wish to "expand or enrich the humanities." For them, the notion of human, signifying a false commonality, gives rise to the notion of the "planet." *Critical* climate change thus is about "deconstruct[ing] the relation between humanity and ecology: there is no ecology that humanity unfortunately comes along to destroy." They judge degradation and redemption discourses to be identical twins joined at the waist from birth. The essays by Gary Tomlinson and Catherine Malabou, in contrast, *do* seek to expand and enrich the humanities in the face of climate change by drawing creatively and critically on the scholarship in "deep history." Tomlinson's essay clearly gives a pass to deconstruction and ends with the remark: ". . . if the expansion of the human imagination—now faced with the imperative to encompass transhuman and inhuman dimensions—is not a productive activism for humanist scholars, it is unclear to me what can be." Malabou's essay argues explicitly about the difficulty of deconstructing the idea of humans as a "geophysical force." David Buckland, Olivia Gray, and Lucy Wood's essay, like Segal's and Castree's, is focused on messaging climate change and outlines through their descriptions of the Cape Farewell project what could be achieved by the cultivation of the faculty of imagination in the face of climate change. Unlike Tomlinson, they oppose imagination to reason, but they all perhaps end up at the same place in emphasizing the importance of humanities in stretching the capacities of that human imagination in the face of planetary climate change. Willis and Astrid Ulloa raise pertinent questions about how the Anthropocene discourse repositions the politics of religion, identity, and gender, while Matthew Burtner's wonderful account gives us a concrete and inspiring example of what a creative musician and academic could do by way of "bridging" changes in "the physical world around us" with conceptual and emotional dimensions of human life.

Altogether, this issue is a splendid collection of essays. And I remain especially grateful for the comments, critical or otherwise, that some essayists have kindly cared to make about my own work. But the simultaneous assonance and dissonance of voices that runs through the essays is typical of scholarship in the human and interpretive sciences. Scientists working for the Intergovernmental Panel on Climate Change (IPCC) try to develop a consensus in spite of the diversity of disciplines they represent among themselves. They can make statements like "x percent of climate scientists believe at y percent level of confidence that contemporary climate change is anthropogenic in origin." Humanities scholars cannot make such statements. They not only produce a plurality of interpretive approaches; they also value and thrive on such plurality. A hermeneutic of suspicion is embedded in their training. To be a scholar in the humanities is to learn to live with differences of perspectives—in reality, this often means the growth of interpretive "churches" that vie with one another for dominance, but the highest ideal still remains that of acknowledging the existence of multiple perspectives on any important question of value and of being able to see an issue from somebody else's point of view (including, these days, points of view of the nonhuman). These are important qualities to bring into the public sphere as global environmental and other crises inevitably sharpen questions of identity, justice, and inequity. But that is also why the humanities do not usually contribute to the development of policy (since answers to questions of value are implicitly assumed in the policy-oriented disciplines). The public role of the humanities cannot be developed by thwarting what the humanities actually are: a collection of scholars who compete intellectually to generate—rationally and on the basis of appeals to necessary bodies of evidence—multiple and vying perspectives on any given issue.

But there are even deeper and structural reasons why "anthropogenic climate change" presents some very peculiar and particular challenges to politically minded scholars in the humanities. First is the question of the temporal scale that the phenomenon of global or planetary warming involves. Climate change is not simply a problem of transitioning to renewables in the next few decades. There are aspects to the science-defined problem of "anthropogenic climate change" that involve swaths of time that are geological in measure, too large for any human intervention. I am not saying this as a humanist. Climate scientists, especially those studying earth system science, themselves say it. Thus geophysicist David Archer, in his much-discussed book *The Long Thaw*, claims, first of all, that "humans are changing the next 100,000 years of Earth's climate." His second claim is that "mankind is becoming a force in climate comparable to the [100,000-year] orbital variations that drive the glacial cycles" (Archer 2009: 6). These are not scales of time over which human politics or intervention can unfold. These are thus real aspects of the problem that governments and political parties simply have to ignore while formulating policies or strategies. Humans address problems that occur over conceivable human scales of time. But our ignoring these very large-scale geological aspects of global warming does not make them disappear. We cannot do much if we have already changed the climate of the planet for the next one hundred thousand years. Such knowledge cannot inform policy. Tomlinson's essay powerfully underlines this point.

But there is an even more fundamental problem, I think, that makes the development of a sense of a human politics adequate to the phenomenon of global warming an extremely difficult, if not an impossible, exercise. Here I find a helpful point of departure in Malabou's observation that the *global* in *global warming* means something different from the *global* in *globalization*. The "globe" of globalization was created through the very process of globalization itself: beginning with European expansion and with technologies of communication and travel giving human beings a growing sense over centuries that their histories had gotten connected, with the process reaching an intense pitch in the second half of the twentieth century. Globalization, a process pushed forward by powerful interests, has been a ground-up process, touching our personal lives and experiences in ways both harmful and beneficial. The hypothesis of "global" warming, in contrast, has come from big science, often American, involving not just Charles David Keeling's recording of carbon dioxide concentrations of the earth's atmosphere at the Mauna Loa Observatory in Hawaii but also satellite observations and examination of ancient air trapped in ice-core samples from the poles, not to speak of the roles of National Aeronautics and Space Administration (NASA) space scientists such as James Hansen and James Lovelock who began their careers studying other planets. Planetary climate science began by looking at this planet from the outside in, as it were, in order to create models of climate for the planet as a whole. As is well known, Lovelock and Hansen developed their interests in "global warming" in the course of researching Mars and Venus, respectively. The "globe" of "global warming" refers to the behavior of the earth as a planet among other planets (that have also seen warming and cooling); it comes out of what may be called "interplanetary studies." The "globe" of "globalization," however, refers to a web of human connections that humans themselves have knowingly created in every step of the process in pursuit of power and profit. The two "globes" are indeed different. I sometimes therefore make a distinction between "the global" and "the planetary."

But this difference has real consequences for what we may think of as politics. Humans today have at their disposal an array of ideas and institutions to engage the process of globalization—these range from international agencies through to national governments and nongovernmental organizations that provide the basis for whatever global regulation or governance is possible. But see what happens in the rhetoric of science when climate scientists attempt to communicate to a global public the "dangers" of excessive warming and the urgency of ameliorative action by picking a number like 2 degrees Celsius. Admittedly, it is not a scientifically picked figure, but the point is that it is a planetary figure, referring to the "*average* surface temperature" of the earth. It means that some places may be well above the average and some well below. Yet one cannot draw up a map of the world setting goals for individual regions or nations—which would also mostly be averages anyway—for the planetary average to be a particular target to be achieved by all the peoples of the world synchronously! The figure makes sense because the science of "global warming" studies the *planetary* climate system *as a whole*. But no politics can follow from it. Will India aim to have an average of a 3-degree rise, and the United States below 1 degree? Can such targets be real? It is one atmosphere, after all. The IPCC can produce "carbon budget" tables for the entire planet—signaling in effect how much greenhouse gas the planet can emit in how much time to reduce by so many percentages the chances (no certainty here!) of climate change becoming dangerous. But such budgets remain only a guideline for the political actors on the global stage.

So the science of global warming communicates "science" and its abstract constructions of planetary climate—big data can create such hyperobjects, as Timothy Morton (2013) says—but this cannot result in any politics that we may legitimately call new or Anthropocene politics, even though the phenomenon of anthropogenic climate change, as many of the contributors have noted, challenges many deeply held assumptions of the humanities. One may go so far as to say that the science of climate change visualizes a climate system that operates on a planetwide scale, and numbers such as the 2-degree threshold or the construction of the so-called nine planetary boundaries are simply shorthand measures devised by scientists to communicate "dangers" of precipitous climatic shifts at the planetary level. But their ideal addressee is a planetary human-subject that simply does not exist or cannot be called into being.

That does not mean that climate science is not useful, even for the humanities. Its insistence on speaking at a planetary level challenges the inherent and deep-set anthropocentrism of the human sciences and calls on humanists to develop new perspectival points from which to comment on the human condition today. But there is no politics that corresponds to planetary perspectives. Humans face the emerging phenomenon of planetary warming from a default position, that is, from within the politics of the institutions that were created to deal with the "globe" of "globalization" with all the assumptions of "stable" Holocene conditions built into them. Thus the process that culminated in nearly two hundred nations signing a nonbinding but peer-reviewed climate treaty in Paris in December 2015 still represents what humans can do by way of coming together to deal with this unforeseen challenge. But this was a process that belongs to the history of globalization, not global warming. What we are throwing at global warming—assuming deep down that humans will somehow adapt to its consequences—are weapons forged in the workshop of capitalist globalization. These weapons carry with them all the logics of inequality and domination that have marked the history of globalization. Jenkins and Ulloa are thus entirely right to raise questions of identity, gender, and indigenous knowledges as so many ways of bringing into the discussion what gets elided or marginalized in mainstream, official narratives.

But there is a welcome change. For all the dissonance of voices in this collection of essays, there is a shared sense that while the inequalities of global capital may get accentuated through the uneven impact of global warming, the story that the scientists tell still requires us humanists to venture forth, intellectually, into areas we never went to before—such as the history of the planet as it was long before humans came and the history of complex life on it. It is through the friction between narratives of globalization, however critically recounted, and the stories that climate scientists tell of the intertwined pasts of the geology and the biology of this planet—narratives that in a Derridean sense supplement one another—that new and bold perspectives will emerge in the humanities. This special issue bears some telltale signs of such a humanities to come.

Reference

Archer, David. 2009. *The Long Thaw: How Humans Are Changing the Next 100,000 Years of Earth's Climate*. Princeton, NJ: Princeton University Press.
Morton, Tomothy. 2013. *Hyperobjects: Philosophy and Ecology after the End of the World*. Minneapolis: University of Minnesota Press.

Environmental Activism across the Pacific

Teresa Shewry, Editor

Teresa Shewry

Introduction

The activism of Indigenous peoples addressed by the essays in this Against the Day section is imperfectly captured by the term *ecological*. It is not really ecological when this term implies a focus on nature as a sphere separate from people's lives.[1] It is ecological, however, in the sense that it involves people engaging, and being engaged by, the land, ocean, atmosphere, and many more things. This activism takes varied beings as having presence, limits, and implications. It thus does not separate ecological struggles from struggles to transform colonizing relations, such as the dispossessions and racisms that underlie military occupation or fossil fuels extraction. As Palauan (Belauan) activist Richard Salvador (2002: 7) put it to the Treaty on the Non-Proliferation of Nuclear Weapons Review Conference Preparatory Committee in New York in 2002, speaking to why Pacific peoples link nuclear-free politics to struggles for freedom from colonialism, "There is little that we meaningfully distinguish between uranium mining and its draconian practices, testing of nuclear weapons AND colonialism."

These essays engage forms of activism in which people seek to protect continuingly creative but ordinary life processes that conflict with imagined or emergent military bases, plantations, tourism infrastructures, and mines. As several contributors note in this section, these activists may reject the term *protest*, if this term implies emergence against, or rejection without an alternative, in a way that elides how opposing is interwoven in ongoing forms of living like fishing, gardening, or visiting sacred places. This activism consequently engages immense ecological upheavals through a focus on relations and territories that are vital to the life of specific Indigenous

The South Atlantic Quarterly 116:1, January 2017
DOI 10.1215/00382876-3749581 © 2017 Duke University Press

communities: a blockade on the roadway to the summit of a sacred mountain to stop construction vehicles; a "swim-in" in a harbor targeted for an aircraft carrier berth. The importance of particular relational existences to this activism reflects the commitments of differing communities to autonomy in shaping the conditions in which they live.

Although this activism is grounded in distinct communities, livelihoods, and territories, it also creates connections between movements across the Pacific. The ocean has long been crucial to the conceptualization of such connections, as is suggested by the complex history of dreams and struggles for a nuclear-free and independent Pacific. The Nuclear Free and Independent Pacific (NFIP) movement, a collective of trade unions, church groups, and other community and environmental organizations, was particularly active in the 1970s–90s, in a climate where colonizing, nuclearized states were exerting extreme economic, physical, and political violence to undermine nuclear-free struggles in countries like Palau (Belau). Describing how the NFIP movement connected freedom and independence movements to antinuclear struggles, Teresia K. Teaiwa (1994: 102–3) argues that it participated in a distinctively Pacific history of resistance informed by "s/pacific n/ oceans" that "honor the specificities of Islander experience, recognize the generic effects of (neo) colonialism on all Islanders, and are committed to political and cultural cooperation at the regional level."

Memories of the NFIP movement and of other histories of oceanic resistance are fanning the sparks of new alliances and activism across the Pacific. Moana Nui (vast ocean), for example, is a gathering of Indigenous and settler activists, practitioners, and scholars from across the Pacific to confront economic hegemony, ecological destruction, and militarized exploitation. Its work has included critical engagements with the Asia-Pacific Economic Cooperation (APEC), a Pacific Rim forum that supports free trade and other kinds of economic integration, and the Pacific Pivot, an Obama administration strategy to refocus US economic and military power on the Pacific through increased military concentration and trade agreements such as the Trans-Pacific Partnership. In 2011, for example, Moana Nui ran an alternative conference timed to confront the APEC meeting in Honolulu, declaring its refusal to cooperate with APEC's efforts to commodify life and land (Moana Nui 2011). Another oceanic collective, the Wansolwara (one ocean, one people) movement, brings together participants through *dances* (a term that replaces *conference* to centralize creative practices) to explore "issues of grassroots sustainability and national self-determination in the face of the relentless assaults of extractive industries, militarization, consumerism and colonialism" (Teaiwa 2014). Teaiwa (2014) writes that the Madang Wansolwara Dance of 2014 involved poets from Hawai'i, visual artists from the University of the South Pacific in Fiji, musicians from the University of Goroka in Papua New Guinea (PNG), yam farmers from PNG and Vanuatu, forestry workers from PNG, social workers from the Federated States of Micronesia and West Papua, landowners from Fiji and Aotearoa New Zealand, tribal chiefs from PNG and Vanuatu, and theologians from West Papua, Australia, Fiji, and Te Ao Ma'ohi (French Polynesia).

These movements draw inspiration from histories of ancestral migrations and navigations and from cosmologies that do not cleanly isolate the saltwater from land and other elements. They associate Indigenous peoples with water, not only with land. Alice Te Punga Somerville (2012: 42) writes of the complex, distinctive resonance of the term *ocean* in Indigenous Pacific theorizations, specifically engaging Epeli Hau'ofa's 1994 treatise "Our Sea of Islands" and Vernice Wineera Pere's 1978 poem "Pacific Note": "The ocean is not solely a body of water but a framework for all the elements; sand, rocks, and the sun are included in the 'ocean,' just as the islands are included in Hau'ofa's Oceania."

These relational, oceanic existences are the site of irreversible loss in this time of global climate change, expanding militarism, and resurgent resource extraction. Saltwater, for example, is seeping up through and surging across the soils and freshwaters of low-lying atolls and islands, where it poisons gardens, floods houses, and washes away land. Pacific peoples contribute little (about 0.03 percent) to global greenhouse gas emissions but face the undermining, and in some places the complete loss, of the material base of their lives in the context of sea-level rise, changing rainfall dynamics, ocean acidification, palm oil plantations, and other climate-related violence.[2]

It may be tempting to tell stories that focus only on the immensity and exceptionality of such contemporary ecological crises, but there are more stories to be told of the Pacific. The essays collected here not only reveal engagement with deeper trajectories of both violence and resistance, but also explore activism that maintains and constructs modes of life and relations of care among humans, the land, the ocean, and other beings.

Acknowledgments

I would like to thank Michael Hardt for thoughtful feedback and editing on this essay.

Notes

1   See Rob Nixon's (2011: 4–5) discussion of tensions between differently conceptual-
     ized ecological politics. He argues that Global South environmentalisms and envi-
     ronmental justice movements have "pushed back against an antihuman environ-
     mentalism that too often sought (under the banner of universalism) to impose green
     agendas dominated by rich nations and Western NGOs."
2   On climate change and the Pacific, see United Nations Permanent Forum on Indig-
     enous Issues (2015).

References

Hau'ofa, Epeli. 1994. "Our Sea of Islands." *Contemporary Pacific* 6, no. 1: 148–61.

Moana Nui. 2011. "Moana Nui Statement." November 29. moananui2011.org/?page_id=675
    (accessed July 1, 2016).

Nixon, Rob. 2011. *Slow Violence and the Environmentalism of the Poor.* Cambridge, MA: Harvard
    University Press.

Salvador, Richard. 2002. "NGO Presentation to the NPT Review Conference Preparatory
    Committee, New York, April 2002: Indigenous Perspective." *Reaching Critical Will.*
    www.reachingcriticalwill.org/images/documents/Disarmament-fora/npt/prepcomo2
    /NGOpres2002/4.pdf (accessed July 1, 2016).

Somerville, Alice Te Punga. 2012. *Once Were Pacific: Māori Connections to Oceania.* Minneapo-
    lis: University of Minnesota Press.

Teaiwa, Teresia K. 1994. "Bikinis and other s/pacific n/oceans." *Contemporary Pacific* 6, no. 1:
    87–109.

Teaiwa, Teresia K. 2014. "'One Ocean, One People'—Interview with Teresia Teaiwa on Self-
    Determination Struggles in the Pacific." *Fightback: Struggle, Solidarity, Socialism.* Octo-
    ber 29. fightback.org.nz/2014/10/29/one-ocean-one-people-interview-with-teresia
    -teaiwa-on-self-determination-struggles-in-the-pacific/ (accessed July 1, 2016).

United Nations Permanent Forum on Indigenous Issues. 2015. "The Pacific Region." www.un
    .org/esa/socdev/unpfii/documents/2015/media/pacific.pdf (accessed July 1, 2016).

Wineera Pere, Vernice. 1978. "Pacific Note." *Mahanga.* Laie, Hawai'i: Institute for Polynesian
    Studies, Brigham Young University-Hawaii Campus.

Michael Lujan Bevacqua

Guam: Protests at the Tip of America's Spear

HACHA: Guam ~~USA~~

Guam is the largest and southernmost island in the Mariana Archipelago, a string of fifteen islands in the Western Pacific. It has been home to the Chamorro people for thousands of years, but for the past century it has been an unincorporated territory, or colony, of the United States. Since it was first taken by the US military in 1898 during the Spanish-American War, Guam has played a key role in linking the United States to Asia, especially in terms of its economic and military interests. While it was first used as a coaling station for US ships, today its strategic location on the edge of Asia makes it ideal for the projection of force against friendly and hostile nations across East Asia. Today, Guam is sometimes known as "the tip of America's spear," a 212-square-mile colony with 29 percent of its land mass composed of US Air Force and Navy bases.

Guam's strategic value to the United States can be broken into two basic parts; the first is its location and the second is its ambiguous political status. Guam lies within just a few hours of all the major nations in East Asia. As such, the island has played a key role in the transportation of troops and weapons to every major US conflict in Asia since World War II. Guam has also acted as a link to the United States in terms of the migration of refugees from US-involved conflicts. Guam was host to more than 100,000 Vietnamese refugees in 1975 as part of Operation New Life. Guam has also hosted refugees from Burma and Kurds from Iraq. The second aspect is Guam's colonial status. Guam is a possession of the United States, a colony, neither a

The South Atlantic Quarterly 116:1, January 2017
DOI 10.1215/00382876-3749592   © 2017 Duke University Press

full part of the nation nor its own independent country. The US military is given more freedom in Guam than they are in other countries in the region. As such the US military does not need to ask permission for many of their activities, as they are required to do for their bases in foreign countries.

The value of this in-between status was first articulated in 1969, in a speech made by President Richard Nixon during a stopover in Guam. That speech became known as the Guam Doctrine and called for "the shifting of the American military perimeter from 'contested bases,' or *contested sites*, in Asia to more secure locations throughout the Pacific" (Hanlon 1998: 219) such as Guam, the Northern Marianas Islands, and elsewhere in Micronesia. According to Admiral Fallon, formerly head of the United States Pacific Command (USPACOM), the advantage of having bases in Guam is that it is an "American territory," and "the island does not have the political restrictions, such as those in South Korea that could impede U.S. military moves in an emergency" (Halloran 2006). In contrast to countries such as South Korea, Japan, and the Philippines where there is sometimes popular and governmental resistance directed to US military presence, Guam's colonial status makes it a vital asset. While those bases are considered to be contested, Guam, as a possession of the United States, is represented as *uncontested*.

In his text *Pacific Passages, World Culture, and Local Politics in Guam*, anthropologist Roland Stade (1998) shares a statement from a Captain Douglas from the US Air Force that further clarifies Guam's value as a colony to the United States:

> People on Guam seem to forget that they are a possession, and not an equal partner. . . . If California says that they want to do this, it is like my wife saying that she wants to move here or there: I'll have to respect her wish and at least discuss it with her. If Guam says they want to do this or that, it is as if this cup here [he pointed at his coffee mug] expresses a wish: the answer will be, you belong to me and I can do with you as best I please. (192)

Douglas continued, making clear the implications of the word *territory*, especially in relation to US military interests: "This is a U.S. territory and not like in the Philippines or other places, where they can kick us out. Here we have absolute right of disposal" (194).

In this essay my goal is to provide an overview of recent US military activities in Guam and the Marianas, not only to inform the reader, but also to challenge the very notion of these islands as being "uncontested." To this extent, I will also provide an overview of popular resistance to these military plans, which are no longer focused only in Guam, but also in the Northern Marianas Islands of Pågan and Tinian.

HUGUA: The Guam Military Buildup

In 1946 Guam was added to the list of international Non-Self-Governing Territories maintained by the United Nations, which are political entities deserving of decolonization and the determining of their own political destiny (United Nations 2016). The United States and other administering powers or colonizers are obligated to help support their colonies toward decolonization. The UN sees increased militarization and the building up of bases as a detriment to decolonization, as it can easily lead to countries ignoring the human rights of colonized peoples in the name of national or regional security and strategic interests. The United States has long ignored its responsibility in this regard, and rather than decrease its military presence in the Marianas, it currently seeks to dramatically increase it (United Nations 2016).

In 2002, then President George W. Bush called the twenty-first century the "Pacific Century" (Bumiller 2002). This was echoed by a number of other political leaders, including US Secretary of State Hillary Clinton (2011). These calls are tied to a changing of US interests and priorities in the world as a result of the rise of several Asia nations, especially China. In US strategic military terms this has been referred to as a Pacific Pivot, a rearranging of US military forces away from a European focus and moving them toward the Pacific Rim (Hudson 2016). As part of this the US Department of Defense (DOD) announced their intention in 2006 to move a significant number of their Marines currently based in Okinawa to Guam (Park 2005). This move was speculated to cost several billions of dollars, as it would require the construction of new housing and training facilities for the troops and their dependents.

In 2009, the DOD released a Draft Environmental Impact Statement (DEIS) outlining their intentions for militarizing Guam. A number of concerns were immediately apparent. The DEIS stated that Guam's population, currently at 160,000, could increase by 60,000 in just a few years with the buildup. Plans to build a nuclear aircraft carrier berth would require dredging seventy acres of beautiful coral reef. In order to create a firing range complex for the Marines, places such as Pågat, which are culturally significant to the island's indigenous people, the Chamorros, were to be closed off to the public and the US military would be required to lease between 1,000 and 2,400 new acres of land.

TULU: Protecting and Defending

Pågat is on the northeastern side of the island and features freshwater caves and limestone cliffs. It was once the site of an ancient Chamorro village and is now a favorite hiking spot and a place where traditional healers gather rare plants. Today Chamorros seeking to reconnect to their ancient ancestors hike to Pågat in order to pay respects among the artifacts and stone ruins of the ancient homes. Pågat became a central point for those critiquing and resisting this US military increase.

At present, the US military controls close to one-third of Guam's land mass and already restricts access to several places on Guam that are sacred and contain numerous artifacts. Frustration over the loss of this site first appeared in social media, primarily through the sharing of Facebook posts and images that contrasted images of soldiers firing and training with cultural symbols important to Chamorros. The images were accompanied by questions like "Do We Want This for Our Island?" (Naputi 2013: 188). A coalition of environmental, cultural, and political organizations banded together to begin taking people on regular tours of the Pågat area, so that Guam residents could experience its historical qualities themselves. Thousands of people were taken to Pågat on what became known as "heritage hikes" meant to illustrate for people what the cost of the proposed military increase might be (178).

From this initial activism, a collection of demilitarization groups stepped forward to protest the military buildup, all of which rallied under the banner of "Prutehi yan Difendi," which is the Chamorro for "Protest and Defend." This coalition comprised older groups that had long sought the return of Chamorro lands that had been taken following World War II by the US military to build their bases to groups made up of younger professionals who felt that Guam's culture and environment were not being treated fairly in this process. The phrase "Prutehi yan Difendi" is drawn from the Chamorro pledge or Inifresi, which is taught to all public school children on the island. Through this idea of protecting and defending Pågat, a wider critical conversation about the US military presence on Guam began to develop (Naputi and Bevacqua 2015).

In talk radio, social media, and public meetings, people began to express more and more discontent over the US military plans. People were unhappy that one of the few places where the public could travel freely to enjoy the natural beauty or to pay respect to their ancestral spirits might soon be blocked off. The idea of a firing range built in the area was also considered offensive. If the US military carried through with their plans, tens of millions of bullets would be fired from a hill above that area, frightening hikers and desecrating the remains of Chamorros that are resting in Pågat. More people were frustrated with the idea that even though the military already controls so much of the island, it was nonetheless seeking to acquire new lands (Underwood 2001).

FATFAT: The Poisons of Militarization

With the proposals for drastic increases on the table, residents of Guam began to see themselves in a wider context and perceive the various ways in which Guam is used by the US military, and how much of this takes place without their knowledge or consent.

For instance, Guam is at the heart of a massive training area known as the Mariana Island Training and Testing Area, or MITT. In the Mariana Islands, the United States routinely holds large-scale multinational training exercises. For example, in 2006, the United States coordinated the largest ever peacetime naval exercises called "Valiant Shield." In all, these exercises included navies of a dozen different nations, and the United States military alone consisted of 22,000 military personnel, 280 aircraft, 28 ships, and 3 aircraft carriers (Batdorf 2006). The exercise was so successful the United States repeated the exercise in 2007 and 2010 with even more personnel and hardware. As the US military uses Guam and the waters around it for training purposes, there is always the possibility for accidents to take place. From 2007 to 2008, there were seven crashes of aircraft in and around Guam (Bevacqua 2008). In 2008 a nuclear submarine also leaked trace amounts of radioactive waste into the waters around Guam.

The heavy militarization of Guam has led to a significant amount of contamination. After World War II, hazardous and toxic chemicals were dumped and buried around the island and are still being cleaned up until today. Currently, there are at least seventy military toxic waste sites on the island (Mitchell 2012). While the US military was conducting nuclear testing in the Marshall Islands, their ships were regularly brought to Guam for cleaning and servicing. It is more than likely that fallout from the radiation tests and also contamination from the cleaning has affected the health of people living in certain areas. Some scientists speculate that the heavy contamination is one of the reasons why people on Guam suffer from incredibly high rates of certain diseases, particularly cancer. For example, someone in Guam is 2,000 percent more likely to get nasopharynx cancer than the average resident of the United States (Natividad and Kirk 2010).

Even the United States' own Environmental Protection Agency strongly criticized the proposal by the US military as "environmentally unsatisfactory," claiming that it "should not proceed as proposed" (Harden 2010). Nancy Woo of the EPA said, "The government of Guam and the Guam Waterworks cannot by themselves accommodate the military expansion. . . . It is not possible and it is not fair that the island bear the cost" (Harden 2010). At the time, Guam government officials put the total costs of the proposed buildup at about $3 billion dollars, including $1.7 billion for infrastructure and $100 million for the already severely overburdened public hospital. On Guam—where a third of the population at the time received food stamps, a massive influx of impoverished immigrants from the surrounding islands was promoted by the United States, and about 25 percent of the population lived below the US poverty level—that price tag could never have been paid with local tax revenue.

LIMA: Public Comments

Using this history and the contemporary reality of military use, community activists worked together during the ninety-day public comment period to build more awareness and outrage over this military buildup. The potential catastrophe of the buildup was clear from the size of the document itself, as the potential environmental impacts to Guam required 11,000 pages to discuss (Aguon 2009). Resistance to the buildup continued to grow as protests, teach-ins, petitions, and lawsuits were all carried out (Natividad and Leon Guerrero 2010). Efforts at international solidarity were made, as Chamorro activists reached out to those with similar struggles in Okinawa, Hawai'i, Australia, South Korea, and the Philippines. But as much of the world considers Guam to be "Guam USA" and just another part of American real estate, other than the start of some strong grassroots links, little came from these efforts.

In addition to hikes to sites threatened by militarization, a "swim-in" occurred in Apra Harbor, Guam's port, and the sites of the proposed aircraft carrier berth. Through the organization We Are Guahan, people were invited to snorkel and see firsthand several acres of the beautiful coral that would have to be dredged in order to carry out the US military's plans (Hauswirth 2010). A Unified Chamorro Statement against the US military buildup was written by a group of professors at the University of Guam, and a diverse group of over four dozen Chamorro organizations signed on expressing their concerns over the US military buildup (Hattori et al. 2010). The US military organized three public comment meetings where the community could make statements and express their concerns. Thousands of people attended these meetings, on one occasion forcing the event to go several hours beyond its scheduled time as hundreds had shown up to express their problems with what was being proposed for Guam.

At the end of the comment period more than 10,000 comments, most critical, had been submitted.

GUNOM: Delays and Diversions

Despite the large number of comments and the critical voices of the people of Guam, the US military's plans were delayed because of outside forces, primarily economic downturns in the United States and Japan. With a price tag in excess of $7 billion, both governments agreed a scaling down of this transfer was necessary. In 2011 in response to a local lawsuit saying that the US DOD had violated NEPA in their selection of Pågat for their firing range, they agreed to temporarily delay their selection and conduct more study or a SEIS (supplementary environmental impact statement) (Camacho 2013). In 2014, when discussions over the military buildup were started again, the United States had changed their tactics and their targets.

When the DOD returned with new plans, proposed troop numbers were reduced and their focus had been moved north of Guam into other islands in the Marianas Archipelago. Guam is the most densely populated of all the Marianas Islands and the one with the longest history of protests against US militarism. As the northern islands are much more sparsely populated and perceived to have fewer economic opportunities, the DOD was certain they would receive a warmer welcome in the islands of Tinain and Pågan. They were wrong.

In April 2015 the DOD announced plans that would radically alter the face of both of these islands and, by using them for a number of different types of artillery and bombing training, would cause potentially irreparable environmental damage. The island of Tinian is most famous historically for its role as a launching point for the Enola Gay during World War II. If the DOD goes through with its plans, the northern half of the island would be off-limits to civilians for an estimated sixteen to forty-five weeks of the year, as training areas would be established that would displace hundreds of farmers and destroy several cultural and historical sites (Zotomayor 2015a). The island of Pågan, with its black sand beaches and twin volcanoes, is known internationally as an ecological treasure. But with the DOD's intent to close the island and use it for bombing and artillery training, its near-pristine beauty is threatened (Olson 2015). Movements to build awareness of the possible destruction of this paradise in the Western Pacific have resulted in small protests throughout the Marianas and an online petition that gathered more than 100,000 signatures. Political leaders in the northern islands have joined with community groups by passing resolutions to protest the DOD's proposals. The DEIS for the military buildup in Pågan and Tinian was 1,400 pages long, but the public outcry over the likely environmental, economic, and social damages resulted in the submission of 28,000 public comments through the NEPA process by October 2015 (Zotomayor 2015b).

As the DOD has spent the last five years shifting their plans in order to make the buildup sleeker and more invisible to resistant forces, the overall process was stalled because of financial concerns from the US Senate. Senators John McCain and Carl Levin put restrictions on funding for Guam/Marianas buildup-related projects until several conditions were met by the DOD, most notably the requirement of a master plan for US force distribution in the Asia-Pacific region. In October 2015, the US Congress approved the first payments for the military buildup, contracts for improving wastewater services in areas where US Marines are soon to be stationed (Dumat-ol Daleno 2015).

Although critical efforts have emerged over each individual island, Tinian, Pågan, or Guam, there has been little success in unifying demilitarized resistance. Where earlier DOD plans had concentrated much of their training activities in Guam, by reducing the overall size of the force to be transferred and redistributing their training facilities throughout three different islands, mounting a campaign against the buildup has proved difficult. Guam's colonial status weighs heavily on its people, helping create a sense of apathy over the perceived impossibility of challenging the most powerful military country in the world.

This military increase to Guam, regardless of whether it signifies a boon or a disaster, is something that is being forced on the people of Guam. As an unincorporated territory, with no semblance of presidential voting power and no voting representation in the US Congress, Guam exists at the whim of the US federal government. When the possibility of moving Marines from Okinawa to Guam was first discussed, representatives of Japan and the United States met, but no one from Guam sat at the negotiation table. Although the people of Guam are occasionally asked to comment on DOD plans for their islands, as a colony, they have no real role in determining their destiny and whether it lies toward peace or war.

As a final note, Guam, like other island bases, provides a good lesson in how militarization works and what must be done in order to counter and disrupt it. The value of places like Guam, Tinian, and Pågan is that their perceived distance and small size means they are invisible or matter little to much of the world. This smallness and this distance are part of the strategic value of island bases, qualities that militaries such as that of the United States count on in order to "protect" the training or activities that are conducted there. When larger, more visible places protest and demand that training be reduced or bases be closed, the United States feels safe in moving their forces to "uncontested" and invisible islands like Guam. For those seeking to dismantle global networks of military power, it is important to keep this dynamic in mind.

Note

The names that appear in the section titles (*Hacha, Hugua, Tulu,* etcetera) are ancient numbers in the Chamorro language, the indigenous language of Guam. As a result of Spanish colonization, they were replaced by Spanish numbers (uno, dos, tres), but there has been a movement to try to bring back the ancient numbers. I try as much as possible to use them in my academic work when outlining my arguments.

References

Aguon, Mindy. 2009. "Guam Gets 90 Days to Review EIS." KUAM News, October 28.

Batdorff, Allison. 2006. "Massive Armada Taking Part in Carrier Exercise near Guam." *Stars and Stripes*, June 21. www.stripes.com/news/massive-armada-taking-part-in-carrier -exercise-near-guam-1.50626.

Bevacqua, Michael Lujan. 2008. "Håfan na Liberasion? #13: Seven Crashes." *No Rest for the Awake—Minagahet Chamorro* (blog), July 22. minagahet.blogspot.com/2008/07/hafa-na -liberasion-11-seven-crashes.html.

Bumiller, Elisabeth. 2002. "Bush Affirms U.S. Role in Asia in New 'Pacific Century.'" *New York Times*, February 19. www.nytimes.com/2002/02/19/world/bush-affirms-us-role -in-asia-in-new-pacific-century.html.

Camacho, Leevin. 2013. "Resisting the Proposed Military Buildup on Guam." In *Under Occupation: Resistance and Struggle in a Militarised Asia-Pacific*, edited by Daniel Broudy, Peter Simpson, and Makoto Arakaki, 183–90. Newcastle upon Tyne, UK: Cambridge Scholars.

Clinton, Hillary. 2011. "America's Pacific Century: The Future of Politics Will Be Decided in Asia, not Afghanistan or Iraq, and the United States Will Be Right at the Center of the Action." *Foreign Policy*, October 11. foreignpolicy.com/2011/10/11/americas-pacific-century/.

Dumat-ol Daleno, Gaynor. 2015. "$399M for Buildup Projects." *Pacific Daily News*, October 1. www.guampdn.com/story/news/2015/10/01/399m-buildup-projects/73131220/.

Halloran, Richard. 2006. "Guam Seen as Pivotal U.S. Base." *Washington Times*, March 11.

Hanlon, David. 1998. *Remaking Micronesia: Discourse over Development in a Pacific Territory, 1944–1982.* Honolulu: University of Hawaii Press.

Harden, Blaine. 2010. "On Guam, Planned Marine Base Raises Anger, Infrastructure Concerns." *Washington Post*, March 22. www.washingtonpost.com/wp-dyn/content/article /2010/03/21/AR2010032101025.html.

Hattori, Anne Perez, Simeon Palomo, and Michael Lujan Bevacqua. 2010. Unified Chamorro Response to the DEIS. February 10.

Hauswirth, Heather. 2010. "Snorkeling Outing Showcases Guam Habitat." KUAM News, February 7.

Hudson, Adam. 2016. "In Pivot to Asia, US Military Reinforces Its Foothold in the Pacific." *Truthout* (blog), February 6. www.truth-out.org/news/item/34694-in-pivot-to-asia-us -military-reinforces-its-foothold-in-the-pacific.

Mitchell, Jon. 2012. "Poisons in the Pacific: Guam, Okinawa and Agent Orange." *Japan Times*, August 7. www.japantimes.co.jp/community/2012/08/07/issues/poisons-in-the -pacific-guam-okinawa-and-agent-orange/.

Naputi, Tiara. 2013. "Charting Contemporary Chamoru Activism: Anti-Militarization and Social Movements in Guåhan." PhD diss., University of Austin, Texas.

Naputi, Tiara, and Michael Lujan Bevacqua. 2015. "Militarization and Resistance from Guåhan: Protecting and Defending Pågat." *American Quarterly* 67: 837–58.

Natividad, LisaLinda, and Gwyn Kirk. 2010. "Fortress Guam: Resistance to US Military Mega-Buildup." *Asia-Pacific Journal* 8, no. 1. May 10. apjjf.org/-LisaLinda-Natividad/3356/article.html.

Natividad, LisaLinda, and Victoria-Lola Leon Guerrero. 2010. "The Explosive Growth of U.S. Military Power on Guam Confronts People Power: Experience of an Island People Under Spanish, Japanese and American Colonial Rule." *Asia-Pacific Journal* 8, no. 3. December 6. apjjf.org/-LisaLinda-Natividad/3454/article.html.

Olson, Wyatt. 2015. "Mariana Officials Bristle at US Military's Live-Fire Plans for Pagan, Tinian. *Stars and Stripes*, April 17. www.stripes.com/news/pacific/mariana-officials-bristle-at-us-military-s-live-fire-plans-for-pagan-tinian-1.340648.

Park, Gene. 2005. "7,000 Marines: Pentagon Announces Shift to Guam." *Pacific Daily News*, October 30.

Stade, Ronald. 1998. *Pacific Passages: World Culture and Local Politics in Guam.* Stockholm: Stockholm Studies in Social Anthropology.

Underwood, Robert. 2001. "Afterword." In *Campaign for Political Rights on the Island of Guam: 1899–1950*, by Penelope Bordallo Hofschneider. Saipan, CNMI: Division of Historic Preservation.

United Nations Special Committee on Decolonization. 2010. "Special Committee on Decolonization Urged to Visit Guam as Petitioners Deplore Militarization of Non-Self-Governing Territory." June 22. www.un.org/press/en/2010/gacol3210.doc.htm.

United Nations Special Committee on Decolonization. 2016. "Non-Self-Governing Territories." www.un.org/en/events/nonselfgoverning/nonselfgoverning.shtml (accessed July 11, 2016).

Zotomayor, Alexie Villegas. 2015a. "Tinian Residents Emphatically Oppose Military Exercises." *Marianas Variety*, May 4. www.pireport.org/articles/2015/05/04/tinian-residents-emphatically-oppose-military-exercises.

Zotomayor, Alexie Villegas. 2015b. "Military Begins Review of 28K Comments on Draft EIS." *Marianas Variety*, December 3.

Noelani Goodyear-Ka'ōpua

Protectors of the Future, Not Protestors of the Past: Indigenous Pacific Activism and Mauna a Wākea

We are trying to get people back to the right timescale, so that they can understand how they are connected and what is to come . . . we are operating on geological and genealogical time. . . . The future is a realm we have inhabited for thousands of years.
—Bryan Kamaoli Kuwada, "We Live in the Future. Come Join Us"

On April 2, 2015, thirty-one *aloha ʻāina* (people who love the land; patriots) were arrested for "trespassing" on government property and "obstructing" the road upon which construction vehicles were attempting to ascend Mauna a Wākea—commonly known as Mauna Kea, the highest mountain in the Hawaiian islands and a sacred *piko* (umbilicus; convergence) for the *lāhui Hawaiʻi* (Native Hawaiian people/nation).[1] The next day, Hawaiian activist-blogger Bryan Kamaoli Kuwada (2015) rejected the copious dismissals of these Kānaka Maoli and our allies as "relics of the past." To be sure, it is a tired colonial trope, representing Indigenous peoples as mere vestiges of a quickly fading and increasingly irrelevant past. But this settler colonial strategy of expropriation and normalization rears its head regularly against Indigenous communities and movements who insist on protecting ancestral connections to lands and waters.

Kuwada instead claimed the future as a realm with which Indigenous people are familiar and highly capable of traversing. His call to "come join us" invited all readers to cast off short-sighted and exploitative notions of prog-

The South Atlantic Quarterly 116:1, January 2017
DOI 10.1215/00382876-3749603 © 2017 Duke University Press

ress that blind us to the inextricable connections between human and planetary health. Indigenous futurities seek to transform settler colonialisms for all who are caught within such relations of violence and exclusion.[2] Eve Tuck and Ruben Gaztambide-Fernandez (2013: 80) posit that whereas *settler futurity* requires the containment, removal, and eradication of original, autochthonous peoples, *Indigenous futurity* "does not foreclose the inhabitation of Indigenous land by non-Indigenous peoples, but does foreclose settler colonialism and settler epistemologies. . . . Indigenous futurity does not require the erasure of now-settlers in the ways that settler futurity requires of Indigenous peoples." In the context of the Mauna Kea struggle, Kuwada (2015) put it this way: "Whenever we resist or insist in the face of the depredations of developers, corporate predators, government officials, university administrators, or even the general public, we are trying to protect our relationships to our ancestors, our language, our culture, and our 'āina. But at the same time, we are trying to reawaken and protect their connections as well."

In this essay, I follow in Kuwada's line of thinking, exploring ways Native Pacific activists enact Indigenous futurities and open space to transform present settler colonial conditions. In particular, I highlight the "Protect Mauna a Wākea" movement as a field of such openings. In this movement Kānaka Maoli and settler allies work together to unmake relations of settler colonialism and imperialism, protecting Indigenous relationships between human and nonhumans through direct action and compassionate engagement with settler-state law enforcement. As Kuwada indicates, this kind of futures-creation is not only in the interest of Indigenous people. Indigenous resistance against industrial projects that destroy or pollute our territories concerns the health of all people.

And yet we should not forget that the violences of exploitative and nonreciprocal practices of imperialisms and settler colonialisms have inflicted harms unevenly throughout Oceania.[3] Struggles against such ecological and social injustice take on an intensified urgency in a time of increasingly rapid global climate change. In 2013, leaders of the Pacific Islands Forum declared, in no uncertain terms, that climate change is "the greatest threat to the livelihoods, security and well-being of the peoples of the Pacific" (Pacific Islands Forum, 2013). Islanders on low-lying atolls are literally losing their ancestral homelands to the encroaching tides. In the high islands of the Pacific, like my own archipelago, sea-level rise may be less pronounced but increasing heat, changing precipitation patterns, and diminished natural resources are all posing new threats to cultural practices and material survival, especially for those who are more dependent on land- and ocean-based subsistence economies. Throughout Oceania, our waters are severely overfished, choked with pollutants, and stressed by ocean acidification. The need for transforming settler enclosures, extractivism, and consumerism could not be more clear.

In October 2014, just six months before the arrests on Mauna Kea, thirty-one Pacific Islanders blocked an important waterway and node in the regional economy—Newcastle Harbor, which serves as the largest coal-shipping port in Australia. The network of islanders from fifteen different Pacific Island nations included representation from islands, like Tuvalu, facing immediate inundation of their homelands by rising tides. And yet their rallying cry was not one of victimhood: "We are not drowning. We are fighting!" Known as the Pacific Climate Warriors, they toured Australia and joined together with settler allies to pose a direct challenge to Pacific Rim countries' extractive and commodifying practices in the form of a flotilla blockade of the harbor. They put producers on notice: "The coal which leaves this port has a direct impact on our culture and our islands. It is clear to us that this is the kind of action which we must take in order to survive. Climate change is an issue which affects everyone and coal companies may expect further actions like this in future" (Queally 2014).

Like the activists on Mauna a Wākea, the Pacific Climate Warriors not only underscored the ways that imperialist industrial projects harm Indigenous Pacific cultures, but they also drew upon those very cultural practices of renewing connections with lands and waters in order to engage in direct action struggle. Long before the confrontation at Newcastle in 2014, young activists had been learning skills of canoe building from their respective elders. Once these canoes were built, the vessels were paddled into Newcastle and joined by Australian settler allies on kayaks to stop several ships and engage police boats. Restoration of ancestral knowledges continues to be an important part of enacting alternatives to settler colonial, capitalist enclosures. When colonial discourses frame blockades at Newcastle or on Mauna a Wākea as obstructions on a march to "*the* future," they miss the ways this kind of activism is actually protecting the possibilities of multiple futures. The assertion of Indigenous epistemologies and practices renews intergenerational pathways connecting watery bodies—human, lake, harbor—and linking ancestors with descendants.

Opening Settler Colonial Enclosures

In many ways the indigenous person's most powerful weapon against further destruction and exploitation is simply *staying*. When the ultimate goal of colonization is to remove ʻōiwi [Natives] from our land in order to access and suck dry the material and marketable resources our ancestors have maintained for generations, it follows that the stubborn, steadfast refusal to leave is essential to our continued existence.
—Kahikina De Silva, "Kaʻala, Molale I ka Mālie: The Staying Power of Love and Poetry"

In Hawaiʻi, as in many other settler colonial contexts, both Indigenous people and settlers are here to stay. There will be no mass exodus of non-Natives from the islands, and although more and more Kanaka Maoli find it necessary to move away from Hawaiʻi, many stubbornly remain in the islands as well. But the problems are not as simple as the fact that Indigenous and settler peoples occupy the same lands and that both typically insist on staying. Our relations with lands and with each other are structured by dominant property regimes that cannot deal with the complexity of our layered and interconnected yet differential interests in the lands on which we reside.

Within settler state government policies and dominant visions of settler futurity, the prevailing models for how to deal with this standoff are inadequate:

> (1) The *allotment* or *assimilation model* aims for a complete enclosure in which the private property system is assumed to be total and Indigenous nations are fragmented as individuals, forever "integrated" or disappeared into settler society;
> (2) the *reservations model* sets aside pockets of land that may be held for the collective benefit of an Indigenous people and polity, while the underlying title often remains with the settler state and while settler society flourishes by commanding the lion's share of lands and resources; and
> (3) the *corporate model* refigures Indigenous nations as private corporate entities that own property and/or development rights that can be capitalized for profit within a globalized capitalist economy.[4]

Thus, if settler colonial relations are built on the enclosure of land as property that can then be alienated from Indigenous peoples, as well as demarcated to privilege certain racialized, classed, and gendered groups of settlers, then we need different ways of relating to land. As Tuck and Yang (2012: 7) argue, decolonization in settler colonial contexts "must involve the repatriation of land simultaneous to the recognition of how land and relations to land have always already been differently understood and enacted." To transform settler colonial relations, we need to do more than transfer ownership. We need to fundamentally shift the system that structures our relations to land.[5] As Candace Fujikane (2015: 9) has pointed out, settler colonial strategies of enclosure try to delink land from water and to cordon off discrete sacred sites from the larger fields of relationality that gives them meaning. She writes,

> Under the conditions of a settler colonial capitalist economy . . . in a system premised on the logic of subdivision, the state and developers draw red boundary lines around isolated "parcels" of land to fragment wahi pana (celebrated places) and wahi kapu (sacred places) into smaller and smaller isolated, abstracted spaces that have no continuities and thus, they claim, "no cultural significance." This is how wastelands are produced as a part of the ongoing process of land seizure in Hawai'i.

To borrow Fujikane's phrase, Indigenous relations to and conceptions of land shatter such "fragile fictions" and settler logics.[6]

Protectors, Not Protestors

The same month that the Pacific Climate Warriors blocked Newcastle Harbor in Australia, the young Kānaka who would later become the most visible in the direct actions on Mauna Kea intervened in the groundbreaking of the Thirty-Meter Telescope (TMT). If built, the TMT would be the largest building on Hawai'i island (popularly called the "Big Island"), eighteen stories high and occupying over five acres of land near the summit.[7] For many years, a hui (group) of Kānaka have been working to assert and protect their genealogical connections to elements and deities of the mountain against an expanding footprint of astronomical observatories and telescopes (Casumbal-Salazar 2014). Those earlier battles were often fought in the courts (Puhipau and Lander 2005). But the disruption of the TMT groundbreaking ceremony and subsequent direct action tactics on Mauna a Wākea brought international attention to these protracted struggles.

The ways the self-described *"protectors*, not protestors" or *kia'i mauna* (guardians of the mountain) conducted the struggle has much to teach us in terms of this essay's central question of how to transform settler colonial relations with land. There were three levels at which protectors challenged the settler state's legitimacy over the permitting of the TMT construction: in Indigenous terms, in national terms and in settler state terms.

Protectors of Mauna a Wākea—the mountain of Wākea—see the mauna, first and foremost, as an ancestor and a home of deities (Maly and Maly 2005). It is the highest point in Oceania. Measured from its base under the ocean to the tip of the summit, Mauna a Wākea is the tallest mountain in the world. It rises above 40 percent of the earth's atmosphere. Kanaka Maoli recognize the mauna as home to numerous akua (gods). As protector, Mehana Kihoi pointed out a few weeks in to her occupation on the mauna "all of the deities on this mauna are wāhine, and they all are water forms" (Moʻolelo Aloha ʻĀina 2015). Mauna Kea's sacredness has to do not only with its remoteness from the realm of regular human activity but also with its significance in collecting the waters that sustain life. The summit is contained within a large land district, or ahupuaʻa, named Kaʻohe. Dr. Pualani Kanakaʻole Kanahele (2015) explains: "In giving the ahupuaʻa the name of Kaʻohe . . . the ʻohe is the product that gathers water in itself. If we live in a bamboo forest, there's always water in the bamboo. This same idea was given to this particular land because the water gathers in this land. . . . It is the ʻohe. It is the place that we will find water, always." Hawaiian efforts to stop construction on the summit have been rooted in the ceremonial honoring of the various elemental forms of *akua* who reside on the mountain and thus give continued life through a healthy water supply. Protectors point out the ways the TMT would impact that water and thus human health.

Protectors have also drawn upon at least two legal regimes in their defense of the mauna: Hawaiian Kingdom law and settler state of Hawaiʻi law. The sacred summit is part of the corpus of lands that were illegally seized from the Hawaiian Kingdom in 1893, when a small group of sugar planters usurped power with backing from the US military. The Hawaiian Kingdom Crown and Government lands—together known as the Hawaiian national lands—remain under control of what protectors on the mauna continue to assert are illegally seized lands, over which the United States and State of Hawaiʻi have no rightful jurisdiction. Thus, on Hawaiian national terms, protectors assert their rights to challenge construction projects permitted by an illegitimate settler government. But protectors have also worked within settler state legal regimes to halt construction, using the settler state's own laws to challenge the construction of a large complex of buildings on lands that the state itself has zoned for conservation. As of this writing, the TMT project was officially put on pause when a state court found that the Board of Land and Natural Resources violated its own rules in issuing the permit and that petitioners against the TMT had not given due process when the conservation district use permit was issued for the project.

In addition to these layered ways of thinking about land and challenging the TMT, protectors further help us to think about ways to transform settler colonial land tenure through the ways they conducted what observers would describe as a blockade of the roadway to the summit and construction site. But the term *blockade* suggests a hard line, a line of exclusion, and what the protectors created was a space of engagement and an opening to "come join us."

Prior to and following the April 2, 2015, arrests of those who used their bodies as barriers against the heavy machinery on its way to the summit, protectors established an "Aloha Checkpoint" for engaging police forces, tourists, construction workers, and others. The Aloha Checkpoint differed from a typical blockade in that protectors were not seeking to establish a border that would exclude anyone besides themselves. This was not a possessive, jurisdictional line. The checkpoint served as a porous boundary that was only intended to block construction vehicles. Furthermore, protectors used the checkpoint as a place to invite opponents and unknowing visitors to talk story. Whether passersby remained in their vehicles or got out to join occupiers in the makeshift tents that served as a kitchen and gathering area, protectors created a space for dialogue and an opportunity to engage in discussion about the ways the TMT project would impact at least five acres of the summit, with its various sites of worship, observation, and hiding places for the bones and umbilical cords of generations of some Hawaiian families. So many supporters donated food during the months-long stand on the mauna that the Aloha Checkpoint also unintentionally became a sort of "soup kitchen." At least one Kanaka relayed that he would pick up houseless people in Hilo and drive them up to the mauna so that hungry folks could eat while also learning about the struggle (Kalaniākea Wilson, pers. comm., April 12, 2016). While the checkpoint was intended to keep construction vehicles out, it was not intended to keep those who operated them off the mountain. Construction workers and police officers, many of whom were also Native Hawaiians, learned through the engagements and in some cases brought their families back up to the mauna when they were off duty, with the intention of learning more and sharing aloha and dialogue with the protectors.

A *kapu aloha*—a philosophy and practice of nonviolent engagement— guided the Aloha Checkpoint and the associated activism on the mauna. Movement leader, *kumu hula* (master hula teacher), and *kiaʻi mauna*, Pua Case describes this kapu as grounded in the teachings of *kūpuna* (elders), and she emphasizes the way the kapu calls one to carry oneself with the highest level of compassion for ʻaina and for all people one may encounter (Maly and Maly 2005). The kapu aloha requires the discipline of empathy, even and especially for those with whom one may disagree. It is not a command to compromise with or assent to harm. The kapu aloha is not intended as a release valve that makes it possible for people to continue enduring intolerable conditions, or to look away from wrongdoing. Speaking to a crowd gathered on the mauna during the occupation, Lanakila Mangauil (2015)—the young leader who disrupted the TMT groundbreaking ceremony in October 2014—expressed that the kapu aloha was particularly important in guiding behavior in a sacred place such as the mountain summit in the wao akua. Such an environment, he explained, reminds people to speak and act with focus, courage, and the deepest respect, even to those who ascend the mountain "on the machines that would rip up our sacred place. We speak to them with the utmost respect and aloha and compassion" (Mele ma ka Mauna 2015). The kapu aloha is a directive to try to understand the circumstances that bring one's opponent to the moment of confrontation.

This kind of aloha manifested, for instance, in protectors greeting law enforcement officials who had come to remove them from the mountain with *lei lāʻī* (garlands of made from ti-leaf, known for its protective and healing qualities) and explicit statements recognizing their interrelatedness. Photographic and video images of law enforcement officers exchanging *hā* (breath), nose-to-nose and forehead-to-forehead with protectors circulated virally through social media channels, underscoring the ways that even when settler colonial relations pit Kanaka against Kanaka, we recognize one another (see figure 1). In many ways, the Aloha Checkpoint and the kapu aloha that ruled it changed the terms of political engagement. Protectors sought not to exclude but to powerfully remind opponents of the ways that the mountain is shared and the ways the mountain connects all in its shadow. While settler state officials cast the kiaʻi as impediments on the road to "progress" (aka settler futurity) and passed regulations that would be used to specifically target and remove protectors from the mauna, kiaʻi stewarded places and practices that invited their antagonists to join them in reaching toward more expansive and sustainable futures.

Kū Kiaʻi Mauna

When you see the possibility of "progress" in this more connected way, you see that we are actually the ones looking to the future. We are trying to get people back to the right timescale, so that they can understand how they are connected and what is to come.
—Bryan Kamaoli Kuwada, "We Live in the Future. Come Join Us"

While Indigenous environmental activism is still often dismissed by the very powers who benefit from exploitative usage of our lands and waters by

Figure 1. The first arrests began on Mauna a Wākea on April 2, 2015, days after the standoff had begun when construction vehicles began ascending the mountain. Photo by David Corrigan, Big Island News

(mis)representing us as fixed in place, pinned in a remote time, we continue to be concerned with the deep time of human survival. As Auntie Pua Case once said, when she guided my *hālau hula* (hula school) up to Kūkahauʻula and Waiau a few years before the highly publicized struggle over the TMT erupted: we know that the Mauna could shake her shoulders and throw these telescopes off. We don't fight for the life of the Mauna, for the Mauna will live far beyond us; we are grateful to celebrate our connection to the Mauna in this way, to remember that we are the Mauna. And so protectors remember and renew connections, inviting others to come join us. Resurgent Indigenous futures beckon.

Acknowledgments

I would like to thank Teresa Shewry for her insightful comments on early drafts of this essay. I am also deeply grateful to Bryan Kamaoli Kuwada, Iokepa Casumbal-Salazar, ʻIlima Long, Candace Fujikane, Dean Saranillio, Noenoe Silva, Noʻeau Peralto, and Auntie Pua Case for conversations that greatly contributed to my thinking.

Notes

1   In his essay on the genealogical connections between the mountain and the Native Hawaiian people, Leon Noʻeau Peralto (2014) explains: "Born of the union between Papahānaumoku and Wākea, Mauna a Wākea is an elder sibling of Hāloa, the first aliʻi.

As such, both the Mauna and Kanaka are instilled, at birth, with particular kuleana to each other. This relationship is reciprocal, and its sanctity requires continual maintenance in order to remain pono, or balanced" (234).

2   *Futurity* refers to the ways groups come to imagine or know about the future(s). Drawing on the work of Benedict Anderson, geographer Andrew Baldwin (2012) argues that certain logics and practices for anticipating and preempting particular futures bolster whiteness. Tuck and Gaztambide-Fernandez (2013) extend Baldwin's usage of this term in order to differentiate between settler and Indigenous futurities, where the former bolsters and extends settler colonial relations of power while the latter challenges them.

3   See Johnston and Barker 2008; Barker 2012; Teaiwa 2014; Goodyear-Kaʻōpua et al., 2014.

4   A fourth, less common, model is a leftist *settler commons model*, which envisions a complete shift to a communal form of land tenure in which all people—without distinction between Indigenous and settler—gain access to all lands before or without simultaneously dismantling settler colonialism. For instance, one such vision in Hawaiʻi proposes a settler reclamation of the commons from the last remaining Native Hawaiian-controlled landed trusts. Such a transition that fails to take into account the differential positionalities with respect to historically rooted systems of wealth and power in the islands would heighten existing inequalities, in which Native Hawaiians have been dispossessed of lands and remain at the bottom of various indicators of social, economic, and physical well-being.

5   As a way to unsettle settler regimes of land tenure, I look to Native Hawaiian understandings and practices of *kuleana* (authority, responsibility, privilege), particularly in relation to land and learning.

6   The phrase "fragile fictions" comes from Fujikane's forthcoming book, *Mapping Abundance: Indigenous and Critical Settler Cartographies in Hawaiʻi*, which will include some of her analysis on critical settler cartography and Indigenous cartography on Mauna a Wākea.

7   The final environmental impact statement of the TMT project acknowledges that the cumulative impacts of all the existing telescopes and related infrastructure on Mauna Kea have already been "substantial, significant, and adverse" on biological habitats. They rationalize the project by saying that further development would add only "incremental impact," thus keeping the level of harm at a continued level that is "substantial, significant, and adverse" (University of Hawaiʻi at Hilo 2010: S-8).

8   *Wahine* refers to women, the feminine, or female elements. See Moʻolelo Aloha ʻĀina 2015 for Mehana Kihoi's explanation.

References

Baldwin, Andrew. 2012. "Whiteness and Futurity: Towards a Research Agenda." *Progress in Human Geography* 36, no. 2: 172–87.

Barker, Holly M. 2012. *Bravo for the Marshallese: Regaining Control in a Post-Nuclear, Post-Colonial World*. 2nd ed. Belmont, CA: Wadsworth Publishing.

Casumbal-Salazar, Iokepa. 2014. "Multicultural Settler Colonialism and Indigenous Struggle in Hawaiʻi: The Politics of Astronomy on Mauna a Wākea." PhD diss., University of Hawaiʻi at Mānoa.

De Silva, Kahikina. 2011. "Kaʻala, Molale I Ka Mālie: The Staying Power of Love and Poetry." Colloquium paper presented at the "Reclaiming CELANEN: Land, Water, and Governance" symposium, University of Hawaiʻi at Mānoa, October 28.

Fujikane, Candace. 2015. "Indigenous and Critical Settler Cartography: Mapping a Moʻoʻāina Economy of Abundance on Mauna a Wākea." Paper presented at the Political Science Colloquium Series, University of Hawaiʻi at Mānoa, November 13.

Goodyear-Kaʻōpua, Noelani, Ikaika Hussey, and Erin Kahunawaikaʻala Wright, eds. 2014. *A Nation Rising: Hawaiian Movements for Life, Land, and Sovereignty.* Durham, NC: Duke University Press.

Johnston, Barbara Rose, and Holly M. Barker. 2008. *The Consequential Damages of Nuclear War: The Rongelap Report.* Walnut Creek, CA: Left Coast Press.

Kanahele, Pualani Kanakaʻole. 2015. "Pualani Kanakaʻole Kanahele on Mauna Kea and Kaʻohe." Big Island Video News. YouTube video, 5:46. April 27. www.youtube.com /watch?v=oxhfJYRFWiI.

Kuwada, Bryan Kamaoli. 2015. "We Live in the Future. Come Join Us." *Ke Kaupa Hehi Ale* (blog), April 3. hehiale.wordpress.com/2015/04/03/we-live-in-the-future-come-join-us/.

Maly, Kepa, and Onaona Maly. 2005. "Mauna Kea: Ka Piko Kaulana O Ka ʻĀina." Prepared for the Office of Mauna Kea Management. Hilo: Kumu Pono Associates LLC.

Mele ma ka Mauna. 2015. "Lanakila Mangauil: 'What Is Kapu Aloha?' Speech." ʻŌiwi TV video, 12:17. April 17. Oiwi.tv/oiwitv/mele-m-a-ka-mauna-lanakila-mangauil-speech/.

Moʻolelo Aloha ʻĀina. 2015. "Mehana Kihoi: The Goddesses That Guide Us." Vimeo video, 00:46. September 13. moolelo.manainfo.com/2015/09/the-goddesses-that-guide-us/.

Pacific Islands Forum. 2013. Majuro Declaration for Climate Leadership. Sept 5, 2013, Majuro. www.majurodeclaration.org/the_declaration (accessed July 1, 2016).

Peralto, Leon Noʻeau. 2014. "Mauna a Wākea: Hānau Ka Mauna, the Piko of Our Ea." In *A Nation Rising: Hawaiian Movements for Life, Land, and Sovereignty,* edited by Noelani Goodyear-Kaʻōpua, Ikaika Hussey, and Erin Kahunawaikaʻala Wright, 233–36. Durham, NC: Duke University Press.

Puhipau, and Joan Lander. 2005. *Mauna Kea: Temple under Siege.* Nāʻālehu, Hawaiʻi: Nā Maka o ka ʻĀina. DVD, 50:16 min. oiwi.tv/oiwitv/mauna-kea-temple-under-siege/.

Queally, Jon. 2014. "'Not Drowning, Fighting': Pacific Climate Warriors Blockade Australian Coal Port." Common Dreams, October 17. www.commondreams.org/news/2014/10/17 /not-drowning-fighting-pacific-climate-warriors-blockade-australian-coal-port.

Teaiwa, Katerina Martina. 2014. *Consuming Ocean Island: Stories of People and Phosphate from Banaba.* Bloomington: Indiana University Press.

Tuck, Eve, and Ruben Gaztambide-Fernandez. 2013. "Curriculum, Replacement, and Settler Futurity." *Journal of Curriculum Theorizing* 29, no. 1: 72–89.

Tuck, Eve, and K. Wayne Yang. 2012. "Decolonization Is Not a Metaphor." *Decolonization: Indigeneity, Education, and Society* 1, no. 1: 1–40.

University of Hawaiʻi at Hilo. 2010. "Final Environmental Impact Statement, Vol. 1: Thirty Meter Telescope Project, Island of Hawaiʻi." University of Hawaiʻi at Hilo. www.mala mamaunakea.org/uploads/management/plans/TMT_FEIS_vol1.pdf.

Eben Kirksey

Lively Multispecies Communities, Deadly Racial Assemblages, and the Promise of Justice

Multispecies ethnographers, from the outset, have worked to get beyond the notion of the nonhuman. Following Susan Leigh Star, we have assumed that "non-human is like non-white—it implies a lack of something" (Kirksey and Helmreich 2010: 555). Recently Alexander Weheliye reinforced this point as it applies to people. Weheliye (2014: 4) describes how "racializing assemblages" divide up groups of people "into full humans, not-quite humans, and non-humans." People who are marked by racial assemblages are routinely abused or killed, and they often have no standing before the law (Weheliye 2014; cf. Wolfe 2013). The notion of the nonhuman often subjects people, plants, and animals to slow violence (cf. Nixon 2011)—marking categories of life as expendable, external to the value system of capitalism. Communities confined to the realm of bare life (*zoe*) are routinely exposed to toxic chemicals and infectious diseases, and they are sometimes targeted for outright destruction.

Indigenous peoples worldwide have lived with racial assemblages that render them killable. Ongoing processes of dispossession, displacement, and genocide are taking place in human worlds as plant and animal communities are rendered into "natural resources" for extractive industry or picturesque backdrops for tourism (Haritaworn 2015: 210). Kim Tallbear (2015: 234) notes that recent critiques of settler colonialism "clearly link violence against animals to violence against particular humans who have historically been linked to a less-than-human or animal status." Despite pervasive

The South Atlantic Quarterly 116:1, January 2017
DOI 10.1215/00382876-3749614 © 2017 Duke University Press

violence targeting "people who are close to nature" many indigenous people continue to recognize other species as "agential beings engaged in social relations that profoundly shape human lives" (234).

I first traveled to West Papua, the half of New Guinea under Indonesian rule, in 1998—intent on studying the intersection of biological and cultural spheres in indigenous communities. After witnessing a series of massacres by Indonesian security forces, I changed the focus of my research. *Freedom in Entangled Worlds: West Papua and the Global Architecture of Power*, my doctoral dissertation and first book, explored the interplay of imagination and collaboration in the struggle by indigenous Papuans for national independence. Drawing on unpublished material from my 1998 notebooks, as well as a 2015 return visit to my original field site, this essay is my first attempt to bring together my research on indigeneity and multispecies worlds.

Power is functioning predictably in West Papua as forests are logged, as natural resources flow out of indigenous lands, as people die from treatable diseases, and as black boys are shot dead by the side of the road. Papuans are searching for opportunities even as deadly assemblages and infrastructures violently collide with lively multispecies communities. Amid ongoing disasters, indigenous groups are pursuing the elusive promise of justice (Derrida 1992).

Life by the Side of the Road

In West Papua I initially lived in a space by the side of the road—listening for stories of people who were getting around and making do, seizing on moments of shock when endangered life ways were suddenly shot through with profound significance (Stewart 1996: 107). Unipo, the village where I lived in 1998, had been built by a logging company at the behest of the government a few years before. Technocrats in distant metropolitan centers hoped to turn the nomadic hunter-gatherers living in the region into a governable population. Unipo sat on the crest of a high, sloping ridge—commanding a view of the surrounding mountains. When I first arrived in the village I was struck by the visual contrast of a huge yellow backhoe against a backdrop of rainforest and simple wooden houses. This machine had been left by a road repair crew six months before.

The indigenous people who lived in Unipo called themselves the Mee (pronounced "May" like the month, meaning simply "the people") of the Siriwo Valley. The Mee saw the new village as an experimental arena of sorts. Novel technologies, emergent infrastructures, and competing dreams were changing human lives and the surrounding ecological communities. Unipo was a place where people were actively testing out strategies for engaging with and leaving modern systems of economic production (cf. García Canclini 2005). Around twenty people lived in Unipo full time, and I came to know about sixty others who were semipermanent residents with other homes in the city, tents at nearby gold panning sites, and hamlets deep in the forest.

Outside of the Amazon, New Guinea has the largest contiguous tracts of old-growth rainforest in the world. Unipo was built as this old-growth forest was being destroyed. The community emerged within a blasted landscape, amid ongoing environmental and social disasters (Kirksey et al. 2013; Tsing 2014).

About one week after I arrived in Unipo, a woman named Marcy came down with the telltale symptoms of malaria—chills with intense shivering alternating with high fever. Malaria was a new disease for the Mee. They historically lived at higher altitudes, in places where there are few malarial mosquitoes. Nomadic lifestyles of Mee groups that ventured into the lowlands, seasonal migrations that disrupted the life cycle of the malarial parasite, had kept transmission rates low. As Mee people settled in Unipo, embracing a sedentary lifestyle, they confronted epidemiological risks as they inhabited a new multispecies world. Alongside these risks also came opportunities.

One sunny Friday morning in 1998 a group of girls tumbled into the tin-roofed shack that was my temporary home. The faces of Melanie, Agatha, and Betty—who ranged in age from eight to eleven—were alive with excitement. "Let's go collect grasshoppers!" they shouted, pulling me away from the notebooks in which I was busy writing. As we walked through Unipo, a five-year-old also got swept up in the enthusiasm of the group. Together these girls showed me a space of autonomy and freedom that persisted along the side of a road, despite destructive forces beyond their control. Foraging for food on the margins of market economies, in the ruins of recently logged forests, they showed me how to exploit opportunities in emergent ecological communities. They taught me how to find fleeting moments of happiness while collecting edible insects.

"Having good 'hap' or fortune," notes Sara Ahmed (2010: 22), was the original sense of the word *happy* in Middle English. While this meaning may now seem archaic—since happiness is not something that money can buy or power can command—Ahmed insists that we return to this original definition, "as it refocuses our attention on the 'worldly' question of hap-penings" (22). Snatching grasshoppers and other insects from the grass that lined the road, the girls of Unipo showed me how to find happiness in the *hap* of what happens in multispecies worlds. As we grabbed prized snacks, the girls taught me the names for their tiny prey: *bigai pugu* (spur-throated grasshoppers), *kekegelke* (giant katydids), *ugapuga* (palm katydids), and *amatape* (leaf mimicking katydids).[1] Quickly darting in and out of the grass, they grabbed insects and quickly killed them by pinching their heads. These small morsels of food were then put inside hollow bamboo tubes that each of the girls carried inside of net bags, made with tree bark string, slung over their backs.

Peals of laughter erupted as I grabbed a praying mantis and then shook it off my hand as it began to needle me with its sharp front legs. The mantis, one of the favorite insect foods of the Mee, is called *egokago*, or fishhooks. As I watched Mary did not even flinch as she deftly picked up another praying mantis and the hooks on its front legs poked into her flesh. After I collected a number of pyrgomorph grasshoppers, I noticed that the girls were ignoring them. I asked why, and Betty said that they were called *didimigo* (hurting head). If you eat too many *didimigo* then you will develop a headache.

We encountered some cicadas on this foraging trip, but we did not collect them. Mary told me that the spirit of her father, a prominent sha-man, entered a cicada when he died. When the bodies of the Mee die a *tene* (departed shadow) is born—if you are on good terms with a *tene* it may pass along critical information from the spirit world, or if you come into conflict with a *tene* it can make you sick. Mary said that her father would warn her with loud cries when trouble was afoot. Thus we did not collect perfectly edi-ble insects since they were regarded as agential beings who maintained ongoing social relations with the living (cf. Tallbear 2015: 234).[2]

On the way home we gathered greens from one of their parent's gardens—leaves of sweet potato, cassava, and taro plants—along with a bundle of bananas. Back at home the bamboo tubes full of insects were pushed into the coals of the fire to slowly steam, while the greens were wilted in a large wok with salt, oil, and red peppers. Crunching through the crispy outer shell of the insects, I found that flavor varied with species: katy-dids and grasshoppers tasted like shrimp and the praying mantises were nutty. A large spider that they called *epe woga*, which had a buttery flavor, was the tastiest of all.

The children of Unipo began routinely taking me on forays to hunt for insects and gather forest products. As we walked they talked about the diverse routes of their parents—the seasonal migrations that drew them up into the mountains and the periodic opportunities for wage labor that pulled families into the coastal cities. Amid unpredictable economic systems and dramatic ecological changes, Mee children were finding new opportunities for foraging. Along the margins of the freshly logged forest, and in the grass by the side of the road, they found happiness and pleasure with the proliferation of grasshoppers, katydids, and praying mantises.

The road also presented an obstacle to deeply rooted indigenous ways of life. Game animals that were once abundant—like wild pigs, tree kangaroos, and other marsupials—were in decline. Logging operations had driven these animals deep into the forest, the men in the village said. Meat rarely found its way to my plate when I lived in Unipo.

Officially the dirt track running through Unipo had a grand sounding name: the Trans-Papua Highway. Construction of this "highway" began in 1979 to support a World Bank transmigration program, which brought landless peasants from overpopulated islands in western Indonesia to establish homesteads in the territory of indigenous Papuans (Monbiot 1989). The portion of the road through the Siriwo Valley, which connected coastal cities with the highlands, was gradually completed in the 1990s, bringing unofficial transmigrants who set up trade stores, opened restaurants under plastic tarps, and prospected for gold.

The Trans-Papua Highway enabled the Mee to participate in market economies by growing cacao and sugarcane for sale in Nabire, a nearby city on the coast. Selling produce generated cash that was used to buy food—like rice, ramen noodles, and canned meat—as well as newly available technologies like chainsaws, kerosene lamps, antibiotics, and hypodermic needles. Market prices were wildly fluctuating during my time in Unipo, and massive landslides regularly halted vehicle traffic along the road. Amid ongoing destructive processes my Mee friends found moments of happiness by living with the contingency of the world (Ahmed 2010: 31). Happiness, however, is fragile like glass. It can shatter at any moment.

Deadly Assemblages

Three years later, on a return visit to West Papua in 2001, I tried to visit Unipo, but landslides had made the Trans-Papua Highway impassable. From afar I learned that the village had been abandoned. Malaria had swept Unipo, killing half of the residents. Melanie, Agatha, and Betty—my insect collecting companions—were among the dead. I was devastated.

The death of my friends was not an isolated incident, but it is part of a systematic pattern. Elsewhere in Indonesia, public health measures have eliminated malaria. According to the Centers for Disease Control in Atlanta there is no risk of malaria transmission to American travelers in the cities of Jakarta and Ubud or in the resort areas of Bali and Java.[3] Malaria continues, however, to kill scores of people in West Papua every week. I became feverish with the disease twelve times myself over the course of my field research—contracting both the low-grade relapsing strain, *Plasmodium vivax*, and the deadly cerebral malaria strain, *Plasmodium falciparum*. The disease is as common as a cold in West Papua. People who miss work as a result are often the butt of playful jokes in Indonesian: "Were you really sick with *malaria*, or were you staying home because of *mala-rindu*, because you missed your girl-friend?" Amid banal jokes, over the years I have lost many of my university-educated colleagues and collaborators—middle-class people living in urban centers—to malaria.

Infrastructures and modern medical practices protect some people in Indonesia from tropical diseases like malaria, while others die. Powerful ethnic groups of Java and Bali pay for public health measures to protect their kin and kind, while leaving the health system of West Papua chronically underfunded. Michel Foucault (1984: 266) would have understood this situation in terms of biopolitics, as the "outcome of a technology of power centered on life." "If genocide is the dream of modern powers," writes Foucault, "it is because power is situated and exercised at the level of life, the species, the race, and the large-scale phenomena of population" (260). By letting malarial mosquitoes live in some regions, the Indonesian government is in effect making Papuans die.

Alexander Weheliye recently criticized Foucault for lacking a cogent account of race. Racism does not emerge from fixed biological phenotypes, according to Weheliye, but is the state-sanctioned exploitation of group-dif-ferentiated vulnerabilities, which produces premature death. As Dorothy Roberts (2011: 51) argues: "Race is not a biological category that is politically charged. It is a political category that has been disguised as a biological one."

In contemporary West Papua, a place where indigenous people are quickly becoming a minority in their own land, light-skinned Indonesian settlers have adapted global racial discourse to turn black people into quasi humans. Carleton Stevens Coon, a professor at Harvard and Penn, pub-lished *The Origin of Races* in 1962, speculating that *Homo sapiens* evolved from five separate subspecies in an identifiable sequence: first from Cauca-soids, then followed by Mongoloids, Negroids, Capoids (southern Africans), and finally Australoids (Papuans and Australian aboriginals). Papuans were thus believed to be the closest living relatives to a missing link between apes and humans (cf. Marks 2002: 75–77). Experts who produced pseudoscientific racism are dying a slow death. A retired professor of anthropology at Yale University told me in 2015: "Papuans are not attractive people. They look like Neanderthals." When I walk on the streets of Indonesian cities like Jakarta, I often hear racial epithets comparing my Papuan friends to nonhuman animals. "We are viewed like we are still evolving according to Darwin's theory," in the words of Filep Karma (2014: 8), an Amnesty International prisoner of conscience. "We are treated as if we are animals in the process of becoming humans. . . . Often Papuans are called 'monkey!'"[4]

When the human genome was sequenced in the year 2000, molecular biologists announced that there is no biological basis for race (Roberts 2011). Nonetheless, black people continue to be barred "from the category of the human as it is performed in the modern west," by sciences, languages, infrastructures, practices, and discourses (Weheliye 2014: 3). Racializing assemblages are elusive. They connect "bodies, forces, velocities, intensities, institutions, interests, ideologies, and desires" (12). In West Papua racial assemblages have produced starkly uneven life chances and vulnerability to premature death (cf. Haritaworn 2015: 212).

Black Lives Matter

Yoteni Agapa, age nineteen, was shot dead on June 25, 2015, during a roadside incident on the Trans-Papua Highway. Black lives matter. But, some black lives matter more than others. Race, nationality, and class all help determine who has full personhood before the law. The shooting of Yoteni Agapa, like so many extrajudicial killings in West Papua before and since, was ignored by Indonesia's national court system. But Agapa's death represents more than just one more example of impunity in West Papua. This killing was the result of a direct conflict among competing modes of life.

The Trans-Papua Highway was repaired in the early 2000s by Indonesian government officials who hoped to promote the flow of regional commerce and to facilitate the movement of military troops. Sections were paved and trucks began regularly to ply the road—carrying clothes, food, gasoline, and construction materials—supporting the lives of Indonesian settlers in the highlands. Countless Mee people who could not afford to ride in vehicles began regularly to use the road as a walking track (Kirksey and van Bilsen

2002). People from multiple social worlds began to share this common infrastructure, even though the road produced a situation of asymmetrical risk and vulnerability (Bowker and Star 1999; Parreñas 2012). Power functioned predictably as natural resources flowed out of indigenous lands—coffee, cacao, timber products, precious metals. Asymmetries were exacerbated; resentment grew (cf. Kirksey 2012: 210–11).

In spaces by the side of this road, the Mee people continued to search through the ecological wreckage left behind by extractive industries. People continued to live within lively multispecies communities—finding opportunities in the face of palpable economic and social inequality. As powerful assemblages collided with the bodies of indigenous people and their beloved companion species, revolutionary moments began to open that were pregnant with possibility.

The evening of the incident, Yoteni Agapa was hunting by the side of the road near the highland town of Dogiyai with a group of teenaged friends. A dog accompanied the boys. She was a companion animal and a carefully trained member of the hunting team, practiced at flushing animals out of the underbrush and treeing them (cf. Haraway 2003). On this particular hunting trip she flushed five *weta*, a terrestrial marsupial with a long snout and small ears, from the grass growing on the margins of a friend's garden. After bagging these *weta*, Yoteni Agapa and his friends started walking home along the Trans-Papua Highway.

As the boys walked along the dark road on June 25, a night like any other, violence suddenly erupted. As a speeding truck bore down on the group, illuminating the scene with its headlights, the dog suddenly ran into the road. The dog was hit by the truck and killed. Rather than stop and offer compensation, or words of apology, the truck driver sped away. The life world orbiting around a beloved hunting companion had been violently disrupted. Passions flared among Yoteni Agapa and his friends. Since the boys did not have the opportunity to seek redress from the driver, they directed their anger toward the infrastructure of inequality that had produced the violence. Long-standing grievances about social and economic inequality suddenly came to a head. They decided to stop the flow of people and goods along the road. These young men, for a moment, disrupted the intense force and velocity of a powerful infrastructure.

The boys set up a roadblock and began asking passing vehicles for money—demanding $2 to $5 from each driver, the price of a meal at a restaurant. After collecting cash from six cars, a black Avanza sport utility vehicle rolled up to their roadblock, at around 10:00 p.m. The SUV arrived from the direction of Waghete, a regional center where there are police and military posts. Yoteni Agapa approached the passenger side of the car, while Melianus Mote, the oldest of the group at twenty-one years, approached the driver's side. Ethnic Indonesians were inside. The other boys—ages fourteen through seventeen—hung back from the car a little bit and watched. They quickly realized that both the driver and the man riding in the passenger seat had guns. As the shooting started the boys scattered and ran.

Yoteni Agapa was shot in the chest twice as he stood beside the car. As he tried to run, the gunman pursued him—shooting him two more times in his right arm. Yoteni managed to stagger away from the car but fell in the middle of the road, about twenty yards away. A group of men came out of the car and began to kick Yoteni's body, stabbing it with bayonets. As they mutilated the body, the holes made by the bullets became larger and less easy to discern. Later, Yoteni's family removed two bullet slugs—one a golden color, the other silver—from his dead body.

Melianus Mote, the young man who was standing by the driver's door, ran as soon as Agapa was shot. As he was bolting, he felt something hot and wet on his upper right arm. Later, after he looked at the wound, he suspected that it was from a bayonet. He told human rights investigators that the driver stabbed him as he was trying to run. The other eight boys managed to escape by jumping in Bakobado River. Police investigators later found twelve bullet casings at the crime scene. The caliber of the bullets was 5.56 mm, which is standard issue for a variety of different Indonesian security forces. After conducting a preliminary investigation, police simply declared that the shooting was conducted by a group of "unknown men." Local human rights investigators alleged that the shooters were Indonesian military troops belonging to the Kostrad Raider 303 detachment that operated a checkpoint nearby. But, no formal legal proceedings ensued.

When whites or Indonesians are murdered in West Papua, the rule of law is applied.[5] But, when black Papuans lose their lives, the cases are systematically ignored by local courts. On September 1, 2015, I joined a coalition of local human rights organizations in West Papua to make a formal submission to the United Nations Special Rapporteur on extrajudicial, summary, or arbitrary executions. We wrote to report the death of Yoteni Agapa as a result of a killing by security forces of the state, or death squads cooperating with or tolerated by the state. The United Nations acknowledged our submission and power continued to function predictably.

Conclusion

"Justice is an experience of the impossible," according to Jacques Derrida (1992: 16). Law (*droit*) is the application of the rules, while "justice is incalculable, it requires us to calculate with the incalculable" (16). As state security forces repeatedly break the rules in many jurisdictions around the globe, violating domestic laws protecting citizens from arbitrary killings and international human rights treaties, there is a growing movement to pursue justice by other means. As the Angel of History continues to be blown backward by the winds of progress (Benjamin 1968), past countless bodies of people and companion animals who never appeared "before the law," a multitude is starting to anticipate "a law not yet existing, a law yet to come" (Derrida 1992: 36). In searching for the elusive promise of justice, Derrida (1994: 82) turned away from what he regarded as the "primitive conceptual phantasm" of community, the topos of territory, native soil, sovereignty, and borders. Rather than pin his hopes on revolutionary events, or historical figures, Derrida waited for nothing—in an abyssal desert—expecting the unexpected (28).

Waiting for nothing in particular resigns the future to fate. As deadly assemblages forestall justice in diverse corners of the globe, it is more important than ever to ground collective hopes. In an era when any claim to sovereignty is quickly undermined by the proliferation of global assemblages, it is important to practice cyborg politics: taking "pleasure in the confusion of boundaries" and making arguments "for responsibility in their construction" (Haraway 1985). As capitalism becomes increasingly nomadic—flitting about with unprecedented speed and intensity, scouring the earth for new resources to exploit (Stengers 2011)—counterhegemonic justice might be best achieved by shutting down flows of commodities, life-giving resources destined for others.

Yoteni Agapa and his friends experienced a moment of justice when they set up a blockade on the Trans-Papua Highway. Recognizing that the driver who killed their dog would never appear before the law, they calculated within the incalculable—forging their own temporary space of sovereignty. Public health officials and technocrats who created the village of Unipo will also never appear before the law to be held accountable for the deaths of Melanie, Agatha, and Betty. The restless spirits of these children are joining legions of others as coalitions of unlikely allies come together in the pursuit of justice beyond existing laws, institutions, and sovereign structures. Struggles grounded in the topos of territory are pushing back against powerful assemblages and infrastructures, creating the conditions for continued life in multispecies communities.

Notes

1   Within Linnean taxonomy these insects were in the Melanoplinae subfamily and Tettigoniidae family of the order Orthoptera.

2   Later I collected two cicada species in Unipo that were identified by Hans Duffels and Arnold Boer as *Cosmopsaltria doryca* Boisduval and *Baeturia bicolorata* Blote. These species are likely not toxic, since *Cosmopsaltria* species are eaten in the highlands (Duffels and van Mastrigt 1991), and *B. bicolorata* is eaten in Papua New Guinea (Arnold de Boer, pers. comm., 1999).

3   Centers for Disease Control and Prevention, "Health Information for Travelers to Indonesia: Clinician View," wwwnc.cdc.gov/travel/destinations/clinician/none/Indonesia (accessed July 22, 2016).

4   My translation.

5   For example, a major international investigation was launched in 2002 following the murder of two white people in West Papua—contract employees of the massive US gold mine Freeport McMoRan. Seven people were given jail sentences for this crime. The masterminds who killed white people in this particular crime, members of the Indonesian security forces, were never brought before a court of law. The seven men who were charged with the crime were black Papuans, some of whom had no connection to the crime (Kirksey 2012: 169–70).

References

Ahmed, Sara. 2010. *The Promise of Happiness*. Durham, NC: Duke University Press.

Benjamin, Walter. 1968. *Illuminations*. New York: Schocken Books.

Bowker, Geoffrey C., and Susan Leigh Star. 1999. *Sorting Things Out: Classification and Its Consequences*. Cambridge, MA: MIT Press.

Coon, Carleton Stevens. 1962. *The Origin of Races*. New York: Knopf.

Derrida, Jacques. 1992. "Force of Law: The 'Mystical Foundation of Authority.'" In *Deconstruction and the Possibility of Justice*, edited by D. Cornell, M. Rosenfeld, and D. G. Carlson, 3–67. New York: Routledge.

Derrida, Jacques. 1994. *Specters of Marx: The State of the Debt, the Work of Mourning, and the New International*. New York: Routledge.

Duffels, J. P., and H. J. G. van Mastrigt. 1991. "Recognition of Cicadas (Homoptera, Cicadidae) by the Ekagi People of Irian Jaya (Indonesia), with a Description of a New Species of Cosmopsaltria." *Journal of Natural History* 25, no 1: 173–82.

Foucault, Michel. 1984. "Right of Death and Power over Life." In *The Foucault Reader*, edited by Paul Ranibow, 258–72. New York: Pantheon.

García Canclini, Néstor. 2005. *Hybrid Cultures: Strategies for Entering and Leaving Modernity*. Minneapolis: University of Minnesota Press.

Haraway, Donna Jeanne. 1985. *Manifesto for Cyborgs: Science, Technology, and Socialist Feminism in the 1980s*. Socialist Review 15, no. 2: 65–108.

Haraway, Donna Jeanne. 2003. *The Companion Species Manifesto: Dogs, People, and Significant Otherness*. Chicago: Prickly Paradigm Press.

Haritaworn, Jinthana. 2015. "Decolonizing the Non/Human." *GLQ: A Journal of Lesbian and Gay Studies* 21, no. 2: 210–13.

Karma, Filep. 2014. *Seakan Kitorang Setengah Binatang: Rasialisme Indonesia di tanah Papua* (*We Are Half Animal: Indonesian Racism in West Papua*). Jayapura, Papau, Indonesia: Deiyai.

Kirksey, S. Eben. 2012. *Freedom in Entangled Worlds: West Papua and the Architecture of Global Power.* Durham, NC: Duke University Press.

Kirksey, S. Eben, Maria Brodine, and Nick Shapiro. 2013. "Hope in Blasted Landscapes." *Social Science Information* 52, no. 2: 228–56.

Kirksey, S. Eben, and Stefan Helmreich. 2010. "The Emergence of Multispecies Ethnography." *Cultural Anthropology* 25, no. 4: 545–76.

Kirksey, S. Eben, and Kiki van Bilsen. 2002. "A Road to Freedom: Mee Articulations and the Trans-Papua Highway." *Bijdragen to de Taal-, Land- en Volkenkunde* 158, no. 4: 837–54.

Marks, Jonathan. 2002. *What It Means to Be 98% Chimpanzee: Apes, People, and Their Genes.* Berkeley: University of California Press.

Monbiot, George. 1989. *Poisoned Arrows: An Investigative Journey through Indonesia.* London: Michael Joseph.

Nixon, Rob. 2011. *Slow Violence and the Environmentalism of the Poor.* Cambridge, MA: Harvard University Press.

Parreñas, R. S. 2012. "Producing Affect: Transnational Volunteerism in a Malaysian Orangutan Rehabilitation Center." *American Ethnologist* 39, no. 4: 673–87.

Roberts, Dorothy E. 2011. *Fatal Invention: How Science, Politics, and Big Business Re-create Race in the Twenty-First Century.* New York: New Press.

Stengers, Isabelle. 2011. *Cosmopolitics II.* Translated by Robert Bononno. Minneapolis: Minnesota University Press.

Stewart, Kathleen. 1996. *A Space on the Side of the Road: Cultural Poetics in an 'Other' America.* Princeton, NJ: Princeton University Press.

Tallbear, Kim. 2015. "An Indigenous Reflection on Working beyond the Human/Not Human." *GLQ: A Journal of Lesbian and Gay Studies* 21, no. 2–3: 230–35.

Tsing, Anna. 2014. "Blasted Landscapes (And the Gentle Art of Mushroom Picking)." In *The Multispecies Salon*, edited by S. E. Kirksey, 87–109. Durham, NC: Duke University Press.

Weheliye, Alexander G. 2014. *Habeas Viscus: Racializing Assemblages, Biopolitics, and Black Feminist Theories of the Human.* Durham, NC: Duke University Press.

Wolfe, Cary. 2013. *Before the Law: Humans and Other Animals in a Biopolitical Frame.* Chicago: University of Chicago Press.

Teresa Shewry

Going Fishing:
Activism against Deep Ocean Mining,
from the Raukūmara Basin to the Bismarck Sea

In late April 2011 the crew of *San Pietro*, a small boat belonging to iwi (kin group, tribe) Te Whānau-ā-Apanui, went fishing near a seismic survey ship, *Orient Explorer*, in the deep waters of the Raukūmara Basin off the East Cape, Aotearoa New Zealand. The government had given Petrobras a permit to search for oil and natural gas in this part of the world where seawater bears down thousands of meters, with crushing pressure, onto ecosystems not reached by sunlight. Earlier that month, swimmers from a flotilla forced *Orient Explorer* to veer off course, and the government responded by deploying police, navy, and air force units to the basin. "You are not welcome in our waters," the crew of *San Pietro* radioed *Orient Explorer*, which was located approximately three hundred kilometers from the coast. They stated they would position the fishing boat directly in the path of the survey ship: "We will not be moving, we will be doing some fishing" (Peace Movement Aotearoa 2011).

Petrobras is among many corporations, in connection with governments and extranational entities like the International Seabed Authority, searching the Pacific Ocean for extractable materials, including fossil fuels, copper, gold, silver, and iron. Mining corporations' interactions with the ocean are expensive, based on processes like core drilling, ROV dive videos, and measuring of electromagnetic fields. They are also highly experimental at their depths (or "out of our depth," as trans-Pacific movement Deep Sea Mining Campaign puts the collective precariousness of ocean mining [Deep

The South Atlantic Quarterly 116:1, January 2017
DOI 10.1215/00382876-3749625 © 2017 Duke University Press

Sea Mining Campaign and Rosenbaum 2011]). In the Raukūmara Basin, Petrobras was permitted to search for oil in water up to 3100 meters deep, including by appraisal drilling. Consider that the Deepwater Horizon drilling rig was working in water around 1522 meters deep when it exploded in the Gulf of Mexico in 2010.

The term *exploration* appears commonly in portrayals of ocean mining. When Petrobras was allocated a five-year "exploration permit" in 2010, Energy and Resources Minister Gerry Brownlee (2010) stated, "Given Petrobras's expertise, and financial and technical pedigree, this is an exciting step into areas of New Zealand until now unexplored." In this story, people have no existing connections with the Raukūmara Basin. We might be led to believe that these waters exist beyond not only the physical but also the imaginative reach of communities in Aotearoa and more broadly the Pacific, many of which already face multiple and severe environmental crises with few resources. Most people have not visited the seafloor ecosystems targeted for mining and almost certainly never will.

Yet, as it turns out, varied Pacific peoples claim close connections with the ocean, including with immensely deep waters far off land. They have been churning the waters of corporate and state aspirations in specific locales, across the Pacific, and beyond. Their struggles expose ocean mining as unevenly localized and expansive ecological violence, including as energy-extraction intensifying global climate change. They also involve Indigenous people's long-standing connections with the ocean and challenges to governments' authority to nationalize and privatize it. Te Whānau-ā-Apanui (2012: 2) stated that in fishing nearby Petrobras' ship, it was "asserting its right to protect its traditional marine territory, and engage in customary fishing practices in waters the tribe has protected and fished for many generations." In this essay, I explore the art and media activism of these struggles, focusing on Greenpeace's photographs (2011) of the Te Whānau-ā-Apanui fishing boat crossing the Petrobras ship in the Raukūmara Basin and Hawaiian artist Joy Enomoto's *Nautilus the Protector* woodcut prints (2015), in which a nautilus battles mining infrastructure in the Bismarck Sea, Papua New Guinea. Through creative tactics—linking fishing to a struggle against fossil fuels extraction, or mobilizing woodcut printing, a fast and inexpensive media form, to animate different imaginaries against a flood of high-tech corporate representations of the ocean—activists find ways to rework conditions of economic disparity and aggressive exclusion from proposed mining sites. They counter corporate and government efforts to condition their relationships with oceanic places targeted for mining. In fishing and other assertions of connection with waters and lands thousands of meters beneath, they challenge mining discourses in which such connections require physically penetrating into and exposing the depths.

Fishing as Activism

Setting out fishing lines ahead of a seismic survey ship, the crew of *San Pietro* positioned fishing as resistance to the violence of fossil fuel capitalism in the Raukūmara Basin. Photographs of the small fishing boat crossing the looming Petrobras vessel circulated in mainstream newspapers and on social media, and they are currently up on the Greenpeace New Zealand website.[1] Greenpeace, which arrived in the Raukūmara Basin at the request of Te Whānau-ā-Apanui, commonly draws attention to occluded oceanic struggles through dramatic photographs of clashes at sea, as in a series of images on its website of French commandoes storming *Rainbow Warrior II* off Mururoa (Moruroa) Atoll amid the antinuclear struggles of 1995.[2]

But far beyond responding to Petrobras's presence, in fishing Te Whānau-ā-Apanui was practicing a different, enduring, and ordinary connection with the ocean. Fishing is not a "protest," Te Whānau-ā-Apanui leader Rikirangi Gage radioed *Orient Explorer* from *San Pietro*, before police boarded *San Pietro* and charged skipper Elvis Teddy with endangering the *Orient Explorer* and resisting arrest (Peace Movement Aotearoa 2011). Petrobras appeared in the ancestral territories of Te Whānau-ā-Apanui and other iwi, interrupting local people, not vice versa. To position a small fishing boat, a source of livelihood, in the path of a Petrobras ship is also to express the deeply uneven allocation of peril bound up in ocean mining. In the East Coast region, more than 85 percent of the people who live along the ocean and on the East Cape, places that would likely be directly hit by oil spills, are Māori (Soutar 2015). By linking fishing to the struggle against offshore drilling, the crew of *San Pietro* pushed associations between people and this oceanic place into view, upending the mining ideology of the ocean as a frontier. Greenpeace's photographic emphasis on the clash between *San Pietro* and *Orient Explorer* seems to both reinforce and be disjunctive with the expressive politics of fishing, which also orient us to more ongoing and ordinary forms of life. The photographs suggest Greenpeace's lens but also differing political engagements within this complex communal struggle.

Fishing could perhaps be interpreted as a competing iteration of the aspirations of capital-intensive extraction evident in seabed mining. Here, it is excessive to, although not sealed off from, the economic upheavals of colonialism and global capitalism. In the Raukūmara Basin, fishing has long been interwoven in a complex communal life based on genealogical and reciprocal connection among all things, including people, the ocean, and fish.[3] For example, the moki, a tapu (sacred) fish caught by Te Whānau-ā-Apanui in these waters, is said to have been carried to the area by an ancestor and is cared for according to protocol, expressed by the moki in a story written by local children: "We will provide tangata [people] with kai [food] as long as they don't beat us with rakau [weapons; sticks] on our tapu heads, mix us with other kai in their boats, cook us on the beach or eat us raw. . . . Our father has warned that if we are ill-treated, we are to return to Hawaiiki forever" (Knight 2011). Moki are ocean travelers who migrate yearly to their only known spawning ground at the East Cape, where they could be disrupted by seismic tests. In an interview, Tweedie Waititi says, "That's the moki's home. . . . Right where they want to drill. Every June, there is a star that shines in the sky and her name is Autahi, and that's our indication that the moki has come home" (Knight 2011). In this area, commercial fishing is undermining small-scale fishing, while near-shore fishing grounds are being smothered by sediment runoff from deforestation and agriculture. By the 1980s, moki had been heavily depleted in a context of trawling and set netting, and their future remains a site of uncertainty and concern.[4] Rather than being an idealized engagement, fishing might speak to people about dilemmas, losses, and openness in their relationships with the ocean at this time.

Mining, too, has a disturbing history in this place. Seven years before Petrobras's arrival, the government passed the Foreshore and Seabed Act (2004), claiming all seabed and foreshore as Crown property aside from some areas held in private title. It overturned a 2003 court of appeals decision that the Māori Land Court could hear Māori claims regarding foreshore and seabed, the implication being that the judicial system might recognize these areas as Māori customary land (*Attorney General v. Ngāti Apa*). In a submission, Te Whānau-ā-Apanui (2010) links the act to the government's aspirations in ocean mining and a deeper history of minerals appropriation, stating it will "continue to challenge the Crown derived fictions that unilaterally confiscated those resources from our future generations." In 2011, after large Māori mobilizations, including a two-week *hīkoi* (march) of thousands of people, the Foreshore and Seabed Act was repealed by the Marine and Coastal Area (Takutai Moana) Act, which restores potential judicial recognition of foreshore and seabed as Māori customary land.

Amid this controversy around tidal and underwater land, the government announced that Petrobras would search the "unexplored" Raukūmara Basin, as one of the country's "frontier basins" (Brownlee 2010). Anna Lowenhaupt Tsing (2005: 27) argues that resource frontiers are made for expansive capitalist extraction: "frontiers create wildness so that some—and not others—may reap its awards." Relying on "unmapping," frontiers erase different imaginative and material engagements, and often seem "sensible and ordinary" (Tsing 2005: 28). Frontiers may seem particularly matter-of-fact in relation to immensely deep waters like the Raukūmara Basin. But applying the term *frontier* here involves a struggle to define, even to dominate, what it means to have a close relationship with the undersea and subterranean world. In its announcement, the government linked such a relationship to two activities planned by Petrobras: (1) physically penetrating into deep water and land through drilling, and (2) exposing such areas, especially to vision, through seismic surveys to reveal depth, seafloor structure, and hydrocarbons (Brownlee 2010). In contrast with drilling (or, indeed, blasting the seafloor with sonic waves) a small fishing boat might not appear to be shaping and expressing a communal space that includes a close interweaving of people and waters and lands thousands of meters beneath. But fishing asserts Māori presence and connects these waters to different theorizations about important linkages between people and oceanic places, including relational networks not predicated on either exposure or penetration. "In relation to the lands and seas from Te Taumata o Apanui to Potikirua the mineral estate is considered part of our tribal territory," stated Te Whānau-ā-Apanui (2010) of the government's aspirations in mining: "Not just for development or exploitation purposes; but because our worldview sees our entire territory as a complete and interconnected biosphere, not something to be legislatively fragmented."

Petrobras faced many reminders of people's presence in the Raukūmara Basin, from bonfires along East Cape beaches to a national movement against drilling, until it gave up its permit in 2012. The following year, the government used *urgency* (a parliamentary procedure to speed up, and bypass aspects of, usual legislative processes) to amend the Crown Minerals Act. The "Anadarko Amendment," as it is popularly known, allows for "noninterference zones" to shield offshore mining structures and ships from people (Crown Minerals Act 1991, sec. 101B). Te Whānau-ā-Apanui fisherman Elvis Teddy's case was thrown out in 2012, but the government appealed and pursued him until 2015, when he was sentenced to community service. As of 2016, the government has not again sought to include the Raukūmara Basin in its yearly offshore offers to petroleum corporations, although it has offered different oceanic basins. In 2016, as I write this essay, the Marshall Islands faces catastrophic drought, the Great Barrier Reef is engulfed in a momentous coral-bleaching process, and the Aotearoa NZ government has offered corporations permits to search for fossil fuels in contested oceanic basins in Northland, Taranaki, the East Coast, and Canterbury.

Oceanic Protectors

Photographs of *San Pietro* clashing with *Orient Explorer* still circulate through labyrinthine social media networks interwoven in people's struggles for alternatives to deep-water mining. Through social media, people share narratives, short films, visual art, and poetry, among other materials, connecting political engagements and shaping radically different imaginaries of the ocean. They counter an immense flood of ocean mining representations that corporations are distributing in investor reports, environmental impact statements, and on platforms like Twitter. As with the direct action of fishing, activist media are created amid deep exclusions, aggressions, and unevenness that mark people's relationships with oceanic places proposed for mining.

In January and February 2015, photographs of woodcut prints from a series called *Nautilus the Protector* (2015) by Hawaiian artist and activist Joy Enomoto were posted on "Nautilus the Protector—Solwara Em Laif" (n.d.), a Facebook page on seabed mining, linked to the Pacific Network on Globalisation, a movement for economic justice. Each work represents a nautilus (a cephalopod who lives in the western Pacific) and in several the nautilus battles with ocean mining infrastructure. Enomoto told me that she used woodcut printing because it is easy and fast to make and has a long history of being tied to struggle (pers. comm., January 8, 2016). The printing ink is made from water and shoe polish, a combination Enomoto described as "sickening" to work with (pers. comm., January 8, 2016). The toxicity of the means of producing the artworks suggests the convoluted ways in which corporations pass damaging impacts of mining onto others, human and nonhuman, as well as the economic and social injustices that mark media engagements with the ocean.

Enomoto's *Nautilus the Protector* works engage Canadian company Nautilus Minerals' efforts to establish the world's first deep ocean copper and gold mine in an active hydrothermal vent ecosystem in the Bismarck Sea, PNG. Beginning in early 2018, Nautilus Minerals plans to move silt and level chimneys, cut and pump material to the surface, separate the material from seawater, and then pump the water back down to the seafloor. It wants to expand in PNG, the Solomon Islands, Fiji, Tonga, Vanuatu, Aotearoa NZ, and the Clarion-Clipperton Fracture Zone, administered by the International Seabed Authority. A speculative image on its website shows a ship connected to a mine far below.[5] Even though no sunlight can reach these depths, the seafloor is lit up and the seawater is transparent, implying that Nautilus Minerals really sees what is down there. As with the representations of the Raukūmara Basin as a frontier, both penetration and exposure to vision implicitly allow for the deep ocean to be known and important. There are no traces of lives and histories in these waters, aside from mining machinery. Mining is an orderly, peaceful future, as suggested by straight vertical lines that represent depth and the mining system.

Enomoto's *Nautilus the Protector* series asks us to engage a very different ocean, one that is contentious, troubling, and enigmatic. In "Great Protector," a nautilus moves through black water, which suggests that "as the sea absorbs nearly the entire spectrum of light that is humanly discernible, it marginalizes human modes of perception," to draw from Stacy Alaimo (2013: 236). The water takes on further meaning in a photograph of the same work, "Great Protector" (figure 1), as a nautilus appears to swim away from a swirling plume of water and sediment toward another plume, seemingly unable to escape the upheavals of the mine below, which is not directly seen. The plumes, which are an effect of light reflecting on the paper when photographed, stretch vertically and horizontally to and implicitly beyond the frame, an aesthetic of inadequacy and incompletion that suggests vast and not well-understood implications of seabed mining as well as people's (even government's) inability to monitor what is happening in such places. The nautilus is linked to deeper waters even though not an inhabitant of those waters and even though these waters are in many ways unknown. As activists expressed in the Raukūmara Basin, people (and other beings) do not need to go down to the deep seabed to be closely connected with it. The black water of "Great Protector" is stirred up by mining and marked by flecks that evoke drifting matter or bioluminescence. This turbulent water suggests the environmental upheavals of mining. To draw from an introduction to Enomoto's works, "To break the foundation of the earth and to threaten those creatures, such as the nautilus that are 2 million years older than the dinosaurs, reveals the continued hubris and naiveté of the western world for the sake of making more microchips for cell phones. . . . The Pacific faces the fastest and most devastating threats from human induced climate change. We must ask ourselves, if we drill a hole through our beginnings, where will we be in the end?" (University of Hawai'i-Mānoa Hamilton Library 2015). The ocean, widely theorized by Indigenous Pacific peoples as where life emerged, a system with which human life is impossibly interwoven, is being radically destabilized.

Enomoto's troubled waters suggest distress but also dissent. In the western Pacific, the nautilus has widely been taken as a symbol of protection. The *Nautilus the Protector—Solwara Em Laif* Facebook page notes, "In PNG, the nautilus shell was hung outside of people[']s homes as a sign of

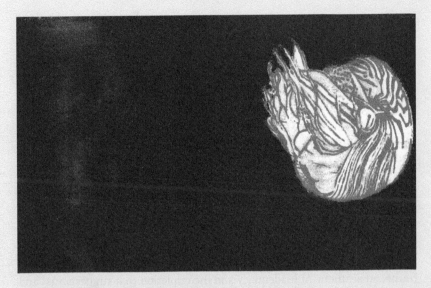

Figure 1. Joy Enomoto, "Great Protector" (2015)

protection against the enemy. While in the Solomon Islands research shows that . . . the nautilus shell is used in the guzuguzu, musumusu, [a] figurehead attached to canoes at the waterline, symbolizing a supernatural protector during voyages." Many nautilus shells were imported to Renaissance Europe for collectors and artworks.[6] Today, this animal is endangered amid a global trade in its shell, ocean acidification, and sea-level rise. The nautilus evokes histories of extraction-driven violence in PNG, including the profound environmental and social injustice already associated with mining in this country. Its histories also suggest vital connections between people and the ocean, expressed by Patrick Kaupun of the Alliance of Solwara Warriors (communities against deep water mining in the Bismarck and Solomon Seas), standing with other activists outside the Fifth Annual Deep Sea Mining Summit in London in 2016: "Our government and Nautilus Minerals have not got the people's free prior and informed consent. The sea is our life. We exist because the sea exists. We will not continue to remain quiet and passive" (Deep Sea Mining Campaign 2016). In PNG and beyond, ocean mining is contested by collectives involving Indigenous people's forums, environmental and legal organizations, church groups, university students and lecturers, and local political figures.

Unlike the fiery nautilus that battles mining machinery in Enomoto's other works, in "Fossil Futures" (figure 2) a gray and white nautilus drifts

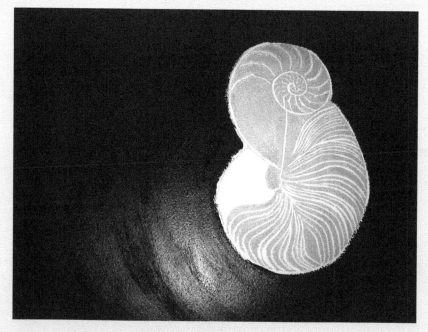

Figure 2. Joy Enomoto, "Fossil Futures" (2015)

in black waters. In "our" context of fossil fuels and climate change, "Fossil Futures" inescapably brings to mind extinctions past, present, and still to come. But the nautilus also appears to emit light into the waters below it, changing how we see these waters, which darken from gray to black as the light disperses. This expressive, creative being churns up seawater to propel itself, but here it can also shape imagination, perhaps as a reminder of unevenly shared peril that extends through these waters to all lives interwoven with them, and as an inspirer in people's continuing struggles for different connections with the ocean.

Acknowledgments

I would like to thank Joy Enomoto for talking with me about her *Nautilus the Protector* artworks, as well as the participants in the Global Environment/Climate Justice Hub workshop at UC Santa Barbara for thoughtful comments on an early presentation of this research.

Notes

1   For one such photograph, see Greenpeace 2011.
2   For one such photograph, see Greenpeace 1995.

3   For an extensive discussion of Te Whānau-ā-Apanui connections with the ocean and
    offshore drilling, see Salmond 2015.
4   For example, see environmental organization Forest and Bird's (n.d.) entry on the
    blue moki in its *Best Fish Guide*.
5   This image is available in the "Technology Overview" section on the website Nautilus
    Minerals: www.nautilusminerals.com/irm/content/technology-overview.aspx?RID
    =329 (accessed June 10, 2016).
6   On this history, see Broad 2011.

References

Alaimo, Stacy. 2013. "Violet-Black." In *Prismatic Ecology: Ecotheory beyond Green*, edited by Jef-
    frey Jerome Cohen, 233–51. Minneapolis: University of Minnesota Press.
Broad, William J. 2011. "Loving the Chambered Nautilus to Death." *New York Times*, October 24.
    www.nytimes.com/2011/10/25/science/25nautilus.html?_r=0.
Brownlee, Gerry. 2010. "Petrobras Awarded Big Exploration Permit." Press release. New Zealand
    Government, June 1. www.beehive.govt.nz/release/petrobras-awarded-big-exploration
    -permit.
Deep Sea Mining Campaign. 2016. "From the Pacific to London: Ban Seabed Mining." Media
    release, May 24. www.deepseaminingoutofourdepth.org/media-release-from-the-pacific
    -to-london-ban-seabed-mining/.
Deep Sea Mining Campaign and Helen Rosenbaum. 2011. "Out of Our Depth: Mining the
    Ocean Floor in Papua New Guinea." Campaign report, November. www.deepseamining
    outofourdepth.org/report/.
Forest and Bird. n.d. "Best Fish Guide: Blue Moki." www.forestandbird.org.nz/what-we-do
    /publications/-best-fish-guide-/blue-moki (accessed June 10, 2016).
Greenpeace. 1995. "A French Vessel Rammed the Greenpeace Vessel." July 9. www.greenpeace
    .org/international/en/multimedia/photos/a-french-vessel-rammed-the-gre/ (accessed
    July 4, 2016).
Greenpeace New Zealand. 2011. "San Pietro." April 10. www.greenpeace.org/new-zealand/en
    /multimedia/photos/2012/July/San-Pietro/ (accessed June 10, 2016).
Knight, Kim. 2011. "Enter the Taniwha." *Sunday Star Times*, April 24. www.stuff.co.nz/sunday
    -star-times/features/4916738/Enter-the-taniwha.
"Nautilus the Protector—Solwara Em Laif." n.d. Facebook page. www.facebook.com/solwaraemlaif
    /info/?entry_point=page_nav_about_item&tab=page_info (accessed June 10, 2016).
Peace Movement Aotearoa. 2011. "Updated—Act Now: Iwi Fishing Skipper Detained on Navy
    Warship." Peace Movement Aotearoa Facebook page. www.facebook.com/notes/peace
    -movement-aotearoa/updated-act-now-iwi-fishing-skipper-detained-on-navy-warship
    /183477711699606/ (accessed June 10, 2016).
Salmond, Anne. 2015. "The Fountain of Fish: Ontological Collisions at Sea." In *Patterns of
    Commoning*, edited by David Bollier and Silke Helfrich, 309–29. Amherst, MA: Com-
    mons Strategies Group and Off the Common Books.
Soutar, Monty. 2015. "East Coast Region." *Te Ara—The Encyclopedia of New Zealand*. www
    .teara.govt.nz/mi/east-coast-region/page-1.
Te Whānau-ā-Apanui. 2010. "Marine and Coastal Area (Takutai Moana) Bill Feedback on
    Behalf of the Constituent Hapu of Te Whanau a Apanui." *New Zealand Parliament*

Pāremata Aotearoa. Select committee submission, November 19. www.parliament.nz /resource/0000133786.

Te Whānau-ā-Apanui. 2012. "Statement of Te Whanau A Apanui: Indigenous Peoples of the East Cape—Aotearoa/New Zealand." *International Maori Affairs*. Submission to the United Nations Permanent Forum on Indigenous Issues. iwimaori.weebly.com/uploads /8/1/0/2/8102509/te_whanau_a_apanui_statement_16_may_2012_1.pdf.

Tsing, Anna Lowenhaupt. 2005. *Friction: An Ethnography of Global Connection*. Princeton, NJ: Princeton University Press.

University of Hawai'i-Mānoa Hamilton Library. 2015. "On Display: Nautilus the Protector." *Hawaiian and Pacific Collections News*, March 4. hpcoll.blogspot.com/2015/03/on-display -nautilus-protector.html.

Notes on Contributors

Ian Baucom works on twentieth century British literature and culture, post-colonial and cultural studies, and African and Black Atlantic literatures. He is the author of *Out of Place: Englishness, Empire and the Locations of Identity* (1999), *Specters of the Atlantic: Finance Capital, Slavery, and the Philosophy of History* (2005), and coeditor of *Shades of Black: Assembling Black Arts in 1980s Britain* (2005). He has edited special issues of the *South Atlantic Quarterly* on Atlantic studies and romanticism and is currently working on a new book project tentatively titled *History 4 Degrees Celsius: Search for a Method*. He served for seventeen years in Duke University's Department of English as a professor and director of the John Hope Franklin Humanities Institute. He has served since 2014 as the Buckner W. Clay Dean of Arts and Sciences at the University of Virginia.

Michael Lujan Bevacqua is an assistant professor of Chamorro studies at the University of Guam. His research deals with chronicling the impacts of colonialism on the Chamorro people and theorizing the possibilities for their decolonization. Most recently he coauthored "Militarization and Resistance from Guahan: Protecting and Defending Pågat," published in *American Quarterly* (2015), and coauthored "Histories of Wonder, Futures of Wonder: Chamorro Activist Identity, Community, and Leadership in 'The Legend of Gadao' and 'The Women Who Saved Guåhan from a Giant Fish,'" published in *Marvels and Tales: Journal of Fairy-Tale Studies* (2016). He has been a longtime activist for demilitarization and decolonization in the Pacific and is a cochair for the Independence for Guam Task Force.

Rosi Braidotti is Distinguished University Professor and founding director of the Centre for the Humanities at Utrecht University. Her books include *Patterns of Dissonance* (1991). *Nomadic Subjects* (1994; 2nd ed. 2011), *Metamorphoses* (2002), *Transpositions* (2006), *La philosophie, là où on ne l'attend pas* (2009), *Nomadic Theory: The Portable Rosi Braidotti* (2011), and *The Posthuman* (2013). She also coedited *Conflicting Humanities* (2016) with Paul Gilroy. Since 2009, she has been an elected board member of the Consortium of Humanities Centres and Institutes (CHCI).

David Buckland is the artist founder and director of Cape Farewell. His publications include the essays "Climate Is Culture," *Nature Climate Change* (2012), and "A Simple and Undeniable Truth" (2012), and the books *Performance* (1999), *Burning Ice* (2006), and *The Last Judgement*, with Sir Anthony Caro (2006). He curated the exhibitions *eARTh*, Royal Academy of Arts, London, 2009; *Burning Ice*, Natural History Museum, London, 2006; *Carbon 12*, Paris, 2012; *Carbon 13*, Martha, Texas, 2013; and *Carbon 14*, Royal Ontario Museum, 2013–14. He has had solo exhibitions at the National Portrait Gallery, London, and in Melbourne, Australia. He produced the films *Art from the Arctic* (BBC 2006) and *Burning Ice* (SundanceTV 2011). He is a visiting fellow at the Chelsea College of Arts of the University of the Arts London.

Matthew Burtner is an Alaskan-born composer and sound artist whose work explores connections between people and the natural environment through avant-garde music. An international award-winning composer, he is professor of music at the University of Virginia, where he teaches courses in ecoacoustics, technosonics, interactive media, and musical materials of activism. He is founder of the environmental arts nonprofit organization Eco-Sono. He worked with the US State Department to create the soundtrack for President Barack Obama's 2015 visit to Alaska, composed music for the National Aeronautics and Space Administration's (NASA) climate change science videos, and premiered *Ice Cycle* at the Smithsonian National Museum of Natural History's Arctic Spring Festival.

Noel Castree is a professor of geography at the University of Wollongong, Australia, and an honorary professorial research fellow at Manchester University, England. Recent publications appear in the journals *Antipode, Dialogues in Human Geography, Geographical Research, Nature Climate Change,* and *Environmental Humanities*. He is managing editor of the journal *Progress in Human Geography*.

Dipesh Chakrabarty teaches history and South Asian studies at the University of Chicago. He is the author of *The Calling of History: Sir Jadunath Sarkar and His Empire of Truth* (2015) and coeditor of *Historical Teleologies in the Modern World* (2015).

Tom Cohen is professor of literary and media studies at the State University of New York at Albany and has recently been Oriental Scholar at Shanghai University of International Business and Economics. His most recent volume is *Twilight of the Anthropocene Idols* with Claire Colebrook and J. Hillis Miller (2016), and he is coeditor with Colebrook of the Critical Climate Change series (Open Humanities Press).

Claire Colebrook is Edwin Erle Sparks professor of English at Pennsylvania State University. She has written books and articles on the philosophy of Gilles Deleuze, poetry, literary history, queer theory, extinction, and gender. Her most recent book is *Twilight of the Anthropocene Idols* (2016), coauthored with Tom Cohen and J. Hillis Miller.

Noelani Goodyear-Kaʻōpua is an associate professor of political science at the University of Hawaiʻi at Mānoa, where she teaches Indigenous and Hawaiian politics. She is the author of *The Seeds We Planted: Portraits of a Native Hawaiian Charter School* (2013), and the coeditor of *A Nation Rising: Hawaiian Movements for Life, Land, and Sovereignty* (2014) and *The Value of Hawaiʻi, 2: Ancestral Roots, Oceanic Visions* (2014).

Olivia Gray is the project and research assistant at Cape Farewell. Her publications include the exhibition catalogs for *Iconos: Sagrado y Profano (Icons: Sacred and Profane)* by Carlos Zapata (2013) and for *Nature of the Life Pavilions* by David Whittaker, cowritten with Joseph Clarke (2014). She curated *Parliament*, an installation by Tim Shaw RA, Cornwall (2005); *"I"—(Passing through the Veil of Solitude)*, Cornwall (2013, ongoing); and *Love at the Poly*, Cornwall (2013).

Willis Jenkins is an associate professor of religious studies at the University of Virginia. He is the author of *The Future of Ethics: Sustainability, Social Justice, and Religious Creativity* (2013), which received a 2014 Award for Excellence in the Study of Religion from the American Academy of Religion, and coeditor of the *Routledge Handbook of Religion and Ecology* (2016).

Eben Kirksey has published two books with Duke University Press—*Freedom in Entangled Worlds* (2012) and *Emergent Ecologies* (2015)—as well as one edited collection: *The Multispecies Salon* (2014). Writing in collaboration with Stefan Helmreich in a special edition of *Cultural Anthropology*, he coined the phrase "multispecies ethnography" to characterize new approaches for studying contact zones where species meet. UNSW Australia recruited Kirksey as a Strategy Hire in 2012 to help found their Environmental Humanities program in Sydney. He was Princeton University's 2015–16 Currie C. and Thomas A. Barron Visiting Professor, where he was researching and writing a new book.

Catherine Malabou is a professor at the Centre for Research in Modern European Philosophy at Kingston University, in the United Kingdom. Her latest book is *Before Tomorrow: Epigenesis and Rationality* (2016).

Matthew Omelsky is a doctoral candidate in the Department of English at Duke University, where he is completing a dissertation on the experience of time in African and diasporic cultural production. His articles on utopian desire, ontology, and the post-Anthropocene in African literature and film can be found in *Research in African Literatures, Nka: Journal of Contemporary African Art, Cambridge Journal of Postcolonial Literary Inquiry*, and, forthcoming, in *Cultural Critique*.

Michael Segal is founding editor and editor in chief of *Nautilus* magazine. Since launching in 2013, *Nautilus* has won over two dozen content and illustration awards. It is also the first magazine ever to earn two National Magazine Awards in its first year. Segal earned his doctorate in electrical engineering from the Massachusetts Institute of Technology and was previously an editor at the academic journal *Nature Nanotechnology*.

Teresa Shewry is an associate professor of English at the University of California, Santa Barbara, where she teaches Pacific literatures and environmental studies. She is author of *Hope at Sea: Possible Ecologies in Oceanic Literature* (2015) and coeditor of *Environmental Criticism for the Twenty-First Century* (2011).

Bently Spang is an independent artist, educator and writer, and enrolled member of the Northern Cheyenne Nation (Tsitsistas/Suhtaio). He has taught at the Tufts University School of the Museum of Fine Arts in Boston (2007–9) and currently maintains a studio in Billings, Montana. His work was featured recently in a traveling group exhibition titled *The Plains Indian: Artists of Earth and Sky* curated by Gaylord Torrence at the Nelson-Atkins Museum, Kansas City, Missouri. The exhibition traveled to the Musée Du Quai Branly in Paris (2014), returned to the Nelson-Atkins Museum (2014), and ended at the Metropolitan Museum of Art in New York (2015). He is the author of *War Shirts I Have Known and Loved* (2014) and *Of Tipis and Stereotypes* (2010). His drawing and video installation *On Fire* debuted at the University of Wyoming Art Museum (2014).

Gary Tomlinson is John Hay Whitney Professor of Music and Humanities at Yale University, where he also directs the Whitney Humanities Center. He is a musicologist whose teaching and scholarship have ranged across diverse fields, including the history of opera, musical thought and practice in early modern Europe, musical cultures of indigenous American societies, and critical and cultural theory. His recent book, *A Million Years of Music: The Emergence of Human Modernity* (2015), offers a new view of the evolution of human musical capacities. This view is developed into a general model of our biocultural evolution in *Culture and the Course of Human Evolution* (forthcoming).

Astrid Ulloa is full professor in the Department of Geography at the Universidad Nacional de Colombia and head of the investigation group Cultura y Ambiente. Her main research interests include indigenous movements, indigenous autonomy, gender, climate change, territoriality, extractivism, and anthropology of the environment. She is author of *The Ecological Native: Indigenous Peoples' Movements and Eco-Governmentality in Colombia* (2005) and *La construcción del nativo ecológico: Complejidades, paradojas y dilemas de la relación entre los movimientos indígenas y el ambientalismo en Colombia* (2004). Her recent essays include "Environment and Development: Reflections from Latin America" (2015), "Territorialer Widerstand in Lateinamerika" (2015), and "Controlando la naturaleza: Ambientalismo transnacional y negociaciones locales en torno al cambio climático en territorios indígenas, Colombia" (2013). She is currently writing about gender and mining and territorial feminisms in Latin America.

Lucy Wood is an artistic producer and currently program director of Cape Farewell. Her articles have appeared in *Writing in Education, Young Writer, Birmingham Post, PQ Magazine,* and *Impact Magazine.* She has been a guest editor for *Run Riot* and *Writing in Education.* She coproduced "Eye of the Storm," an audiovisual project with director Mark Silver (2008) and *Tongue and Grove,* a spoken word European show, European tour (2008).

DOI 10.1215/00382876-3858910

Printed and bound by CPI Group (UK) Ltd, Croydon, CR0 4YY

13/04/2025

14656471-0004